DOROTHY DAY, THOMAS MERTON

AND THE GREATEST COMMANDMENT

Radical Love in Times of Crisis

Julie Leininger Pycior

Paulist Press
New York / Mahwah, NJ

Photograph permissions may be found with the captions, pp. 92–102.
Cover images: Dorothy Day photo by Bob Fitch. Used with permission of the Bob Fitch Photography Archive, Department of Special Collections, Stanford University Libraries. Thomas Merton photo, see caption credit p. 93. Background image by IndianSummer/Shutterstock.com.
Cover design by Sharyn Banks
Book design by Lynn Else

Library of Congress Cataloging-in-Publication Data
Names: Pycior, Julie Leininger, author.
Title: Dorothy Day, Thomas Merton and the greatest commandment : radical love in times of crisis / Julie Leininger Pycior.
Description: New York : Paulist Press, [2020] | Summary: "Catholic worker leader Dorothy Day and monk/author Thomas Merton, who gave radical witness to love of God and neighbor in the tumultuous 1960s, together come center stage in this compelling account of the visionary duo spotlighted by Pope Francis in his historic address to Congress"— Provided by publisher.
Identifiers: LCCN 2019043756 (print) | LCCN 2019043757 (ebook) | ISBN 9780809155156 (paperback) | ISBN 9781587688157 (ebook)
Subjects: LCSH: Day, Dorothy, 1897-1980. | Catholics—United States—Biography. | Social reformers—United States--Biography. | Catholic Worker Movement. | Merton, Thomas, 1915–1968. | Trappists—United States—Biography. | Monks—United States—Biography. | Church and social problems—United States—History—20th century. | Church and social problems—Catholic Church—History—20th century.
Classification: LCC BX4705.D283 P93 2020 (print) | LCC BX4705.D283 (ebook) | DDC 282.092/2—dc23
LC record available at https://lccn.loc.gov/2019043756
LC ebook record available at https://lccn.loc.gov/2019043757

ISBN 978-0-8091-5515-6 (paperback)
ISBN 978-1-58768-815-7 (e-book)

Published by Paulist Press
997 Macarthur Boulevard
Mahwah, New Jersey 07430

www.paulistpress.com

Printed and bound in the
United States of America

To Betty Sue Flowers, Eileen O'Neill,
and all the dear sisterhood that sustained me in this work

Contents

Illustrations follow page 91.

Foreword

Rowan Williams

PERCEPTIONS OF THE mid-twentieth century vary wildly. For some people, it is the beginning of the end, the period when Western civilization lost its nerve, its discipline, and its depth; for others, it is a "land of lost content," a utopian era when peace and progress seemed set to prevail over the war-torn memories of the century's first half. And for Christians, not least for Catholic Christians, the same duality is clearly at work: was Vatican II the first step toward a paralyzing spiritual decadence or a new dawn that was never fully realized?

Thinking in vast binaries like this is actually not very helpful in understanding history, and it may be more productive to look at the detail—the biographies, the personalities, the specific conflicts and convergences. This may at least make it possible for us to recognize that, whatever else may be said about the Church of the mid-twentieth century, it saw a revival and rediscovery of all sorts of deeply buried resources, in theology and ethical vision, in art and spiritual formation. And what emerged was not an archaeological curiosity, a new Gothic revival, but a sharply challenging picture of what the Church might be if it recovered a depth of spiritual and imaginative integrity and a level of sheer moral courage in the face of the unhappy Cold War standoff between drab mercantile modernity and homicidal totalitarianism. The great figures who form the subject matter of this profoundly welcome and significant book are precisely figures who embodied this search for spiritual and imaginative integrity and a richness of Christian and Catholic understanding that could offer a living alternative to the sterile social pieties of the age.

Dorothy Day and Thomas Merton were friends—often uneasy friends, critical friends, even exasperated friends—for a long time. Merton's early experience working in Harlem with Catherine de Hueck meant that he had an instinctive sense of what Dorothy Day's mission was about, and her deep, contemplative hinterland meant that she knew why monks and nuns existed, in a way that not every mid-century activist did. They understood one another, and they understood that their Catholic faith offered them not only riches for cultivating prayer but riches for grounding a critique of contemporary capitalist society that was far more than fashionable, progressive posturing. (Both could be scathing about the blandness of modern liturgy and the Pollyanna-ish brightness of sentimental modernism.) Both were ultimately unable to look away from the face of the suffering Christ in the poor, the racially excluded, the unrespectable, the victims of war, the napalmed children, and the despairing homeless. This holding together of the wealth of spiritual tradition and the destitution of contemporary human experience was what most deeply and lastingly united them, despite all the tensions.

Readers of Dorothy Day's journals will know what I mean when I say that she comes across consistently as a radically *converted* person, submitting all her crotchets and prejudices and uncharities to the light of Christ's love, without any hesitation or deviation. Readers of Merton's journals will know what I mean when I say that his almost embarrassing honesty about his emotional ups and downs, his reckless exposure of wounded ego, fantasy, obsession, and absorbed enthusiasm shows his deep *trust* in a God who is free to see and hear and accept and transform this flawed, complicated experience. As has been said, just when you feel most impatient with Merton, he turns around and expresses that impatience for you in a moment of raw self-recognition. The two heroes of this book are in no way paragons of straightforward religious achievement (there is no such thing, of course); they are Christian disciples in the making, which is another matter entirely.

And that is what makes their stories so compelling—and so necessary at a time when sterile pieties, destructive binaries, compulsive ungenerosity, and shrinkage of spiritual imagination once again haunt the life of a Church profoundly not at peace with itself in a society just as profoundly diseased. This book invites us to look to their lives not for solutions or good examples but for *epiphanies*, for moments when the veil is torn and the face of Christ appears, when we know we are judged and loved as we could never have imagined. Lovers of Dorothy Day and Thomas Merton will find new perspectives here; those coming fresh to these two giants will find a new world opening up, cutting across tribal divisions, and pressing the question of whether we too want to be disciples in the making.

Prologue

IT'S THE MIDDLE of the night, and you're lying in bed, stewing. Here you are, in your comfortable suburban home, even as you consider yourself a follower of someone who said, "Sell all you have and give it to the poor." You think of Catholic Worker leader Dorothy Day, who tried to live out this call of Jesus literally, having begun her work simply by welcoming into her apartment people needing a place to stay. "Let us be fools for Christ," she wrote, quoting St. Paul. "Let us rejoice in poverty, because Christ was poor. Let us love to live with the poor, because they are especially loved by Christ....Even the lowest, most depraved, we must see Christ in them, and love them to folly." She would sometimes say that if each of us welcomed a needy person into our home, and if each parish community took care of "the least" in their midst, we would go a long way toward ending destitution.[1]

What a challenge! But when an interviewer asked her that same question—what about those comfortable suburbanites?—Day turned the tables on herself. We need to always guard against judging the other person, she replied to the television host, for in pointing out the splinter in their eye, we may miss the beam of wood in our own. Indeed, she did maintain that we all are called to center our lives on the Works of Mercy, but when people asked her if she thought everybody should join the Catholic Worker, Day replied that each of us has our own call to bear witness to God's love. For many people, living at the Catholic Worker turned out to be a temporary experience: a sort of school, she called it (even as some of those departures were painful for her). And no one was more aware than Day herself that the Houses of Hospitality she inspired are populated by very human people, full of weaknesses—volunteers as well as guests—or that the soup line and clothing room depend on donations from supporters with conventional occupations. We all, she said, participate in this unjust economic system. Still, Day did live out the Christian call more literally than most of us, even as she would say that, flawed though we all are as we struggle to honor "the least," we can gain hope from the fact that all of us are members of the Mystical Body of Christ.[2]

But, then, why believe in this Christ anyway? In our scientific, analytical, skeptical age, why believe that the universe was created by a God who then sent his child to redeem us by rising from the dead and is present—really present—on the altar; in each one of us; in all of Creation? "The Hound of Heaven," Dorothy Day called it: finding oneself pursued by a God that we are at a loss to explain adequately in words.[3] Plumbing this paradoxical phenomenon, the Trappist monk Thomas Merton reflected,

> While I am asking questions You do not answer. You ask me a question which is so simple that I cannot answer. I do not even understand the question. This night, every night, it is the same question.... But there is greater comfort in the substance of silence than in the answer to a question. Eternity is in the present. Eternity is in the palm of the hand. Eternity is a seed of fire....The things of Time are in connivance with eternity. The shadows serve You. The beasts sing to You before they pass away. You who sleep in my breast, are not met with words, but in the emergence of life within life and wisdom within wisdom. You are found in communion: Thou in me and I in Thee and Thou in them and they in me....There are drops of dew that show

> like sapphires in the grass as soon as the great sun appears, and leaves stir behind the hushed flight of an escaping dove.[4]

Merton's deep but quasi-existential approach to the divine would inform his trailblazing pieces on the spiritual roots of nonviolence, notably as published in the *Catholic Worker*.

But many of those path-breaking insights would only come to me later, in the process of writing this book. As I lay awake that night in the 1990s—on Christmas Eve, as it happened—the question of how to live out the Greatest Commandment very much hung in the air. Suddenly my funk was punctured by an intriguing question: Which one was more inspiring? Was it Dorothy Day, attempting literally to live out the command of love of neighbor? After all, in the years after she and co-founder Peter Maurin first began aiding their indigent New York neighbors in 1933, Catholic Worker communities spread across the country, and tens of thousands of people subscribed to the *Catholic Worker*. Or was it Thomas Merton? He was famously devoted to love of God as the most celebrated monk in American history, thanks to his 1948 bestselling autobiography, *The Seven Storey Mountain*. He sealed this reputation with scores of books and articles capturing the nature of our spiritual anxieties better than we ourselves could do, and then he often transcended them. This priest with the protean mind also made clear that, to be a Christian—to love others as oneself—required openness to others' beliefs: not despite one's faith, but because of it, and with meditation an especially fruitful path toward such communion.

But, then, the Catholic Worker leader herself meditated daily and was a vowed affiliate of a monastery, with her Catholic Worker Houses of Hospitality modeled on the monastic Rule of St. Benedict, which calls for offering hospitality to the stranger as "another Christ." For his part, Merton's was a life of vowed poverty, and although Day was the person manifestly of the world—living in her cacophonous Manhattan community when not traveling around the country lecturing and visiting other Catholic Worker houses—and Merton was the one praying at least six times a day in a rural Kentucky cloister, it was Day, with her natural authority and self-disciplined prayer life, who was sometimes nicknamed "the abbess," while Merton was the charming, best-selling author who corresponded with everybody from Soviet Nobel laureate Boris Pasternak to Henry Miller, whose novels had been banned by U.S. Customs as obscene.[5]

Suddenly it hit me: what mattered was Day and Merton together. Did they themselves recognize their powerful synergy? Curious, I tiptoed down the dark staircase and into the living room, where I pulled out of the wooden bookcase *The Hidden Ground of Love: The Letters of Thomas Merton on Religious Experience and Social Concerns*. The entire back cover was taken up with Merton messages to one correspondent: Dorothy Day. Sitting down on the couch, I opened to those letters and found myself caught up in their world as they strove to bear witness to love of God and neighbor.

"It was a pleasure to get your letter, and of course I keep praying for you and the Catholic Worker....Again, I am deeply touched by your witness for peace," Merton's first message began. If this letter challenged me to bear witness to dangerous public policies—even overwhelmingly popular ones—his next letter spoke to the concern that had been keeping me awake: how to respond to the radical devotion to the poor evidenced by Day and her Catholic Worker cohorts. "O Dorothy," he wrote, "I think of you, and the beat people, and the ones with nothing, and the poor in virtue, the very poor, the ones no one can respect. I am not worthy to say I love all of you....I am not worried about all this and am not beating myself over the head. I just think for the love of God I should say it and for the love of God you should pray for me."[6]

Suddenly I felt a pull—a magnetic pull, like none ever before—to go into the dining room. I found myself on my knees in front of our little crèche, a simple affair: cardboard stable, plastic figures (purchased by my late mother-in-law at the dime store). As my eyes traveled above the manger scene, through the window I beheld a solitary star. A spiritual peace came over me as Christmas Eve turned into Christmas Day, my doubts not so much answered as trumped—overwhelmed by something greater.

"Inspired," my eight-year-old daughter wrote about this epiphany—even if today, like so many people, she is basically agnostic. Or take the case of author and psychiatrist Robert Coles, who wrote in the preface to his biographical profile *Dorothy Day: A Radical Devotion*: "When my wife became seriously ill, she prayed long and hard for her…and wrote us every single morning for a while.…My wife miraculously—the doctor's word—survived the illness."[7]

That a Harvard academic and prominent author who has not publicly stated any religious affiliation would write such a thing emboldened me to reveal this, the only spiritual epiphany of my life. Meantime, as a historian, I found myself called to tell their powerful story. During the totemic 1960s, Day and Merton together gave compelling witness to love of God and neighbor in a world seemingly spinning out of control. This witness resonates anew in our own perilous times; no wonder Pope Francis chose Day and Merton as the two American Catholics to spotlight in his historic address to Congress.

Amazingly, that celebrated reference likely resulted from my research, for the then-president of the U.S. Conference of Catholic Bishops (USCCB), Cardinal Timothy Dolan, had suggested the Day/Merton topic to the pope after I had recommended it to the cardinal for a speech of his own. But as Merton and Day used to remark with regard to the Church hierarchy, "God writes straight with crooked lines." In fact, I had originally suggested that Cardinal Dolan speak on Dorothy Day and Thomas Merton out of concern about what he otherwise might say when he spoke at my college's graduation ceremony.[8]

The choice of Cardinal Dolan as the commencement speaker was not surprising, given that my institution, Manhattan College, identifies itself as Catholic. The Chapel of

Saint Jean Baptiste De La Salle dominates the college quadrangle, and many if not most of the students were raised in Catholic families. Most students do not attend Mass regularly, however, while the majority of the faculty is non-Catholic. The graduation speaker is not always Catholic, and like the vast majority of higher educational institutions, both Catholic and non-Catholic, Manhattan College subscribes to the intellectual freedom guidelines of the American Association of University Professors. It also could be argued that Catholic teaching mandates full use of one's talents, which in the intellectual realm means following the evidence wherever it leads.

Still, the announcement of Cardinal Dolan as the commencement speaker prompted me to wonder: would he, as one of the most prominent spokesmen for the Church's stance against same-sex marriage, say something that would offend my gay colleagues? I wrestled with the issue. The stakes were high, with so many loving gay unions, even as the Church holds that marriage, as traditionally defined, is a sacrament: nothing less than "an outward sign, instituted by Christ, to give grace." But Catholicism does teach that the Greatest Commandment is love God, love your neighbor, in particular the poor, the marginalized, the ostracized, the vilified. At any rate, the prospect of what this leading prelate might say was making me almost sick with worry—even if it is also true that the views of the typical liberal arts faculty member in fact align with virtually all of the Church's policy positions except those related to sex/gender.[9]

As graduation day approached, and as I reflected on all of this, I recalled Day and Merton's own responses to Cardinal Francis Spellman, the most powerful U.S. prelate of their era—and, like Dolan, the archbishop of New York. Spellman famously supported military actions in general and the escalation of the Vietnam War in particular, but despite her near despair over his labeling as God's will a war that she considered immoral, Day did not cease to love him in Christian charity—or fail to note her own human flaws. Deeply touched by Day's Spellman essay, Merton praised her for pointing out "the moral insensitivity of those in authority," but in words marked by love.[10]

Still, history doesn't repeat itself, it rhymes; as of 2012, Spellman's successor was leading the sainthood cause of none other than Dorothy Day. True, some Catholic Workers feared that this might be an attempt by the bishops to use her canonization cause to buttress Church teaching on abortion at the expense of her peace stances. But although she supported all the Church's sex-related teachings, peace and economic justice were so much the center of her identity that they framed the discussions even before Pope Francis showcased these priorities in his famous 2015 reference to her.[11]

Meantime in 2012, even as I worried about that upcoming commencement speech by Cardinal Dolan, I took note of his evident admiration for Day and the Catholic Worker, and I wondered if he held the same opinion of Merton. I doubted it, as a committee of bishops had removed the famous monk from a U.S. Catholic catechism for young adults, citing him as passé, plus Merton's openness to Buddhism was a cause for concern among many in the hierarchy. However, the USCCB had never criticized Merton. Indeed, the same year that Merton was removed from that catechism, Dolan published a book that included a brief reference to the monk, along with three saints, as "great ascetical writers [who] have left us a legacy of spiritual reading to help us enhance our relationship with Christ."[12]

Suddenly an idea dawned on me: to write to Cardinal Dolan suggesting that in his Manhattan College speech he focus on Day and Merton's call to love. In that letter, after telling him of my research on them and thanking him for his own interest in these two figures, I noted, "Now you will be speaking to us at graduation. Your Eminence, when you speak to us, please speak to us of love: 'The Hidden Ground of Love,' as Merton put it, or as Dorothy Day wrote, 'The final word is Love.'" Indeed, throughout the letter I strove to emulate the candid but loving approach they had used with regard to Cardinal Spellman. When bringing up politics, I acknowledged that if I were to cite Day and Merton on the issues, I might do so selectively, "especially in the current climate." Making reference to the 2012 presidential contest, I added, "In this campaign year we are all tempted to—what?—help the team we prefer, even as we know that our Church transcends mere partisanship, viz. the USCCB's lobbying more forcefully on behalf of 'life' issues than anything else, obviously, but at the same time lobbying, in sheer numbers, for more things on the other side of the political spectrum, it would seem."

At the same time, I did not shirk from making the point that "most people seem to think the USCCB only lobbies in favor of one side"—at least at that time before the Francis papacy, with its emphasis on the much more numerous Church teachings unrelated to sex/gender. Doubtless this savvy prelate grasped my implication that the bishops were responsible for this widespread misperception: this ignorance of the fact that the USCCB actually lobbied on behalf of everything from gun control to campaign finance reform to national healthcare to decreased military spending to a living wage and labor rights to environmental protection and renewable energy, as well as immigration reform and an end to the death penalty. Also, Dolan likely assumed, correctly, that I disagree with some official Church teachings (e.g., the exclusion of women from the priesthood), even as such "disobedience" is complicated by another official teaching: that Catholics must follow their (faithfully informed) consciences. Still, this cardinal known for his pastoral manner made time to send me a gracious response, thanking me for the Day/Merton speech suggestion.[13]

Now, however, any reference to the hierarchy takes on a darker, almost menacing cast in the wake of the innumerable revelations of their scandalous mishandling of clerical sexual abuse cases. How would Day and Merton have responded? No doubt she would have cried out in grief to her readers and prayed before the Blessed Sacrament with renewed vigor, storming heaven on behalf of the victims, while Merton would have named that institutional sin for what it is and would have found the right words to honor the injured little ones that Jesus so loved. Would Day and Merton have approved of my offering Dolan my prayerful best wishes? I suspect that they would have wanted me to treat him with the respect owed any child of God, and would recognize that he works devotedly in service to the people of God, but they would have looked for me to acknowledge that, while archbishop of Milwaukee, he had transferred to a cemetery fund money that otherwise would have been available for payment of legal claims—and with most of those lawsuits having been made by victims of clerical abuse.[14] What is certain is that the Catholic Worker leader and her monk soulmate would have prayed for the cardinal and his episcopal colleagues, recognizing their great need for prayer (even as Day and Merton, aware of their own sins, constantly asked each other for prayers).

If the revelations had come to light as of 2012, it is unlikely that Manhattan College would have offered the cardinal an honorary degree. Meantime he graciously responded to my letter, thanking me for the Day/Merton idea; in fact, it constituted the framework of his speech at graduation. "Can I spend just a couple of minutes speaking about love?" he began. "After all, love is our origin and love is our goal," he added as he invoked Merton and Day: "Two real giants when it comes to love."

> I mean it, new classmates, when I tell you that I believe that I am now looking out with love and admiration upon today's Thomas Mertons and Dorothy Days. Because, you know what? As Archbishop of New York, I meet alumni of Manhattan College helping in our soup kitchens and homeless shelters. I see them teaching in our inner city Catholic schools, I see them wheeling kids with cancer to their next MRIs or blood tests. I see them soothing the face of the dying at Calvary Hospital. I see them as policemen and women walking the beat

> as a dedicated cop or advising a client on a morally upright way to invest his or her money. I see them as engineers helping us repair St. Patrick's. I've seen the data folks. Manhattan College teaches love.[15]

Later in the day, when I ran into our president, he said that the cardinal had inquired after me.

So where does that leave things? As the Day/Merton story reveals, the answer is simple—simple, but not easy. The answer is love, as made evident in their hard-won breakthroughs bearing witness to radical love. Take Pope Francis, who asks all of us, whatever our beliefs, to practice love in action. The traits that brought him worldwide recognition are the same ones that make Day and Merton continue to signify, especially in a time of crisis such as our own: social justice witness, deep spirituality, and loathing of sanctimony. Like this figure from our own era who constantly says, "Pray for me," Day and Merton knew in their bones that considering oneself holier than other people is the occupational hazard of religious adherents.

The Day/Merton relationship also reveals a frequently overlooked but central aspect of the pope's message. Yes, he is saying that we should have compassion for those on the margins, but, beyond that, he argues that in fact they are the most important people of all: that we are called to love everyone as children of God, but that it is the poor, the wounded, the ostracized, the victimized who especially deserve our respect and favor, not because we think they are more virtuous than anyone else, but because they are especially beloved of God. Like his namesake—so famously identified with the dispossessed—like Day and Merton, and like those Day/Merton admirers making a difference today, Francis bids us strive to effect a radical reordering of our own priorities and those of society at large.

And yet the pope is himself under a cloud for having been too slow to call out those in the hierarchy complicit in covering up clerical sexual abuse, and slow to bring laypeople into the investigations and oversight implementation. With so many children scarred for life, where is his championing of "the least"? On a different plane, one could say that, in calling for us to practice radical love, the pope might be opening up a challenge for himself to the extent that people in the LGBT community consider the Church the source of much of the opprobrium they feel. Here Day and Merton would seem to provide few if any insights, for on the rare occasions that they referenced sex/gender issues, they did not challenge Church teaching.

Nonetheless their emphasis on love is something that Pope Francis echoes in his desire to interact compassionately with people who are gay. Thus, the person he named as the first cardinal archbishop in the history of Newark, New Jersey, Joseph Tobin, CSsR, welcomed a pilgrimage of LGBT people into the sanctuary of his cathedral, greeting them with the words, "I am Joseph, your brother." In one of his first interviews, Cardinal Tobin underscored the need to "develop a spirit of discernment among us, reading the signs of the times and places in the light of the faith, and being able to talk about that and asking ourselves, what is God's will? Where is God opening a door?...That isn't a fancy name for relativism or changing timeless doctrine, but a way of thinking of what it means to follow or lead a life of discipleship today." Like his papal mentor, Tobin seems to respect what Pope John Paul II called the "countercultural" mission of the Church—bearing witness to its values, regardless of whether opposed by the Right or the Left—but Tobin and Francis are especially focused on loving accompaniment. In this they echo Merton, who reflected, "Love knows, understands, and meets the demands of life insofar as it responds with warmth, abandon, and surrender," while Day famously said (quoting St. John of the Cross), "Love is the measure by which we will be judged."[16]

But what about this religion marked by cascading scandals of priestly abuse and episcopal cover-up? It would seem that the Church itself is the cross on which Christ is crucified. Extreme as that sounds, it assuredly is what Dorothy Day would say if she were alive today, for when confronted with ecclesiastical sins she sometimes did remark, "The Church is the cross on which Christ is crucified"—citing a writer that Merton himself regularly referenced: Romano Guardini. At the same time, Guardini is hardly a renegade author. This priest theologian is regularly cited as one of Pope Francis's favorites and even was a mentor to the more conservative Benedict XVI.[17]

So, again, where does this leave things? Catholicism is facing its gravest crisis in centuries. Nonetheless, were they alive today, Day and Merton still would place their faith in their Church, even though Merton had a somewhat dyspeptic view of the hierarchy, while Day wrote to a mutual friend of theirs, the Catholic sociologist and peace activist Gordon Zahn, "I never expected much of the bishops." She drew strength from Holy Communion and from "the saints that keep appearing all thru history who keep things going." If they were with us today, Merton and Day would remind us to look to St. Francis, who inspired them both. He lived at another time marked by clerical corruption, but the person we remember is the poor friar of Assisi.[18]

This amazing pair, with their loathing of sanctimony, would have us recognize another uncomfortable truth: that whatever our views, none of us are God, that all of us have our blind spots (as with some abortion rights/pro-choice folks being slow to acknowledge the scientific studies reporting advancements in the viability of human life at ever earlier stages of fetal development). Even professional findings are not infallible, of course: take the historical example of so many social scientists in the first half of the twentieth century having advocated eugenics.[19]

Even while wrestling with their own personal demons, Dorothy Day and Thomas Merton gave visionary, spiritually informed social justice witness to the crises of the 1960s. In our own time of great crisis, this compelling duo signifies anew, challenging us to stake our lives on the fact that when Jesus was asked, "What is the greatest commandment?" the reply was, "Love God, love your neighbor": Love.

Acknowledgments

WHERE TO BEGIN? Ever since the idea for this story first came to me in that epiphany over two decades ago, countless amazing people have aided this book's path to fruition. From the world of Dorothy Day, these folks include Cathy Breen, Bill Griffin, and Jane Sammon of the New York Catholic Worker, Mary Anne Grady Flores of the Ithaca Catholic Worker, and former Catholic Worker Robert Ellsberg, publisher of Orbis Books and editor of Dorothy Day's published diaries and letters. From the world of Thomas Merton, they include Judith Emery, Brenda Fitch Fairaday, Anne McCormick, and Gael Mooney of the International Thomas Merton Society's Corpus Christi (New York City) chapter; the pastor of Corpus Christi Church, Rev. Daniel O'Reilly and the former pastor, Rev. Raymond Rafferty; Merton author Rev. George Kilcourse, and the members of the Contemplative Outreach meditation group that meets at Immaculate Conception Church, Irvington, New York.

Dear friends who have sustained this work in countless ways include the late Joseph Ascherl, Gerald F. Cavanagh, SJ, Simon Hendry, SJ, Thomas Quinn—and, especially, that amazing sisterhood of supporters: Barbara Abrash, Sidney Callahan, Betty Sue Flowers, Nancy Gallant, Mary Ann Gohr, Grace Higginbottom, Mary Jane Lilly, Eileen O'Neill, and Jill Sen. Others who have helped light my way—from varied, sometimes contrasting perspectives—include Michael Baxter, Regina Bechtle, SC, Marina Cunha, Adele Dahlberg, Luke

Duchemin, Rev. John P. Duffell, James T. Fisher, Rev. Robert Henry, Matthew Janeczko, Elliot Martin, Margaret Murphy, OP, Angela Alaimo O'Donnell, Rev. Thomas Oppong-Febiri, Linda Terracosta, and Raissa Wu.

Members of the Manhattan College community—students, faculty, staff, administrators, and alumni—who served as valuable sounding boards include Kevin Ahern, Robert Berger, FSC, Alannah Boyle, Joan Cammarata, Katherine Clyde, Thelma Collado, John Evans, Lois Harr, the dearly departed Rev. George Hill, Jeff Horn, Mary Ann Jacobs, SCC, Stephen Kaplan, Mary Ellen Malone, Claire Nolte, Brennan O'Donnell, Michele Saracino, Claudia Setzer, Andrew Skotnicki, Derek Smith, and Gregory Zajac.

Deep gratitude goes to the many people (a number of them no longer with us) whose memories and reflections in oral history interviews helped bring this amazing story to life: Eric Anglada, Ade Bethune, James Conner, OCSO, Rev. John Dear, Monica Durkin Cornell, Eileen Egan, Mark Filip, OCSO, Patrick Hart, OCSO, Anna Koop, SL, Robert Lax, William Meninger OCSO, Jeanette Noel, Roger O'Neill, and Rev. William H. Shannon. Special thanks to the interviewees who knew both Dorothy Day and Thomas Merton: John Eudes Bamberger, OCSO, Mary Donald Corcoran, OSB, Thomas C. Cornell, Ned O'Gorman, John Stanley, Robert Steed, Mary Luke Tobin, SL—and, in particular, Jim Forest.

Archivists far and wide provided invaluable assistance, notably Phillip Runkel, director of the Dorothy Day/Catholic Worker Collection at Marquette University; and Paul Pearson, director, and Mark C. Meade, associate director, of the Thomas Merton Center, Bellarmine University. Other archivists who proved extremely helpful include Bonnie Staib of Madonna House archives, Combermere, Ontario; Tara Craig, head of public services, and Jocelyn Wilk, university archivist, Columbia University Rare Books and Manuscript Library; Dennis Franks, university archivist, and Paul Spaeth, rare books and special collections librarian, St. Bonaventure Library; Andrew Isidoro, public services specialist, Archives and Special

Collections, Burns Library, Boston College; Scott S. Taylor, manuscripts archivist, Booth Family Center for Special Collections, Georgetown University; as well as the archivists at the Cornell University Archives, the Nazareth College Archives, and the University of Notre Dame Archives.

At Paulist Press, the devotion and expertise of senior academic editor Donna Crilly and marketing and sales director Bob Byrnes were crucial for the success of this project (while editor Trace Murphy and former Paulist Press editor Paul McMahon contributed helpfully at the early stage).

But what to say of my family? My husband Stan and our two children, Robert and Anna, supported me in so many ways that thinking about it makes my head spin. In the midst of writing these words I got up from the desk—which Stan built, actually—and walked out to the back yard. Beholding our beloved Hudson River in the distance, my heart overflowed with gratitude and love for this crew of mine that supported me even while not really sharing my passion for this subject. To take but one example: on our sole European trip as a family, they all gamely went along with the notion of detouring to visit the little town in rural France where Merton, as a ten-year-old, had resided with his father. Back home they navigated around my piles of *Catholic Worker* back issues and stacks of Merton books; they helped me with computer glitches—on and on. Anna, now grown and living in Oregon, introduced me to a typical Portland twenty-something who happens also to be a Day/Merton fan. Bob, on my most recent birthday, made a generous donation in my name to the Catholic Worker house in his adopted town of Rochester, New York. Meantime my sister and brother have never flagged in their support, while my ninety-five-year-old mom, Joan Leininger, was a pillar of love, always interested in the book, always pulling for me to see it through. And as I wrote to Rowan Williams, his foreword arrived "on the very day that the book's biggest booster, my mother, left this earthly life. Can't help but think that Mom was looking out for me."

"Love is its own reward," Merton tells us. I learned that

quote from the brother of our campus chaplain, the late Fr. George Hill, who had shared the practice of meditation with many appreciative students at Manhattan College and who knew Dorothy Day and a Trappist colleague of Merton's. I posted "love is its own reward" on my office door when it became increasingly apparent that darkness threatened to consume our nation and our world. A colleague posted on her own office door this inspiring rejoinder from Martin Luther King Jr., "Darkness cannot drive out darkness: only light can do that. Hate cannot drive out hate: only love can do that." Indeed, as Dorothy Day reminds us, "The final word is love."

List of Illustrations

CHAPTER ONE

The One Thing Necessary

"WE ARE ALL INTENSELY grateful to you for all your writings, and it delights me especially to see them in bus stations and drug stores as I travel about the country," Dorothy Day wrote to Thomas Merton in 1959. Indeed, many people—including many in her Catholic Worker Movement—were inspired by Merton's best-selling conversion narrative, *The Seven Storey Mountain*. In luminous prose, the author brings to life his journey from New York sophisticate to a member of the cloistered Cistercian Order of the Strict Observance, better known as the Trappists: a silent but powerful sign of contradiction to the greed and sterility in much of modern life. Meantime, for her part, Day "was always considered to be, like, the lunatic fringe, and hanging onto her place in the Church by her fingernails. That wasn't true, but that was the perception," recalled longtime Catholic Worker Tom Cornell, who also knew Merton. Still, it would be the famous monk, rather than the controversial laywoman, who would feel the need to initiate this historic relationship.[1]

By the time Day and Merton began exchanging letters in the late 1950s, some two hundred fans of his spiritual writing had entered the monastic community that he had characterized as the center of the world: Our Lady of Gethsemani Abbey in rural Kentucky. One of these novices, future Catholic Worker Robert Steed, had found himself so captivated by *The Seven Storey Mountain* that it was instrumental in his becoming a Catholic. "And what better way to be a Catholic than to be a monk?" he thought, as he headed to Gethsemani Abbey. Still, nobody pointed out the famous Trappist to him until one day a monk who was giving Steed some tailoring instructions happened to comment, "Oh, here comes Father Louis (Merton's religious name)," as he passed by their workshop. "He always seemed in a good humor, cheerful, pleasant," Steed recalled, "sober like a monk should be, but not stiff and morose."

Before long, however, the young man returned home. "I just wasn't happy there," Steed recalled years later. "As soon as I got out of the monastery," he added, "one of my relatives told me, 'There's this Catholic Worker place...' and I thought, 'There's a place right here in Memphis? My God!'" Since his teenage conversion, Bob Steed had been reading the *Catholic Worker*, inspired by its witness to the Works of Mercy, and now it turned out that in his totally segregated city, an African American woman, Helen Caldwell, had founded an integrated Catholic Worker house! After a spell, she suggested to Steed that he might like to visit the movement's headquarters, and the young man decided to join the New York community in 1955. After a decade, however, Steed left the Catholic Worker and, eventually, Catholicism itself, for reasons he would share publicly only much later. Still, he kept in touch with his Catholic Worker friends. In the new millennium Steed still writes the occasional review for the *Catholic Worker* and even would be interviewed by the archdiocesan committee supporting Dorothy Day's cause for sainthood. As he himself noted, "If I had stayed in Memphis, what I would have missed!"[2]

The same year that Steed entered Gethsemani monastery, so did another future Catholic Worker, John Stanley. He sometimes served Mass for Fr. Louis/Merton, and years later recalled that the famous monk was "so gentle...very considerate....He knew that a lot of us were new at serving, and that a lot of us had read his book," and thus regarded him with a bit of awe. When Stanley was hospitalized while Merton was being treated for bursitis, the monk stopped by and gently inquired after him: leisurely chats that conveyed genuine, warm interest in the novice. Stanley had been weeping in church—"conversion hysteria," the psychiatrist called it—and in retrospect, he thought that Merton looked in on him in part to send back an assessment to the superiors, which was fine, Stanley thought. The novice master suggested that Stanley might find the Catholic Worker worthwhile, as it was one community, out in the world, that embraced many Trappist values, from daily Vespers to the monastic rule of offering hospitality to strangers.

At the Catholic Worker Dorothy Day "kept things fairly in hand," Stanley recalled. Even if community life could get a bit crazy at times, "You did not fool around with Dorothy Day....She never had to raise her voice—ever—but she ran the place as she wanted it run." At the same time, he characterized this tall, quietly impressive woman as "charming.... She spoke very softly, and she had a very sort of sweet, gentle smile....And when she laughed it was more of a very quiet chuckle." She was a good conversationalist, he added; even her public lectures felt conversational.

Like his friend Bob Steed, John Stanley eventually left the Catholic Worker and the Catholic Church. In his case this was partly due to clashing philosophies; he embraced Communism for a time—and at one point even labeled Merton's writing "Birchite" (as in the right-wing John Birch Society). On the other hand, in his old age, John Stanley "came all the way back to the Catholic Church," as he put it. Steed and Stanley agreed that he did so out of fear of death and, said Stanley, despite the hierarchy living like princes, "which can't last—or shouldn't last." The *Catholic Worker* obituary for John Stanley, in 2016, would be written by Robert Steed.[3]

In 1959, a decade after *The Seven Story Mountain* had changed the lives of these men, another young seeker, Jim Forest, was passing through the New York City bus terminal when the cover of Merton's autobiography grabbed his attention with its promise of a surprising spiritual journey. Mesmerized by the saga, Forest himself considered entering a monastery, but in the meantime, he read Dorothy Day's own spiritual memoir, *The Long Loneliness*. Her vivid personal account of a Greenwich Village radical hounded by God, who went on to fuse deep spirituality with committed social justice witness, prompted him to join the Catholic Worker. Aware of his admiration for *Seven Storey Mountain*, Day handed Forest a letter from Merton and suggested that the young man answer it in her stead.

Day, for her part, had mixed feelings about Merton's autobiography. She appreciated its great spiritual power but considered its concluding section somewhat triumphalist, with its lauding of the monastery over "the world." Merton himself arrived at that opinion in the late 1950s, the same point at which, not coincidentally, he reached out to Dorothy Day. In the meantime, she did not indicate whether the tremendous national impact of *The Seven Storey Mountain* influenced her to publish her own, now-classic conversion saga four years later, in 1952. *The Long Loneliness* did draw some national attention, notably a two-part feature in the *New Yorker*.[4]

But for all her religiosity, Day's pacifism, and her dyspeptic view of capitalism, caused FBI agents and American bishops alike to eye her warily at a time when most Americans saw the world as divided between "free" and "Communist." Whether Democrats or Republicans, bishops or laypeople, they perceived as threatening the anticapitalist Soviet government that had pressured Eastern European countries to set up dictatorial Communist regimes, and they were uncomfortable with China becoming Communist in 1949, the very same year that Stalin acquired the bomb, perhaps partly with the aid of American spies. Of course, historians note that the Soviets would have produced the bomb in any case. More important, most of the anticommunist "free" world was unfree—from colonial powers trying to hold on in Asia and Africa to Latin American military dictatorships—while unbridled capitalism posed its own problems. By 1959 the two superpowers were engaged in a nuclear arms race that threatened human existence itself, a situation that Day and Merton felt called to oppose as followers of the Prince of Peace.

"Some readers, and old friends too, ask us why we do not protest Russian tests as well as English and American. We can only say that we have—over and over," Day wrote in a 1957 newspaper column. "In the two talks I gave on May Day before left wing groups, I stressed the numbers of unannounced nuclear tests made in Russia," she noted, before coming to her main point: "We believe in taking the beam out of our own eye, we believe in loving our enemy, and not contributing to the sum total of hatred and fear...already in the world." Doubtless Merton read that column, for his monastery subscribed to the *Catholic Worker*, which regularly featured reviews of his books (invariably written by admirers, such as Bob Steed). And two years later she would tell him some editors of the Communist *Daily Worker*, after reading *The Seven Storey Mountain*, had forsaken the Party![5]

That was in 1959, when he had just begun writing to her. Merton was attempting to respond with integrity to an epiphany he had experienced the previous year, and nobody appreciated that struggle better than Dorothy Day. While on a monastery errand in downtown Louisville, Merton was struck by an insight so famously moving that the city would erect a historical marker on the spot. "Yesterday, in Louisville, at the corner of 4th and Walnut, I suddenly realized that I loved all these people, and that none of them were, or could be, totally alien to me," he wrote in his journal, "as if waking from a dream—the dream of my 'separateness' of the 'special' vocation to be different." The thought hit him that every person is beloved: that no matter how flawed, or even depraved, each of us was created by the Maker of the entire universe, the One who actually became a human being out of love for us.[6]

Now Merton would reach out to this woman who, for a quarter century, had been giving radical witness to society's most marginalized and despised "others": not despite being a Catholic, but because her faith taught her that all of us, most especially "the least," carry within us the spark of the divine. Her own epiphany had come three decades earlier, through a personal crisis made even more excruciating because she was torn between two opposing loves: a long loneliness, indeed.

In the pit of the Depression Dorothy Day was in Washington, DC, on assignment for the Catholic lay magazine *Commonweal*, reporting on the mass marches of the desperately unemployed. She was struck by the idealistic selflessness of the lead organizers; in fact, some of them were friends of hers from her preconversion years as a Greenwich Village radical (when she edited socialist magazines and drank with literary lights, notably Eugene O'Neill). But why were the Catholics not marching alongside "the least"—those most beloved of God? Why instead were Catholics excoriating the organizers for their Communism? She loved her faith: the faith of the immigrant poor; the faith of the saints; the faith that finally hit her with full force when she was able to conceive a child despite having feared that she could never become pregnant after an abortion. This was the faith that she believed gave her the transcendent gift of God himself in Holy Communion, but now she stood on the sidelines, alone, torn apart. Fighting despair, she made her way to Mass, for it was a holy day of obligation: December 8, the Feast of the Immaculate Conception. At Washington's Basilica of the Immaculate Conception, the young woman threw herself at the feet of Mary. "I offered up a special prayer," she wrote, "a prayer which came with tears and with anguish, that some way would open up for me to use what talents I possessed for my fellow workers, for the poor."

When Dorothy Day returned to her New York apartment, she "found waiting for me a short, stocky man…as ragged and rugged as any of the marchers I had left." The *Commonweal* editors and a Communist organizer both had recommended to Peter Maurin that he look up Dorothy Day. Now this garrulous character with the thick French accent proceeded to talk excitedly of the Church's many longstanding social justice teachings and his plan for radically living out the Works of Mercy: feed the hungry, give drink to the thirsty, clothe the naked. They would welcome "the least" in Houses of Hospitality. They would create cooperative enterprises and farms and handicraft centers. They would engage in roundtable discussions "for the clarification of thought." They would found a newspaper. They would worship at Mass, and they would recite the monastic vespers around their own plain table. In sum, they would work toward creating "a new society within the shell of the old," he said, "a society in which it is easier for people to be good." To broadcast their call, Day, the journalist, immediately seized upon the idea of publishing a newspaper. "But where do we get the money?" she asked. Peter Maurin blithely responded, "In the history of the saints capital was raised by prayer.... You will be able to pay the printer. Just read the lives of the saints."[7]

That was in 1933. By 1960, Catholic Worker Houses of Hospitality extended across the United States and beyond. Now the leader of this improbable network would provide Merton with crucial encouragement as he sought to combine a life devoted to prayer with writing that, while spiritually rooted, would directly challenge injustice. Although he corresponded with many other people who strove to bear witness to injustice—writers, artists, social scientists, activists—more than a few of them were urging him to forsake his religious community and join them in the public square. For their part, many Catholics, both within and without the monastery, argued that a monk should not weigh in on public issues, period.

Dorothy Day not only understood Merton's vision of spiritually rooted social justice witness, she also knew what it meant to be misunderstood on that very point. People on both the Left and the Right tended to downplay her spirituality, with both sides mainly noting her criticism of war and capitalism: those on the Left lauding it, those on the Right lambasting it. From seemingly opposite perches, the contemplative and the movement leader began encouraging each other in their lonely call: contemplation and action in the service of love of God and love of neighbor. As the crises mounted in the coming decade, their shared witness would prove critical to others seeking to heed that same call—and with lessons for facing any time of great crisis with integrity.

Merton's loving esteem for Day shines through from his very first surviving letter to her. That 1959 message centered on…toothpaste. Promising to send her numerous tubes that had been donated to the monastery, this monk who lived in voluntary poverty under the monastic vow of "conversion of life" paid tribute to this woman who welcomed into her house virtually anybody who was not a physical threat. As he dryly put it, this gift would help keep his community true to its life of poverty, "what's left of it." In an age of rampant commercialization, even his monastery used slick brochures to advertise its cheese, and Merton's frustration with the Madison Avenue techniques of his abbot, a Harvard Business School graduate, would eventually reach the point that Merton would compose the satirical verse "CHEE$E, by Joyce Killer-Diller: A Christmas Card for Brother Cellarer."[8]

Seriously, though, Merton made clear that he was "very touched by your witness to peace." He knew that she was among the lonely handful of demonstrators going to jail rather than participate in civil defense drills that ordered people into subway stations, purportedly as protection in the event of a thermonuclear attack. And in characterizing her passive resistance as "Satyagraha"—the "argument of suffering" made famous by Gandhi—he was citing to Day someone she had eulogized as "a modern Francis, a pacifist martyr." He also knew that his writing, in contrast to hers, was praised in many official diocesan newspapers, and he assured her that even if such Church sources scored her movement's criticisms of war and capitalism, she could take heart from the fact that her work reflected some fundamental truths.[9]

He also shared with her, in confidence, his new vocation idea: to become a hermit who would live among a people marginalized by the dominant society. He would be able to contemplate God—meditate on the divine—more constantly than was possible in his monastic community, with its many hours of community prayer and assigned tasks. Establishing such a hermitage amid people far from the seat of power would give radical witness to love of neighbor. He must have assumed that she would applaud his idea of this silent witness among the oppressed. After all, this person who herself lived among the oppressed was, first and foremost, a spiritual pilgrim—one whose own newspaper reported a new hermitage founded by the Camaldolese Benedictines in California that same year.

Instead, however, she responded, "May you be faithful unto death." Almost twenty years his senior and possessed of a less mercurial personality, Day viewed his vocation with a kind of reverence. She persisted in addressing him by his monastic name, "Fr. Louis," even though he quickly shifted to signing his letters "Tom"—and she to "Dorothy." For Dorothy Day, Merton's vow of stability—promising to stay with one's monastic community unto death—was a promise that mattered. At the same time, she made clear to him that she worried about her ability to remain faithful to her own way of life. Day experienced her own wanderlust at times, with Catholic Worker stalwarts sometimes grousing when she headed off on one of her extended lecture tours and they were left handling the inevitable crises on the home front. The problems she faced were never ending, but she trusted in God "to take me by the hair on my head...and set me where he wants me." Merton agreed that perseverance means not striving desperately to hang onto our calling so much as faithfully allowing ourselves to be carried along toward its realization.

"I am coming to think that God (may He be praised in His great mystery) loves and helps best those who...had gradually lost everything, piece by piece until there was nothing left but God," he wrote to Day. That she welcomed into her life those very people sparked a sentiment on his part that was nothing short of incandescent. "O Dorothy," he wrote,

"I think of you...and the ones no one can respect. I am not worthy to say I love all of you." Calling himself a "big, dumb phony" for desiring national prominence, he asked her for the ultimate gift: that she intercede for him to God. Not surprisingly, in her reply, Day ignored his implication that she was a living saint, instead pouring out to her new Trappist friend her many woes.

Writing from the Catholic Worker farm on Staten Island, she begged his prayers for some of the people living with her, including a problem-ridden family and a former Trappist prone to erratic if affectionate behavior. She even confided her anguish over the trials of her daughter, Tamar Hennessy, who lived a hardscrabble life in rural Vermont and was expecting her ninth child. Her husband David "tho strong in faith has many problems mental and physical," as Day put it to Merton. She well knew that her son-in-law was struggling with a drinking problem, and the following year she would be anxiously reporting to Merton that David had entered a mental institution. At the same time, it is highly unlikely that she had any inkling that he evidently was haunted by a deep, longstanding emotional wound that dared not speak its name.

Still, Day believed with all her heart that Jesus, who himself suffered so excruciatingly in this life, is especially present in our brokenness. Merton admired her for that insight, pronouncing himself "deeply moved" by her account. Society worshiped "bursting smiles and the radiance of satisfied bodies," he told her, but it is precisely the lost, the broken that God loves best. Thus, it is when we are failing that the divine especially touches us. "He will catch you without fail and take you to His Heart. Because of *the prayers of the poor* [very much his emphasis], you are the richest woman in the world, with such prayers behind you."[10]

Still, with many of his correspondents he was not about to focus on prayer. This Trappist wordsmith was a pleaser, a charmer, a connector, who met you where you could best meet him, going as far as he could to try and make his faith intelligible to those of other persuasions. In his introductory letter to Jewish psychologist Erich Fromm, Merton likened the best psychological thought to the Christian belief that we are called to discern our true identity and destiny.[11] Of all his correspondents, however, no one better represented for Merton the one thing necessary—love of God and love of neighbor—than Dorothy Day.

What other social justice activist lovingly evokes Compline, the evening prayer that has been recited for centuries by monastics worldwide? Writing to Merton from the Catholic Worker farm in New York's Hudson River Valley, she noted that they had just concluded their daily recitation of Compline and the Rosary in their chapel, "heavy with the smell of the cow downstairs," and added that his prayer intention was posted on their bulletin board. In this, her second letter to him, she again put in a plug for perseverance, noting that Merton's spiritual insights, as a monk of Gethsemani, inspired people across the land. "It is the work God wants of you, no matter how much you want to run away from it," she candidly wrote, adding for emphasis that through the decades she herself had received many a prayer from his religious community for herself and her own community.[12]

In fact, from the start, the Catholic Worker Movement had been influenced by Benedictine monastic spirituality as it developed in medieval France. Peter Maurin hailed from that land where "to walk through those streets was to walk through the Middle Ages," as Merton said of the French village in that general region where he had resided briefly in his youth. "The whole landscape, unified by the church and its heavenly spire....Oh, what a thing it is, to live in a place that you are forced, in spite of yourself, to be at least a virtual contemplative! Where all day long your eyes must turn, again and again, to the house that hides the Sacramental Christ!"[13]

The Rule of St. Benedict teaches that monasteries should offer hospitality to the stranger, as "another Christ," and this dictum inspired Dorothy Day and Peter Maurin to christen their Catholic Worker communities Houses of Hospitality. Also since its inception, the Catholic Worker has received regular donations from monasteries, and for years the most supportive community was Our Lady of Gethsemani in Kentucky: "For your great and noble work," as the abbot, M. Frederick Dunne, OCSO, wrote to Dorothy Day in 1939, three years before Merton entered that community.[14]

Indeed, in 1955, Day herself had become officially affiliated with a monastery. Taking the name Dorothy Benedicta, she was professed as an oblate, or lay associate, of the Benedictines, the religious order that spawned the Trappists. Even as she was deepening her contemplative life in the late 1950s and early 1960s, Merton was finding himself increasingly compelled to address "the big issues, the life-and-death issues," as he put it to her. The following month Merton sent Day his breakthrough social justice piece, "The Root of War Is Fear," which the *Catholic Worker* featured on the front page in October 1961. Indeed, Dorothy Day's newspaper would serve as the main platform for his trailblazing essays on the spiritual implication of the Cold War.

He had had enough: even his own monastery was building a fallout shelter, as was the monastery they had founded in upstate New York. "On all sides we have people building bomb shelters where, in case of nuclear war, they will simply bake slowly instead of burning quickly or being blown out of existence in a flash," he wrote in "The Root of War." He had even heard of people—followers of Christ, no less—saying that they would defend their shelter with a machine gun. The Kennedy administration, with the enthusiastic support of the Republican opposition, reserved the option of a nuclear "first strike." Characterizing this crusade against atheistic Communism as "madness," even "diabolical," he wrote that "the duty of the Christian... is to work for the total abolition of war." Acknowledging the issue as one of "terrifying complexity and magnitude," Merton argued that nonetheless "the Church...must lead the way on the road to nonviolent settlement of difficulties." And to the readers themselves he posed this challenge: "Christians must become active in every possible way," from prayer to patient explanation of nonviolence as an active, practical—potentially potent—force in the world. "This implies," he noted, "that we are also willing to sacrifice and restrain our own instinct for violence and aggressiveness in our relations with other people." As for those who might consider such a nonviolent peace campaign foolish: "Whether we succeed or not, the duty is evident. It is the great Christian task of our time...for the survival of the human race depends upon it."[15]

On the front page of a national newspaper, this cloistered monk renowned for his spirituality suddenly was criticizing military policies promulgated by a Catholic president and blessed by the bishops—and people noticed. Daniel and Philip Berrigan had long found spiritual sustenance in Merton's meditative writings, but this new turn on the part of their fellow priest, in the paper published by antinuclear activist Dorothy Day, prompted the two brothers to seriously rethink their support of war, even a defensive war. Their response would bind Dan, especially, to Merton and Day, with both Berrigans soon to make history as prominent, if controversial, peace activists.[16] Mostly, however, the *Catholic Worker* received letters accusing Merton of violating his monastic calling. "I am one of the few Catholic priests in the country who has come out...for the use of nonviolent means to settle international conflicts. Hence by implication...against all violence," he wrote to himself, noting that his life had now taken a decisive turn. For her part, Day reported to Merton that they were under increasing attack, and she asked for his prayers.

Soon after Merton's article appeared, the *New York Times* noted on its front page that a Catholic theologian had challenged the Trappist's argument. Jesuit ethicist Reverend L. C. McHugh defended the right of a fallout shelter owner to fire a weapon to keep others from entering if their presence would result in life-threatening overcrowding. "Nowhere in traditional Catholic morality," McHugh wrote in *America*, "does one read that Christ, in counseling nonresistance to evil, rescinded the right of self-defense which is granted by nature and recognized in the legal systems of all nations."

Merton fired off a rebuttal for publication in the next issue of the *Catholic Worker*. Interestingly, although Dorothy Day's newspaper took a pacifist stance, he nonetheless stated that families had the right to self-defense before quickly scoring "the poisonous attitude that one is being noble and dutiful if one is ready to shoot his neighbor." Squaring the two arguments, he noted, "Our rights certainly remain, but they do not entitle us to develop a hard-boiled, callous, selfish outlook, a 'me-first' attitude...which is so unchristian and which modern movements in Catholic spirituality have so justly deplored." United with Day in emphasizing love of God and neighbor, Merton declared, "A Christian is committed to the principle that Love and Mercy are the most powerful forces on earth....We must strive, then, to imitate Christ and His sacrifice insofar as we are able."[17]

Even so, Day evidently was unhappy with his defense of a violent response under some circumstances, arguing in her next *Catholic Worker* column that those "who justify a man's right to defend himself, are preaching *casuistry*, dealing with *cases* which should be dealt with in the confessional, not in the pulpit or the press." Saying that no one would go to hell for practicing self-defense if they were ignorant of what she considered the moral bankruptcy of that approach, she stressed the Christian call of every person to "non-violence, love of enemy, bearing wrongs patiently, doing good to those who despitefully use him, giving up his cloak when his coat is taken, laying down his life for his brother, in other words, living the Gospel way."

Merton immediately wrote to her apologizing for what he allowed was the unfortunate tone of his shelter ethic piece, adding that instead of thwarting their neighbor with a gun, someone who was radically living out the Greatest Commandment might well cede their place in the bunker to the person seeking entrance. Nonetheless, like most people, Merton was not ready to forswear self-defense altogether, telling her that he thought a parent would be justified in violently stopping a lunatic who was attacking their children. Trying to bridge the gap between her principled pacifism and his more pragmatic approach, the monk concluded by telling her that, in fact, his analysis was largely informed by that famed apostle of nonviolence, Gandhi. For her part, Day viewed Merton's qualified approach to nonviolence with skepticism, and this wariness would not help their relationship amid the national crises to come.[18]

In the meantime, McHugh's machine gun defense was receiving national attention, with the Jesuit even interviewed on CBS Television News in this era when virtually everybody tuned in to network newscasts. Merton responded by allowing his rebuttal to be published in any periodical that wished to reprint it. Equally crucial, he had worked to see that the piece appeared in a timely manner. This was no easy task: as a priest—never mind a cloistered monk under a solemn vow of obedience—he was required to obtain the official *nihil obstat* certifying that the manuscript contained no doctrinal error (regardless of whether his superiors agreed with the argument). Although squirreled away in rural Kentucky, Merton sent a steady stream of messages to top Trappist officials in the United States and Rome—and, at the same time, made sure to keep *Catholic Worker* editor Jim Forest apprised of the censorship process. Crucially for Merton, one of the two Trappist censors assigned to ascertain the dogmatic fidelity of "The Shelter Ethic" was a former Catholic Worker: Dorothy Day's old friend Jack English, now Trappist Father Charles. He and the other censor issued the publishing permission barely in time for the November issue. On their end, Jim Forest and the other *Catholic Worker* editors had delayed sending the issue to press for as long as they could.[19]

"I must set everything aside and work for the abolition of war," Merton wrote in his journal. But even in these private entries he did not entertain any thoughts of quitting the monastic life. In fact, more than ever the nation's most famous monk wanted to live as a hermit, even as, yes, he saw his prayer life to be increasingly devoted to the cause of peace, with his latest article on monasticism even called "The

Vision of Peace." It appeared in the September 1961 issue of *Jubilee*, the innovative periodical of Catholicism founded by some of his friends from his student days at Columbia.[20] The following month "The Root of War" appeared on the front page of the *Catholic Worker*, and over the next twelve months Merton fired off one hundred antinuclear letters. Predictably, Dorothy Day and other Catholic peace movement figures were prominent among the recipients, although this network included a wide variety of creative, influential people.

Merton planned to publish his correspondence as a book, *Cold War Letters*, but he was not about to share any of his creative lobbying strategy with his abbot, Dom James Fox, who subscribed to the crusading anticommunism promoted by *Time* magazine. Still, this complicated monk sent one of his Cold War letters to the wife of *Time*'s publisher—and a leading conservative in her own right—Clare Boothe Luce. Much more than Day, Merton consciously tried to influence leading Catholics who held more conventional views. To this Cold Warrior and fellow convert who admired his spiritual writing, Merton invoked the religion that constituted the epicenter of their lives. He used the argument that salvation itself was on the line to make the point that Christians like themselves were called to work for peace in every way possible at this time when the world stood on the brink of nuclear disaster. Doubtless he hoped that his message would reach the powerful *Time* publisher, Henry Luce, much as the monk used his correspondence with President Kennedy's sister-in-law, Ethel Kennedy, to convey his fervent wish that the president continue the nuclear test ban indefinitely.[21]

Cold War Letters would not be published in Merton's lifetime, nor would a book of essays he compiled in early 1962, *Peace in a Post-Christian Era*, for at that time the abbot general of the worldwide Trappist Order issued an edict from Rome forbidding him from publishing anything on war and peace. That he was increasingly associated with Dorothy Day didn't help matters, as when a Trappist censor blacked out Merton's reference to Catholic Workers as leaven in the peace movement.

A few months before the ban went into effect, Trappist censor Fr. Charles English had managed to persuade the other censors to allow the *Catholic Worker* to publish one of Merton's meditations on war and peace after he had agreed to modify the title. As English put it to his old Catholic Worker cohort Dorothy Day, "Actually I feel he is able to express what is a traditional Catholic position in fresh language." He also confided in frustration, "This being a censor is a delicate (and thankless) business to say the least." Delicate, indeed: it seems he never sent her the letter. His work was not made any easier by the fact that her newspaper published a Merton piece before English and the other censors had ruled on it. Likely both Merton and Day were at fault. The monk was prone to sending the *Catholic Worker* drafts without making clear that they were still at the preliminary stage, while the young editors were long on energy and talent but short on time and experience.

Merton wrote, in French, to Abbot General Gabriel Sortais, apologizing for the article having been published without the Order's permission and saying that he had arranged for a clarification to appear in the *Catholic Worker*. He also promised to publish a post-censored version of the piece in *Jubilee*. Merton couldn't resist adding, however, that British Trappists had received approval for a publication that made the very same arguments, and he noted that the United States had many more monks who criticized peace efforts as naive. Indeed, he had heard that evidently a warning about his publications had been sent to Sortais by a U.S. abbot who had been informed by one of his monks, a former FBI agent, that the Catholic Worker was connected to the Communist Party. How a Catholic movement could be considered an affiliate of an atheist organization was something never explained to Merton by his Order.[22]

Still, he accepted the ban. On one level Merton was a bit relieved to be freed from the role of "Peace Monk," but fundamentally he obeyed as a Trappist faithful to his call, telling the abbot general, "I obey willingly and with great joy." Not that this was easy. As Merton would tell religious studies scholar Huston Smith: the voluntary poverty was no problem, really, and chastity could be handled, but obedience—ah, that was the challenge![23] At the same time, Merton thought himself well within his rights, as a faithful monk, to hold a dissenting opinion in his heart. After all, Catholics are required to follow their faithfully informed consciences, and in this case, he thought it nothing short of scandalous that his religious superiors did not consider military aggression a sin worthy of comment by monks. He set up that Cold War letters network, which also served as an outlet for his growing number of unpublished peace essays, notably the mimeographed version of *Peace in the Post-Christian Era,* which would not see publication until many years after his death.[24]

Merton created a pseudonym, Benedict Monk, in order to publish an article scoring clergymen for passively accepting the nuclear threat that he considered a social sin. The piece appeared in the *Catholic Worker*: predictably, just as it was predictable that Dorothy Day would confide to him the latest challenge she faced. In an incident that would become part of Catholic Worker lore, Day informed several young people that they must move out of the Catholic Worker after they had published *F--- You: A Magazine of the Arts*. That the periodical's main founder, Ed Sanders, would play a significant role in linking the Beat generation to the Hippie generations mattered not a whit to Dorothy Day, who shared with Merton her anguish over this publication that she considered scandalously pornographic. Trying to be sympathetic, he expressed his sadness that she was having her "usual interminable troubles" with volunteers in her community, and he mused that for such young people, the Catholic Worker experience constituted "a temporary phase," as in the case of "offbeat" literature that sometimes emanated from there.

Dorothy Day was not amused. "I'm rather hurt at Merton, who talks about 'witless pacifists' and 'notorious CW,'" she confided to Fr. Charles English. But despite her use of quotation marks, there is no evidence that Merton ever wrote those words, and they do not sound like him, given his high regard for her movement, as reflected even in his private journal entries. Indeed, when he spoke of the Catholic Worker volunteers as often living there temporarily, he was echoing Day, who sometimes remarked that, for many people, the Catholic Worker was a kind of school. As for his airy reference to literary works, Merton allowed wide berth when it came to creativity. He wrote most of his correspondence to his closest friend, Robert Lax, in zany free verse, and other old friends included such creative types as the abstract expressionist artist Ad Reinhardt.

Of course, Day had to be careful, as a single woman responsible for an entire community—one that included impressionable young volunteers and near-desperate street people—but it is also true that she forbade *F--- You*'s publication on principle: as a scandalous affront to the sacrament of matrimony. She fired off a letter to Merton saying that Catholic Workers were not Beats but, rather, responsible people, many of them with professional backgrounds. Merton, for his part, did not equate Beats with irresponsibility so much as creativity, and he had not even used that term to describe Catholic Workers, but Day could sometimes shoot from the hip, at least in private: a trait that she well recognized, with her diaries peppered with prayers for patience.

Thus it was that the New York City activist evidenced much less sympathy with artistic rebellion than did the cloistered monk who yearned to be a hermit. At this time, she also groused to Fr. Charles English that Merton seemed to consider Pax the first Catholic peace organization in U.S. history, when the Catholic Worker had been carrying on such work since 1933. "I sure am an innocent," she wrote bitterly. "It is hard for me to realize how despised we are." This judgement must have hurt English, who loved her but who had joined Trappists in part due to Merton's writing. Doubtless what he meant was that he considered Pax the first Catholic organization totally devoted to the peace issue, even as the Catholic Worker—to its credit—emphasized not just peace but also economic justice and solidarity with the poor as well. In fact, it was Day who had insisted to Peter Maurin that their new organization be called the Catholic *Worker* (rather than the Catholic Anarchist).

To Merton himself, however, Day voiced a much more important reason for her discontent: that Pax seemed to exist "to take care of the fearful souls who did not want to be associated with the Catholic Worker"—presumably in its staunch pacifism. She did not need to mention that she knew Merton himself refrained from calling himself a pacifist. What she did not know was that he felt it necessary to state to the abbot general his support of the Catholic teaching allowing "just" wars. Now to Day he hinted at this predicament but made the point that while he did not oppose the Church's Just War doctrine, he did not see a single, solitary war that fit those criteria, nor did he anticipate one materializing. And although he thought that rigid pacifism could engender an overreaction on the part of the general public, he made a point of telling her that the real "scandal" was that so few Christians supported her efforts to curb war-making; indeed, her witness was absolutely "precious" to him. While not as effusive, Day did emphasize that his prayers kept them going and that they loved to distribute copies of his *Catholic Worker* peace articles to the many people requesting them.[25]

In the meantime, she told Merton that her application for permission to visit Cuba had been approved by the State Department and she asked for his prayers "that the U.S. planes do not bomb nor saboteurs blow up buildings," as the media had been reporting. In a remarkable series of articles, she brought her readers along with her to literacy programs, to health clinics, and even to daily Mass. Catholics could worship freely, she noted. And although Catholic schools had been closed, seminaries continued to operate. Regarding this delicate religious dance—one that neither Cuban nor U.S. officials acknowledged—she wrote of "my Catholic friends in Cuba who...are Fidel Castro's good cooperators, but first of all, God's servants." That she was quoting a statement that took its cue from Thomas More, the Catholic who lost his head to Henry VIII, shows that her admiration of Castro's social reforms, while real, was not naive. Merton was deeply moved by Day's accounts of life in Cuba, telling Dan Berrigan that her candid, lovingly Christian witness made him want to join her there.

Dorothy Day returned home on the eve of the October 1962 Cuban Missile Crisis. Soviet ships that were bound for Cuba laden with construction materials for Soviet-sponsored nuclear missile sites headed home rather than confront the naval vessels President Kennedy had sent to deter them, and most U.S. citizens reacted with a mixture of relief and pride. Once again Day and Merton found themselves nearly alone among American Catholics. She raised with her readers a question few Americans were asking: "Where did the Cuban people stand on the issue?" Day reprinted a letter from a friend she had made in Cuba, who reported that the island's residents were more united than ever in opposing what they considered Yankee meddling (even as she also quoted a Cuban priest to the effect that lay Catholics must "penetrate" the government programs: offering true service, but without supporting atheism). For his part, Merton was among the very few U.S. citizens who recognized that the United States itself was pointing missiles at the USSR from bases in Turkey. Only later would historians note that the Kennedy administration did in fact quietly promise to remove those missiles if the Soviets dismantled the ones being constructed in Cuba. Meantime, Merton's insight remained confined to his personal journal, given the ban on his peace writing.

Despite all the crises, Merton and Day found a glimmer of hope: the opening of the Second Vatican Council, with its promise of reform. Indeed, the Trappist abbot general had been persuaded to allow Merton to send some of his peace writings to the Council fathers, while Day would prayerfully lobby them in Rome itself. In this perilous nuclear era, with so much at stake, could the world's largest religion be persuaded to officially promote peace?[26]

CHAPTER TWO

Hopes and Fears

IN THE EARLY morning hours, before the soup line or a newspaper editorial meeting or the inevitable run to the emergency room with an ailing guest—or even before heading out to morning Mass—Dorothy Day would steal an hour or two for prayer and spiritual reading. And in the spring of 1963, that meant Merton's *The Wisdom of the Desert*, the latest book he had sent her way. This window on the ancient Christian mystics provided a lifeline for her. She had long admired the writings of these early hermits, but as she explained to her readers, Merton "brought the desert fathers closer."

She who did not shy away from an anarchist's skepticism of party politics must have appreciated Merton characterizing as anarchists these ancient spiritual writers who remind us of the "primacy of love over everything else in the spiritual life," as Merton put it, noting, "Love in fact *is* the spiritual life, and without it all of the other exercises of the spirit, no matter how lofty, become mere illusions. The more lofty they are, the more dangerous the illusion." *Wisdom of the Desert* makes clear that these hermits, with their "paradoxical lesson for our time," remind us to "liberate ourselves, in our own way, from involvement in a world that is plunging to disaster" by striving "to ignore prejudice, defy compulsion and strike out fearlessly into the unknown."[1]

Such bracing insights prompted Day to thank Merton for his "loving kindness to us." She looked forward to reading the material he shared with them, but his books often went missing in her chaotic community of vulnerable, indigent guests and fluid cast of volunteers who were often out protesting civil defense drills. When Day was jailed for refusing to seek shelter in a subway station, Merton was heartened that this faithful Catholic was highlighting the absurdity of a policy, blessed by the U.S. bishops, that purported to protect the public in the event of a nuclear attack. "There Has to Be a Jail for Ladies," he called his bold poem for the *Catholic Worker*.

This controversial protestor is the same person who offered Merton, of all things, a spare copy of the book by the ancient spiritual writer John Cassian—and this, at the very same time Merton was preparing to lecture on this desert mystic for the monastery's novices. No wonder he characterized Dorothy Day to his students as an exemplar of the ideals set forth by Cassian: that prayer should be devoid of artifice and that we should bear witness to God's hope, not facile optimism. Actually, a few years earlier, Day had been reminded of that same desert hermit when she observed a group of bedraggled Catholic Worker residents bent over in recitation of the Rosary. "Their lives do indeed contrast with that of the world," she explained, "their baggy clothes which never fit, their complete lack of self-consciousness....Who paint the house, put new pipe in it, who see improvements to be made and make them." Such insights led Merton to tell his students that Dorothy Day was akin to the medieval woman mystic Julian of Norwich, who famously wrote that, by the grace of God, "All shall be well."[2]

Not that either of these modern spiritual sojourners fell for the fallacy that desert hermits—or traditional saints, for that matter—were somehow perfect. That would be idolatry. Besides, Day and Merton both were privately wrestling with the fact that some medieval saints trumpeted conquest in the name of Christ. In his journal Merton wrote in grief of famed fellow monk St. Bernard's support of the crusades that sacked Muslim towns, and this modern-day monk vowed to make amends by advocating for peace. At that very time, in her own personal entry, Day bemoaned the crusader mentality of one of her favorite saints, Catherine of Siena.[3]

Having long admired each other's work, now as the 1960s were heating up, Day and Merton were forging a shared prophetic witness of contemplation combined with radical witness, as they confided in each other their hopes and fears. In her letter to Merton about *The Wisdom of the Desert* she took the opportunity to share her latest litany of woes. The most recent Catholic Worker retreat had been led by a priest who "was duller than ditchwater—actually put people to sleep," and she requested Merton's prayers for a young Catholic Worker who praised God for Merton's writings but who now was suffering from the complications of a miscarriage. She had married in a civil ceremony, one of several young people who recently had married "outside the Church," Day noted, reflecting her concern over the tension that was growing between her religion and many of its members regarding lifestyle issues.

Change was afoot in the Sixties, reinforced for Catholics by the historic Second Vatican Council, which opened in late 1962. Day and Merton were heartened by Pope John XXIII's call to "open the windows of the Church," but change could be difficult to contain. A growing number of men were leaving the priesthood despite the Church's teaching that the sacrament of Holy Orders confers that state for life: "Thou art a priest forever, in the order of Melchizedek." It was in this context that Day informed Merton in early 1963 that there was talk of him quitting the monastic life. She also was well aware of his restless nature, for his letters to her were replete with notions of relocating to a hermitage in New England or New Mexico or Latin America. Plus, she was just old enough to be his mother, even as she also understood the currents that had drawn him, like her, to the bohemian life in their youths. But she quickly added that his words to her indicated "that you will hold fast." Merton replied, with a tinge of exasperation, "You often mention my perseverance. I am no stronger than anybody else, but it seems to me that I am almost bound to stay here." Dismissing the rumors, he stated that the monastery might well be the only community that would accept him. "Tramp though I am…I am here unless the Lord pulls me out by the hair of my head (and there is no hair left.)"[4]

On the other hand, Day had no problem with Merton, as a priest, speaking out on controversial public policy issues. She called his antinuclear writings nothing less than "a gift from God." Much like people clinging to a raft in choppy seas, Day and Merton supported each other's lonely positions as deeply devoted Catholics upset by what they considered a dangerous American Cold War consensus. No wonder she confided to him that she was headed to Rome with Mothers for Peace to thank John XXIII for his peace statements and to request that he speak out against nuclear weapons.[5]

At the same time, as a savvy New Yorker with a journalism background, Day considered it the height of folly for Mothers for Peace to think that they could obtain a private papal audience, and she sought alternate suggestions from this monk who shared her sophisticated background but who, unlike her, also possessed something of a continental sensibility. However, he did not receive that letter until she had already returned from Rome, as the abbey censored the incoming mail. Day did not mind this policy, for she admired the monastic emphasis on keeping a distance from the outside world so as to focus on God. To her, more important than any timely tips was the sure knowledge that her Trappist correspondent was praying for her intentions, as were the novices under his charge.[6]

Meantime, in his monastery's copy of the *Catholic Worker*, Merton could read her report that the Mothers for Peace had arrived in Rome soon after the publication of John XXIII's historic peace message. In her words, their delegation represented "the 'first fruits' of the pope's great encyclical *Pacem in Terris*." Merton, for his part, also lauded this proclamation, which called for all nations to stop engaging in war altogether and for each one of us, in our own way, to promote peace. Indeed, he marveled at the pope's emphasis on dialogue with the Communists at a time when so many Americans, notably Catholics, were characterizing them as evil incarnate. Citing these points to the abbot general in Rome, Merton argued that if *Pacem in Terris* had faced the scrutiny of the Order's censors, the encyclical would never have been approved for publication! The letter was met with stony silence.

Merton's religious superiors forbade his publishing the antiwar article that he had written for the July 1963 *Catholic Worker* unless the essay appeared under a pseudonym. "Benedict Moore" was the byline for his piece "Danish Nonviolent Resistance to Hitler." This meditation on courageous nonviolent resistance as practiced by an entire nation points out that, although individuals in many countries actively opposed the Nazis, only one country offered official, total public opposition: Denmark. "The entire Danish nation simply refused to cooperate with the Nazis and resisted every move of the Nazis against the Jewish people," he wrote, noting that this response came not from some civic education program in nonviolent methods, or from any sort of nonviolent cultural heritage, but (as he emphasized) "*simply by unanimously and effectively expressing in word and action their deeply held moral convictions*."

That the Danes were able to save nearly all of their Jewish compatriots addressed the most telling criticism aimed at pacifists. Surely, it was argued, they would at least support a military response to the Nazis. Likely Merton was thinking of Dorothy Day, who had faced just such opprobrium for her lonely pacifist stance during World War II. As a young man during that conflict, he had been torn between his hatred of war and his sympathy for the British defending themselves against Hitler's bombs as they rained down on the country where he had lived as an adolescent and where his beloved father had died of cancer. But in the nuclear age, with the future of the entire world at risk, Merton was drawn increasingly toward the Catholic Worker position.

In censoring Merton, the Trappist authorities perhaps found inconsistent his lauding of resistance to the Nazis while calling for dialogue with the Communists, but, then, the pope himself was calling for just such a dialogue. And in an exchange that mirrored Merton's with his superiors, a Vatican prelate accused Day and the other Mothers for Peace of harboring Communists. She "could only reply," Day told her readers, "that if we understood the Holy Father's last plea, he wished a closer association, a seeking for concordances, and the opportunity to discuss oppositions. I would like to go through the encyclical on peace and count the number of times the word 'trust' was used." She had no more luck with this high-ranking priest than Merton had with his abbot general. This Vatican official thought the "trust" she spoke of "would be used for political purposes by the Communists," she wrote. In effect, this laywoman accused of abetting the Communists was aligned with the pope's thinking far more than was this papal bureaucrat. That such a fact would discomfit both the Curia and the Communists was an irony likely not lost on Dorothy Day, and one Merton would have appreciated.[7]

At the same time both were very aware of their own shortcomings, but it was Day who regularly remarked on hers in public. In that column criticizing the Vatican official, she went on to quote a reader who had criticized Day herself. Could the money for her trip not have been better spent on the poor? Even if Day pointed out that "that was the question asked of our Lord when he was anointed by Mary Magdalene just before he was betrayed," still, she took the charge seriously, writing that her voyage had been paid for by two donors, and she described the cell-like room she shared with a fellow pilgrim. Not that the Catholic Worker leader was complaining. Much as Merton's austere monastery was set amid great natural beauty, so this simple hostel was graced with "a delightful garden full of singing birds...and also some very active turtles," and she was writing that article in a sitting room that featured "French windows wide open on the fading light of evening."

That their peace delegation had secured decent, affordable housing during Holy Week in Rome was something of a miracle—or, one could say, was thanks to the resourcefulness of a Catholic Worker studying theology in Rome, Jim Douglass.[8] On fire with the cause of peace, Douglass had the temerity to ask Merton to lobby the bishops from his cloister by sending his latest peace writings to an American prelate who promised to distribute the material to every member of the Council.[9]

In the meantime, Day's prediction proved accurate: the hopes of Mothers for Peace for a private papal audience ran afoul of Vatican procedures, not to mention bureaucratic suspicions regarding the non-Catholics in the delegation (un-Christian though such an attitude might be). To complicate matters, Rome was full of rumors about John XXIII's rapidly deteriorating health. In the end, Mothers for Peace garnered an invitation only to the pope's weekly public appearance in Saint Peter's Basilica.[10]

Joining ten thousand other people, the disappointed women waited in line, unaware of the drama about to unfold. Once inside, they found themselves standing in the rear, their view blocked by the crowd. Suddenly a young Italian woman who spied their "Madri Per La Pace" buttons motioned to Day and two others in the delegation—pulled them, even—toward a small elevation. Clambering up, they found that they could see part of the speaker's platform and had a clear view of the main aisle. Now they stood and waited. And waited. After two hours "there was a surge in that vast mob and a sudden silence followed by almost a roar of greeting," Day reported to her readers. The procession slowly passed through the vast space, the pope in his raised chair blessing people in every direction.

One by one the delegations were announced, from Italian villagers to German schoolchildren to a group of U.S. visitors, but "our pilgrimage was not mentioned!" Why had they come to Rome? What was the point? Suddenly, as the pope spoke, she found that "the words that fell from his lips seemed to be directed to us, to our group." He referred to "Pilgrims for Peace" and expressed thanks to them for their "gratitude and encouragement." Their young Italian supporter "kept beaming at us" as she scribbled down the English translation for them. With John XXIII's words, "All those around us, seeing our buttons...smiled," gesturing back and forth between the Mothers for Peace and the white-cassocked figure in the distance. As one writer would note years later, "The pope—a peacemaker—was one of them. It felt like a miracle."

The next day a newspaper article linked John XXIII's statement to Mothers for Peace, and later that week Day was invited to meet with the head of interreligious affairs for the entire Catholic Church, Cardinal Augustin Bea. His outreach to other faiths had heartened Merton, and now this top Vatican official welcomed Dorothy Day to his private living quarters. They talked alone for a solid hour, and the cardinal asked her all about the Catholic Worker, adding that he hoped to visit the Catholic Worker on his next trip to New York. But when she inquired about the Council more clearly stating, in her words, "the theology of war and peace today," the prelate's vague response made her more determined than ever to nudge the bishops in that direction.[11]

Among her personal experiences in Rome, meantime, doubtless the most moving was the Mass in memory of Peter Maurin, with the event providing a glimpse of the deep, abiding, but very private spirituality that for her centered on the Bread of Life. As it happened, the priest who arranged for this liturgy, Fr. Urban Snyder, was a Trappist stationed in Rome who had been ordained alongside Merton and who had immediately preceded him as novice master.

On the fourteenth anniversary of her Peter's passing, Day walked down the quiet streets of early morning, headed for her very own service at Saint Peter's. In the dark, quiet basilica her heels clicked on the old stones as she made her way to the designated chapel tucked underground near the tomb of that other Peter, appropriately enough. After saying the Mass, Fr. Urban showed her Saint Peter's crypt and the resting places of recent popes, including Benedict XV, "the pacifist pope," as she boldly characterized him to her readers. But she wrote nothing of the thoughts that had passed through her mind during the Mass itself as she knelt at this spot at the heart of the Church, praying the liturgy that constituted the heart of existence for the two Catholic Worker founders. The prayers she offered before the tabernacle stayed locked in her heart—or, as she might have said, were shared with Peter and God alone.[12]

In her quasi-stream-of-consciousness style, writing amid the near chaos of her Catholic Worker community, Dorothy Day shared the lessons she had gleaned from the trip. "My general impression," she told her readers, "was…that the clergy did not know too much about any lay movements in the world that questioned either the injustices of the social order by direct action, or that tried to educate the people in the ways of peace, which would include refusal of conscription or the payment of taxes for war…and in the racial struggles…and a sharing of poverty which would be the beginning of true courage, the readiness to face suffering and death."

But while many a disgruntled Catholic might mount a protest when faced with obtuse hierarchy, or might leave the Church entirely, the Catholic Worker leader redoubled her efforts to organize at the grassroots, trusting the Spirit to do the rest. "I came away from Rome," she noted, "more convinced than ever that the particular vocation of the Catholic Worker is to reach the man in the street, to write about… the great adventure of the spirit, which can effect so great a transformation in the lives of men if they would consent to the promptings of the Spirit."[13] (In using "men" to mean "people," Day—and Merton, for his part—was conforming to the stylistic conventions of the time.)

John XXIII did soon pass away, and on hearing the sad news, Merton reflected on the boldness of *Pacem in Terris*, with its clear statement that "war is inhuman." The liturgical stole that the pope had given him hung on a nail in Merton's hermitage, and this monk who had lost his father in his teens considered Pope John something of a father figure. The grieving Trappist mused to himself that this towering but very human figure would be recognized as a saint eventually—that is, if the human race did not annihilate itself first. And according to Dorothy Day, the pope's own deathbed concern was that people were "not listening to his cries of *Pacem in Terris*." He offered up his pain, she wrote, for the success of the next Council session and, especially, "for peace in the world." She ended on a more hopeful note than Merton, for she seldom engaged in sardonic asides. "Seek concord, not discord," Peter Maurin told her, and in this newspaper column she concluded with the thought that "in his love, John XXIII will be watching over us." Still, hanging in the air was this question: What would become of the Catholic peace activists' attempt to move Church teaching in their direction, absent their most powerful advocate?

Dorothy Day had no interest in the speculation running rife over who would be elected pope, but in his journal, Merton compiled a list of likely candidates, including his favorite: "Montini." Cardinal Giovanni Montini was elected pope and took the name Paul VI. Merton sent him a letter of congratulations and, having corresponded with him occasionally over the years, received a personal reply.[14] Making no reference to the papal election in her columns, instead Day talked yet again about *Pacem in Terris*. This was no exercise in nostalgia, however, for the power of nonviolence was being tested. Lives were on the line. She used the encyclical for the frame of her talk at a civil rights rally in Danville, Virginia, last capital of the Confederacy and home to one of the most vicious police departments in the entire South, according to Dr. Martin Luther King.

Day had been asked to speak in place of the mother superior of a local convent, who had withdrawn under pressure from her pastor. He was scandalized by this sister's participation in the antisegregation demonstrations, not to mention her radio comments critical of police attacks. The priest threatened to censure the sisters and, worse, to request that the bishop shut down the projects they had painstakingly established over two decades to serve the poorest Danville residents of both races. When the mother superior turned down the speaking invitation, the person she chose to replace her was a woman who had been reporting on racial justice issues in the *Catholic Worker* for thirty years.[15]

At the next rally/prayer service, Dorothy Day joyously joined in "the Freedom songs, many of which have been composed in jail, coming from the heart," she told her readers, "from the suffering, from the open bleeding wounds of a people who have known indignity and sorrow for generations." Speaker after speaker gave wrenching testimony, often ending with a call to register for the vote even in the face of intimidation and threats. Then this tall, pale woman in the plain dress took the stage—this journalist who dreaded speaking in public. Day told herself that at least she was representing an admired local figure in the mother superior. She also was buoyed by the spirit alive in the room, plus you could not beat the material: "There was no end to what you could say about the Encyclical…the rights of conscience; about unjust laws; about the place of women, the part they had to play in the world." Referencing her work with Mothers for Peace, Day underscored the link between peace activism and the struggle for racial justice. She noted that the civil rights movement was leading the way in this regard, words that proved prophetic: Martin Luther King Jr. would be awarded the Nobel Peace Prize the following year. Finally, she drew attention to the pope's ringing call for equal rights, his declaration that anyone "who possesses certain rights has likewise the duty to claim those rights as marks of his dignity, while others have the obligation to acknowledge those rights and respect them." Later that night she wrote that theme on a placard to carry aloft at the next day's demonstration.

Upon returning to New York City, Day reflected that each person could contribute something to the struggle, be it demonstrating or donating or even providing technical assistance to places like Danville, whose textile workers were suffering the effects of job losses from automation and, increasingly, from competition with overseas factories that paid starvation wages. At the same time, Day felt as if she and other white people were responding pitifully slowly—almost too late—to the "people whom we have injured."[16]

Or, in the words of a publication issued at that time by Martin Luther King Jr.'s organization, "The purpose of non-violent protest, in its deepest and most spiritual dimensions, is then to awaken the conscience of the white man to the awful reality of his injustice and his sin." That pamphlet was written by Thomas Merton. Like Dorothy Day, and ahead of most white Americans, he recognized the providential nature of the hour. He had written an endorsement for *The Fire Next Time*, James Baldwin's searing meditation on racism, which the monk considered "tremendous." Also like Day—and like King himself—Merton linked the struggle for racial justice to the peace struggle. Civil rights activists, he wrote, recognized that whites' delusional fear of nonwhites contributed to the delusional nuclear tactics of the Cold War. And despite his cloistered existence, Merton was among the few in the dominant society to recognize that the rising generation of African Americans sought not integration so much as self-determination.

Thus his booklet was entitled "Black Revolution." Merton sensed that members of the Student Nonviolent Coordinating Committee (SNCC) were becoming impatient with situations such as that in Danville, where even the legendary human rights attorney William Kunstler could not obtain the release of hundreds of people; they had been convicted under an 1859 law enacted in response to John Brown's raid. Racial segregation and disenfranchisement were ebbing much too slowly for many in SNCC, who now were beginning to chant, "Black Power!" Merton warned that if white Americans did not learn from the civil rights movement, frustrated, trapped ghetto youth might well riot, overshadowing the heroic non-violence of civil rights demonstrators and even overshadowing the idea of violent self-defense as a last resort promulgated by the emerging Nation of Islam (more commonly known as Black Muslims). The monk fervently hoped otherwise, and he illuminated with care—affection, even—the sacrificial love of the civil rights movement: united with the suffering God of the Christian faith and offering whites "*a message of salvation*" through union in love: "*a providential reciprocity* willed to us by God."

Merton made no mention of white racists invoking the name "Christian." Perhaps he thought their religious views beneath mention: retrograde and seemingly in decline. Like most observers at that time, Merton and Day made little note of the Christian fundamentalism that would experience a great resurgence as a national movement in the coming decades. At any rate, his prediction about violence was realized just a few weeks later in Harlem. The following year, on learning of full-scale revolt in Harlem, Merton could not help noticing that he had lived on one of those very blocks while a student at Columbia University.

Whatever might happen, for Thomas Merton—as for Martin Luther King Jr. and Dorothy Day—to be a Christian meant to love, to suffer, to serve, bringing one into deep communion with others, regardless of belief. "The purpose of this suffering, freely sought and accepted in the spirit of Christ," Merton wrote, "is what Gandhi called *Satyagraha*—the struggle first of all for the *truth*, outside and independent of specific political contingencies." But the monk harbored no illusions that such love would be easy. Whites needed to respond to the injustices spotlighted by African Americans, otherwise "there will be no more hymns and prayer vigils. He will become a Samson whose African strength flows ominously back into his arms. He will suddenly pull the pillars of white society down upon himself and his oppressor": powerful stuff, and clear-headed in its warning to the "oppressor," but an unfortunate metaphor, given the racist characterization of African American men as dangerous brutes. His conclusion, however, was as nuanced as it was powerful, invoking

Martin Luther King Jr. and James Baldwin as prophets whose challenges readers should weigh for themselves.[17]

Merton also was well aware of the racial dynamics in his own monastery: like so many places at that time, it was not overtly racist but was structured in a way that privileged whites. Trappists certainly did not exclude nonwhites, but few African Americans were Catholic, and in his journal Merton made reference to the handful of nonwhites in their community with affectionate concern. Seeing the lone African American monk at work cleaning out a big box reminded Merton that the lone monk of Mexican heritage had recently left. Evidently he had some emotional problems that had surfaced, but Merton was sad that the young man would not remain a Trappist, adding that this devout monk had embodied for the rest of the community "what it means to be poor, pushed around by the police."[18]

And with words that resonate in any time of great crisis, Merton offered advice to someone yearning to make a difference in the face of injustice. Daniel Berrigan, SJ, a cohort of both Merton's and Day's ("our favorite poet," she called him), had written to Merton out of frustration—grief, even—over his religious superiors having denied his request to join the civil rights movement on its front lines: Birmingham, Alabama, where children faced the attack dogs and firehoses unleashed by segregationist police chief Eugene "Bull" Connor. The Jesuit's heart had been seared by King's recent "Letter from a Birmingham Jail," with its ringing call for his fellow clergy to place their bodies on the line—that justice delayed is justice denied. The same day that Berrigan wrote to Merton, the monk wrote to his publisher requesting that his new poem, "And the Children of Birmingham," be shoehorned into his soon-to-be-published anthology.[19] Indeed, Merton's reply to Berrigan echoed his outrage and frustration. Supposedly in the name of "contemplation," his abbot often assigned the monks meaningless tasks, but if one tried to hew to the message of the Holy Spirit as outlined in *Pacem in Terris*, one was liable to be chided for supposedly engaging in political activism. In a gesture of solidarity with his angry friend, Merton added that some members of his religious community actually were fascist.

Still, Merton was able to maneuver around many of the abbey's strictures; more important, he had made a solemn commitment to the monastic way of life, and it was in this spirit that he moved gently toward his main, cautionary point. Merton speculated that if Berrigan disobeyed his superiors, public attention would focus on the "disobedience" issue, distracting from the civil rights cause, with some people even likely to erroneously infer that his Jesuit provincial somehow supported the segregationists. Merton also questioned wedding oneself to a movement that soon enough was likely to turn violent and spin out of control. "Most important of all, you have to consider the continuity of your work as a living unit," he concluded, noting that Berrigan's writings were influencing some members of the hierarchy to seriously weigh including social problems in the official definition of *sin*. He advised his fellow priest that his lecturing and publishing would be more effective than acting as one demonstrator among many.

The Jesuit did not quit his campus assignment in favor of full-time civil rights demonstrating, although later in life, after Merton's death, Berrigan would spend much if not most of his time as a controversial peace activist. Meantime, his superiors did not object when Berrigan and some of his confreres participated in the historic August 1963 March on Washington. "Dan Berrigan will be in the big march on Washington I hear. Good for him," Merton wrote to a friend, and he noted in his journal that he offered a Mass for the marchers, citing in particular Dan Berrigan and his brother Phil.[20]

In that same journal entry, he chided himself: not for too little activity, but for too much. Despite his monastic vocation, Merton carried on correspondence akin to the barrage of emails experienced by people today, and in effect he agreed with Dorothy Day that he was called to prayer and solitude. But hadn't people he greatly admired encouraged him—as when Day called his writing a gift from God? Should he be responding to all these people, and take on all these writing projects, or withdraw into prayerful solitude? As he wrote in his journal, "How do I know?"[21]

In one of the innumerable writing chores that he undertook, Merton agreed to endorse Dorothy Day's *Loaves and Fishes: The Story of the Catholic Worker Movement,* and he reported back to the editors that he had read the proofs "with great pleasure." For her part Day was less than thrilled with the edits made by the publishing house, but she did not go public with her complaints, instead telling her readers that she was grateful to have an editor, for "When I am turned on, a flood of words come and hundreds of new pages pour out." Regarding his own compulsive, stream-of-consciousness tendencies, Merton confessed in his journal just a few weeks later, "It would be so much better if I just wrote what was really in my heart to write. But I find the other things spilling out continually....And I suppose I am as attached as the alcoholic to his bottle. Breaking it will not be simple."

For one thing, so many people appreciated his writing. Dorothy Day's publisher devoted the entire back cover of *Loaves and Fishes* to just one endorsement: "A letter from Thomas Merton." The savvy editors knew that he was a best-selling Catholic cleric whose good word could encourage people to take seriously this book by a controversial laywoman. (As Day put it at this time to Trappist Fr. Charles English, "We have been getting plenty of attacks....Birchites, of course, and diocesan papers....If it is not attacks, it is silence.") Moreover, this endorsement by the nation's most famous Trappist was a powerful one.

"Every American Christian should read Dorothy Day's *Loaves and Fishes*, because it explodes the myth that we have solved the 'problem of poverty' in our affluent society," Merton began.

> But poverty, for Dorothy Day, is more than a sociological problem: it is also a religious mystery. And

> that is what gives this book its extraordinary grace, and gentleness, and charm. It is a deeply touching and delightfully humorous record of experiences.... But that does not mean that we can afford to enjoy them and forget them. This is a serious book, about matters of life and death....Yet Dorothy Day never preaches, never pounds the table: she remarks quietly on the things she has seen....We would do well to take her seriously....It is a great pity that there are not many more like Dorothy Day, among the millions of American Catholics.[22]

Loaves and Fishes plunges the reader into the world of the Catholic Worker, starting in 1933 with the arrival on Dorothy Day's doorstep of Peter Maurin, "good as bread. Peter slept in his clothes, as the Trappists do." He assured her that, as she put it, "in the Catholic Church, one never needs any money to start a good work....People are what are important." She noted that when Catholic Workers gave away what little they had, more came in: providentially, and because "our readers feel called upon to give, and to help us keep the work going." Feeding hundreds of people each day was a constant "exercise in faith and hope," she added, recounting how Mike Wallace of CBS News asked, "With wonder rather than irritation...'How can you be so sure?'" She simply responded,

> If I were ever visited by doubts—either religious ones or doubts about my own vocation in this movement—I would accept it as a temptation, as a great suffering that I must share with so much of the world today. Even then, deep within, I would be sure, even though I said, "I believe because I want to believe, I hope because I want to hope, I love because I want to love." These very desires would be regarded by God as he regarded those of Daniel, who was called a man of desires, and whom God rewarded.

Not that any of this was easy. "Daily, hourly to give up our own possessions and especially to subordinate our own impulses and wishes to others—these are hard things." Just the simple fact of people living in community posed challenges. But citing the monastic communal rule as laid down by St. Benedict, she noted, "One man is in charge.... His authority is accepted because he has won the respect of the others around him." Of course, she was using the word *man* in the generic sense. The leader of the Catholic Worker unquestionably was Dorothy Day.

She also laid bare the horrific experience of serving jail time: the lack of light and space; the callousness of "officials who do the best they can" in a heartless system; the reality of "drug addiction, prostitution," topped off by the "apathy of the great masses of people who believe that nothing can be done." But she found solace in the "Little Way" of St. Thérèse of Lisieux: performing even the smallest acts with great love.[23]

Dorothy Day's quiet but deep witness drew people to her. "The impression was quite overwhelming: that she was *so* dedicated, and so much of a strong and fighting personality," recalled Merton's best friend, Robert Lax. He reported on Day's arrest for *Jubilee*, the magazine founded by some of Merton's old Columbia friends that took a fresh, wide-ranging approach to Catholic topics. Some of his photographs for that piece became illustrations for *Loaves and Fishes*, and he gave poetry readings at the Catholic Worker.

Lax found that these folks who were striving to live out the Works of Mercy were, in fact, also "very interested in art, and in developing their own arts, and in the arts....I did thus hit it off with that crowd," he recalled years later. In the *Catholic Worker* piece on his 1962 book *The Circle of the Sun*, the reviewer noted, "Lax has written a long poem which gracefully unites...the aesthetic and the religious, within a circus metaphor, because his concept of 'grace' functions both as an attribute of the acrobat, and as a gift of God." The next year Lax got double billing in the February issue of the *Catholic*

Worker. He was one of the leaders cited in a piece on the Catholic peace movement, and his latest book of poetry was reviewed. Channeling Lax's poetic voice, the reviewer wrote the piece in free verse!

For her part, Dorothy Day was known for her aesthetic sensibility, from her enraptured attention to radio broadcasts of the Metropolitan Opera to her delight at a geranium on a fire escape. "The world will be saved by beauty," she liked to say, quoting Dostoevsky. "She certainly did invite poets and artists to work with her at the Worker," Lax recalled. "She loved us and we loved her."[24]

At one point Lax and the other editors at *Jubilee* even permitted her to publish a request for donations, so great was their admiration for the Catholic Worker. "Beloved: That is what you are to the Lord, and to us, too," she told the readers of *Jubilee*. She and her cohorts owed the grocer $2,000 and had only one dollar to their name, but "I like writing an appeal when we literally have nothing...and then joyfully open the letters to see whom we are hearing from."[25]

Such nothingness echoed the "Little Way" of St. Thérèse so beloved by Day and Merton—and the charism of the Little Brothers and Sisters of Jesus. Peter Maurin had explained to her that these Christians led hidden lives of prayer as they worked and resided alongside the poor. After he visited some of the Little Brothers in Europe, "Bob Lax of *Jubilee* spoke at... the Catholic Worker...of the Little Brothers of Jesus of Charles de Foucauld," Day wrote in her column. She spotlighted Lax's point that "their whole life is based on that hidden life of Nazareth in poverty, hard work, and living with the poor, with no outward works, like institutions, but in silence."[26]

The next year, 1960, she began the process of formal affiliation with the Jesus Caritas Fraternity of Charles de Foucauld, as they are officially known. This woman who engaged in protests and speaking tours, this editor of a national newspaper and leader of a national movement found herself taken by their deep if humble devotion to love of God and neighbor in action. Merton was one of the people she informed of this quiet decision, for Foucauld, who lived in radical solidarity with Muslims, was a Trappist who then became a hermit. Unlike Merton, this early twentieth-century Frenchman severed his affiliation with the Trappists prior to becoming a hermit. But it should be recalled that in modern times, the Trappists did not allow their members to become hermits—at least not until Thomas Merton.

He praised the selfless generosity of spirit showed by the people of Jesus Caritas, as in a letter to Dan Berrigan. Perhaps by way of advice for the intensely idealistic Jesuit, Merton added that in his view the typical big protest movement alas all too often eventually took on a reckless life of its own. Concerned about this possibility, the following year he would organize a historic retreat for Christian peace activists, "the Spiritual Roots of Protest," which would tap Thérèse of Lisieux and Charles de Foucauld's vision of selfless, often unseen acts of love, drawing from the wellspring of God's loving mercy.[27]

"We must lay one brick at a time, take one step at a time....We can be responsible only for the one action of the present moment," Dorothy Day wrote in the concluding section of *Loaves and Fishes*. "But we can beg for an increase of love in our hearts that will revitalize and transform all our individual actions, and know that God will take and multiply them, as Jesus multiplied the loaves and fishes." Her book could well have ended with that poetic evocation of its title, but instead the Catholic Worker leader issued a direct challenge: "If those who read this will pray for the prisoners—if New York readers, when they pass the Women's House of Detention, will look up, perhaps wave a greeting, say a prayer," she wrote, "there will be the beginning of a change."

This call was echoed in Merton's blurb: "I hope," he wrote, "that those who read her book will be moved by it to serious thought and some practical action: if only to do something to support the Catholic Worker movement, which is a credit to American democracy and to American Catholicism." In the spirit of Jesus Caritas, Day sends the reader off with these words: "The greatest challenge of the day is: how to bring about a revolution of the heart, a revolution that has to start with each one of us. When you begin to take the lowest place, to wash the feet of others, to love…with that burning love, that passion, which led to the Cross, then we can truly say, 'Now I have begun.'"[28]

CHAPTER THREE

Straight but Crooked Lines

AFTER A SUMMER full of visitors, autumn came none too soon for Thomas Merton and Dorothy Day in 1963, even though they had no way of knowing that that same fall would end with a national tragedy of cataclysmic proportions. To his relief, no out-of-towners would be allowed stay at the abbey guesthouse in September, while Day, for her part, reflected, "How wonderful are those first days in September, when the summer is over and gone, with its conferences, its stream of visitors, vacationers, parents with children, students, the sick, the lame the halt and the blind—all energized by the warmth of summer to set out in search of something."[1]

Among these searchers were unmarried young people engaging in sex. The Catholic Worker leader considered "this profound force" the purest union with another and even akin to the beatific vision when exercised within the sacrament of marriage, but otherwise, "I can only consider that woman is used as a plaything, not a person," she told her readers. The exploitation that she named would find echoes fifty years later in the #MeToo movement, with its spotlighting of sexual assaults long underplayed by most people, but certainly not Dorothy Day. On the other hand, even as most people still look askance at extramarital relations, over the past half century premarital sex has become widely accepted, and this attitude was gaining traction among young peace activists.

After demanding that the unmarried searchers cease sleeping together or leave the community, a frustrated Dorothy Day vented to Merton, "The peace movement seems to be plagued by such. 'And what's wrong with it?' six young freedom fighters asked me."[2]

Merton reflected to Day on many points she had shared with him but made no comment on this one; he had chosen the monastic life over that of a parish priest in part to avoid having to deal with such issues. The wisdom of having eschewed an active vocation was brought home to him vividly a few months later when a young woman masquerading as a relative finagled a meeting with him. His personal entry described her as "a beat" who came onto him sexually, and he nearly succumbed to her allure, he added, calling her a "nymphomaniac" (one of the questionable descriptions of women—e.g., "hysterical"—common at that time).[3]

That September he put the finishing touches on the poetry collection *Emblems of a Season of Fury*. That title would prove tragically appropriate, for the book appeared on the heels of President Kennedy's assassination. *Emblems* featured several stark poems related to Dorothy Day, notably "There Has to Be a Jail for Ladies," which was inspired by her civil disobedience, but also "Advice to a Young Prophet," which offered warnings to their mutual friend Daniel Berrigan, SJ, that his own witness would cost him dearly—perhaps in blood. Then there was the ominous "What to Think When It Rains Blood" and the momentous "Chant to Be Used in Processions around a Site with Furnaces." In "Chants," Nazi functionary Adolf Eichmann describes his chillingly efficient management of mass murder. Merton's ominous warning struck a chord, as when comedian Lenny Bruce concluded his nightclub performances by reciting "Chant." Over the years, however, as memory of the Eichmann trial faded, Merton's words became less timely—or so it seemed, until the recent resurgence of violent white supremacy groups.[4]

Still, hope abides, Merton reminds us in "Love Winter When the Plants Say Nothing." It first appeared in Day's newspaper, for she drank deeply of nature, as in her stays at the Catholic Worker farms: bucolic if precarious outposts of Peter Maurin's vision of a society that promoted small farms, crafts, and cooperatives. And while the central work in this poetry collection, the epic poem *Hagia Sophia*, would seem far from the gritty realities of the Catholic Worker, in fact this paean to the mother of God has her crowning her child with the grace to be found in the poor and the dispossessed.[5]

The fall of 1963 also brought big news from the Second Vatican Council: wholesale changes in the Mass. The Roman Catholic Church's four-hundred-year-old liturgical rite would be recited in the vernacular, not Latin, with the priest no longer facing the altar but, rather, the congregation. Day, Merton, and their circle nonetheless remarked little on this radical (if gradual) shift. Changes in form, no matter how major, did not matter to them nearly as much as changes in substance: especially regarding the Church's stance on war and peace.

True, some of Day and Merton's mutual friends relished the opportunity for a more down-to-earth ceremony emphasizing God's immanence, the Spirit's intimate presence among us. Dan Berrigan celebrated a Mass at the Catholic Worker using a ceramic coffee cup from the kitchen cupboard, but Dorothy Day was not impressed with this kind of immanence. She felt that it came at the expense of an equally important value: transcendence. As she explained to her readers, "I am afraid I am a traditionalist, in that I do not like to see Mass offered with a large coffee cup as a chalice. I believe too that when the priest offers Mass at the altar, and says the solemn words, 'This is my body, this is my blood,' that the bread and the wine truly become the body and blood of Christ, Son of God, one of the Three Divine persons." This, even as she quickly added, "I speak impetuously, from my heart, and if I err theologically in my expression, I beg forgiveness."[6]

Moreover, the Catholic Worker leader took pains to make clear that "the Mass, high or low, is glorious, and I feel that though we know we are but dust, at the same time we know too, and most surely through the Mass that we are little less than the angels." Indeed, she "would not dare write or speak or try to follow the vocation God has given me to work for the poor and for peace...if I did not have this constant reassurance of the Mass." And although she found the traditional rite inspiring, with its candles and incense and ancient, universal Latin chants, Day was not wedded to any particular format. Even more, she had been drawn to the Church as a religion of the poor, of immigrants, so she welcomed a more accessible language for the people in the pews.[7]

At this time Merton sent her a compilation he had put together of liturgically themed sermons, *Seasons of Celebration*.[8] As the title implies, the author thought that many of the liturgical updates made sense, and as someone with an artistic sensibility, Merton certainly was no cultural reactionary. But he also was fluent in Latin and drew inspiration from the traditional rite, and he had his aesthetic standards. In his journal he vented about "the constant effort to achieve new liturgical 'effects,' new vessels, new vestments....Sincere no doubt in a way, but also vapid."[9] Moreover, he presciently anticipated the rebellion likely to brew among the most traditional Catholics—precisely those who deferred respectfully to Church authority—when faced with this reform issued from the top down. Still, for Merton and Day, such debates paled in comparison to lives on the line—and to Christ made incarnate in the breaking of the bread.[10]

The announcement of these planned changes, as officially issued by the Second Vatican Council in September 1963, was overshadowed by the shock of President Kennedy's murder. In fact, earlier in November 1963 another head of state had been assassinated: South Vietnamese leader Ngo Diem. Noting that this Catholic dictator's repression had led to a wave of protests by monks—Buddhist monks—Merton wrote of his disgust at "these corrupt 'Catholic' bosses...running little countries supported by American guns." Even as he asked God to forgive his nation for this policy, he found that the U.S. Catholic press was defending the Diem regime to the hilt.[11] Merton did not speak of these concerns. Most members of his monastic community, starting with the abbot, supported the South Vietnamese regime as a bulwark against Communism, an attitude typical of Americans at the time, especially Catholics. If Merton saw Diem's growing repression as violating Jesus's call of love, the U.S. hierarchy trumpeted this former seminarian as a champion of Christianity and pointed to the Catholics fleeing the North Vietnamese dictatorship of Ho Chi Minh. But these refugees were a small group, even as the typical American prelate refused to acknowledge that Catholicism was seen by the vast Buddhist majority as reflecting the legacy of French imperialism. No wonder Merton was corresponding with Catholic Workers such as Tom Cornell, who the previous year had been one of the organizers of the first nationally televised anti–Vietnam War demonstration.[12]

In November 1963 Merton was recuperating from back pain and numbness in one arm, even while praying in the cold, unheated hermitage he had finally obtained from the abbot two years earlier: the first Trappist hermit in modern times, but not the last. He eventually would obtain heating, indoor plumbing, and his own little chapel. In the meantime, he continued his many activities: the innumerable writing projects, the mountain of correspondence, the many visitors, his participation in the communal monastic prayers six times a day, and his teaching and advising duties as master of novices.

One day Merton was walking from the woods to teach his class when a Trappist brother ran up to say that President Kennedy had been assassinated in Dallas. "Of course it had to be some idiot place like that!" Merton vented in his journal. "The country is full of madness and"—he prophetically noted—"we are going to know this more and more." To Dorothy Day he wrote of the "terrible warnings" signaled by this catastrophe. She also viewed the tragedy as a warning to society, but she never failed to include herself among the culpable: in this case remarking to her readers on "the struggle in which we are each one of us engaged, a struggle between the forces of good and evil."[13]

That tragic season also marked a sad personal circumstance for Day and Merton, the illness of her old friend, and his admiring fellow Trappist, Fr. Charles English. A member of the community in Georgia, he visited Gethsemani Abbey in December 1963. There he addressed the monks, referencing Merton's works, then was making his way to Merton's hermitage when he was stricken by a heart attack. As Merton explained to Day, he had been waiting, wondering why English had not shown up. Now Merton was in charge of arranging for her to visit her ailing friend. Merton promised her a very warm welcome from the monks and made clear that he himself had long been anxious to meet her. In the end she decided against the trip, however, explaining to Merton that she had been traveling for months and needed time with her "CW family" now that Christmas was approaching.[14] They could not know that Merton's untimely death exactly five years later would mean they would never meet. Now, as the sad year of 1963 came to a close, Day emphasized the importance of Merton's writing, telling him, "A drifter came into the room to tell me he was reading your latest paperback. You will never know the good you do. I pray the Lord will continue His inspiration. It truly is your vocation."[15]

Like Merton, Day was suffering from physical ailments, but of an even more debilitating nature. Painful arthritis in her knees forced her to increasingly use a cane. More troubling, early 1964 saw the flaring up of a heart ailment that would only worsen in the intense years to come. "Cardiac problems," she noted tersely in her diary, even as Fr. Charles (Jack) English called her in a depressed state after she had not come to visit him in the hospital. Such a telephone conversation was extraordinary, given the Order's rule of silence, but nonetheless he soon finagled a way to call again, even if only to tell her that she needn't rush down to his monastery. The Catholic Worker-turned-monk missed this woman he so admired—loved, even. He didn't want to be one of those possessive types. He understood that Day was not able to write frequently; still, he carried around a photo of her, taken when she was in her late thirties. "It is very beautiful," he told her, signing off, "Love, Jack." We will never know whether she herself shared those feelings, given her amazing discipline in avoiding any hint of any romantic attraction.[16]

At this time, just as the Sixties were about to explode, it was no coincidence that the Day/Merton network was gaining traction. In early 1964 their mutual friend Daniel Berrigan, SJ, on a visit to Rome, made a "tremendous" impression on former Catholic Worker Jim Douglass, who was studying the theology of peace at a Vatican-affiliated university. As Douglass recounted to his mentor Dorothy Day, the Jesuit struck him as "one of those people (like you) who opens up all your horizons. You have the feeling that if he could only be put in everyone's living room, the world would be converted. Which is, of course, nonsense—there will always be a resistance to grace—but still some indication of the impression he made." The feeling was mutual, with Berrigan suggesting that Douglass be the Vatican representative to the upcoming Prague Christian Peace Union meeting.

The papal offices did not send anyone, while the Jesuit's own religious superiors had given him this European sabbatical to exile him from teaching at their college in Syracuse after he said Mass more informally than officially prescribed and especially after he accused some of the college's benefactors of engaging in racial discrimination in their real estate dealings. It didn't help that a few years earlier the local bishop had accused Berrigan of contradicting Catholic Just War teaching by encouraging his war resister friend Karl Meyer to set up a local Catholic Worker House of Hospitality.[17]

Berrigan complained to Merton that Vatican officials resisted any talk of peace. Not that the Jesuit was giving up. He hoped to spend the following year in Eastern Europe, albeit unofficially, and he suggested that Merton petition the pope or the Jesuit superior general—somebody—to make it happen. Merton replied that it seemed his friend had been struck by the "paralysis" engendered by religious life. The strict prohibitions against Merton's peace writings made him feel almost drugged: immobilized precisely at a time when he sensed that society was about to take a dangerous turn. From his cloister, Merton even speculated about a radical notion: that perhaps eventually the organizational Church might fade altogether.

But mostly he took a more detached, even spiritual approach to problems with Church authorities. Telling his priest friend not to get discouraged but to trust in the Holy Spirit, the monk advised Berrigan against vituperative outbursts. "First there is the problem of communication, which is impossible. Then there is the fact that God writes straight on crooked lines anyway, all the time, all the time." In his own life, the monk observed this mysterious phenomenon at work. The new abbot general of the Trappists quietly lifted the publication ban on Merton's peace writings. Quickly he collected the boldest pieces in an anthology, *Seeds of Destruction*. For the centerpiece he had a strong antiwar essay—available precisely because he had not previously been able to publish it![18]

Day also referred to God writing straight with crooked lines—and, like Merton, she was responding to a friend angry over Church policies regarding war and peace. "Of course, conscience comes first," she explained to her then–Catholic Worker cohort Ammon Hennacy, "but just the same, nothing would ever drive me from the Church.

> No pronouncements from the Pope or Bishops, no matter how wrong I thought them, would cause me to leave the Church. I would rather stop the work, keep silent and wait. The spiritual weapons of prayer and sufferings would do more to further any cause than protest and defiance. God writes straight with crooked lines, and arrogance and pride would do more to wreck a cause than any pronouncement from the hierarchy. Not that I anticipate being stopped, being suppressed by the Church.

To illustrate these straight but crooked lines in action, she pointed to a stark doctrinal paradox: that the central Catholic dogmas emanated from the faithful themselves. Citing the only teachings officially labeled by the Church as "infallible," she wrote, "All dogma such as the Immaculate Conception and the Assumption is first of all believed by the masses of the people before it is pronounced a dogma." And "it would be the same with war," she assured him.[19]

For his part, Berrigan would recall years later, "It came to something like this…gradually, and with clumsiness, through friends: Dorothy Day, Merton….Obedience, time and again, in the most painful and unpromising circumstances, shed a momentary light on the way I must go. Something happened, over which the authority had no control: the crooked line straightened." This was starting to be evident to him in 1964. Thanking Merton "for the beautiful letter…from the heart," which arrived just as his Jesuit superiors had rejected one of his articles for the second time, he added, "A long loneliness indeed," in a touching reference to Dorothy Day's autobiography, *The Long Loneliness*. In the end his religious order approved his trip behind the "Iron Curtain" to the Prague Peace meeting.[20]

At this time Merton heard from another priest who was tangling with Church authorities. Fr. William Dubay made headlines when his archbishop, Cardinal James McIntyre, banned him from preaching about civil rights. In his response to Dubay, Merton made clear that he thought the prelate's action was scandalous: making it appear that racism was not a sin. But he refused to support Dubay's call for Paul VI to remove McIntyre and advised the California cleric not to become a "rebel priest" media caricature and risk playing into the hands of the right wing.[21]

In her article "The Case of Cardinal McIntyre," Dorothy Day also took a complicated, nuanced approach to the controversy: in her case, speaking respectfully, even gratefully, of the cardinal before criticizing him. She noted that as a young priest in the Archdiocese of New York, Monsignor McIntyre had given her helpful spiritual counsel prior to her baptism. Occasionally he asked her to come into the chancery to answer criticism from the latest person complaining about the Catholic Worker, but he always treated her in a courteous, even friendly manner, she recalled, at most shaking his head and saying, "'There is the necessity of course to inform one's conscience.' And I assured him that that was what we were trying to do." As she explained to Merton, one time McIntyre told her that they held her responsible for the work of her organization, even while on a long retreat, and she chose to focus on the fact that he was implicitly acknowledging the Catholic Worker as a Catholic organization operating in the archdiocese.[22]

At the same time, in that essay she did not mince words regarding the McIntyre/Dubay controversy:

> The way I have felt about Los Angeles is that the lay people had to make their complaints directly, to priest and cardinal, demanding the leadership, the moral example they are entitled to....How can any priest be prevented from preaching the gospel of social justice in the labor field and in the interracial field?[23]

Day noted that papal encyclicals—and the words of Jesus himself—supported the struggle for respect for every person, and she spotlighted Catholics working for racial justice, including many Catholic Workers. But like Merton, she worried about criticisms hurled at the hierarchy in anger. She prayed that folks would strive for the spirit of St. Francis, who responded to obdurate prelates "with love and with respect." Thus, again like Merton, she never mentioned Dubay's name in public, let alone his demand that the pope fire a cardinal. Rather, she cited a bishop, no less, who, she said, called for "the laity to plough ahead, to be the vanguard, to be the shock troops....And to make the mistakes." She did not mention that this bishop was something of a rarity, but she did conclude by stating that the people in the pews should demand strong moral leadership from the hierarchy. Day and Merton loved the Church that so often gave them scandal, for they believed that their religion, despite so many venal human aspects, nonetheless was of God.[24]

At this time God's straight-but-crooked way was driven home to Merton personally. Suddenly his abbot surprised him by approving his request to visit Zen master D. T. Suzuki in New York City. True, Merton had argued that the opportunity would not come again; the Japanese scholar, ninety-four years old, was staying for only the month of June and could not visit Gethsemani. And, yes, the two spiritual figures had wanted to meet ever since Merton had sent him *Wisdom of the Desert* four years earlier. Still, the abbot, Dom James Fox, had rejected Merton's previous travel requests, and the Order had refused to allow Suzuki to contribute to a Merton anthology at this time when the Church still viewed with suspicion any attempts to link Catholicism with other beliefs, let alone those of non-Christians.[25]

One Catholic who did appreciate the value of such interchange was Dorothy Day, who characterized Suzuki's works and Merton's *Wisdom of the Desert* as "strangely alike," both having "done us a service." She had encountered the Zen master back in 1957, at the New Knowledge in Human Values conference at the Massachusetts Institute of Technology. She told her readers that Suzuki outshone all the other "extraordinary" presenters. Day was captivated by this slight, elderly figure, "just a layman trying to promote unselfish behavior." He warned against the worship of technology, and she could not help noting that he made this point in "an auditorium that rises like a mushroom from an unadorned newly planted acre." Suzuki's ability to connect Zen with ancient Christian beliefs really struck her, as when he compared the Zen teaching "when alive be as a dead man and then act as you will" to St. Augustine's "love God and do as you will." Merton himself came across Suzuki's description of that MIT conference, and the Trappist noted that the "consummate wit and latent humor" of the Zen master punctuated the sponsors' hyperrationalist presumptions. Reflecting on Suzuki's conference essay, Merton wrote, "If anything new can come out of human values it is from the cup of tea taken by two monks."[26]

In June 1964 the two monks sipping tea would be Suzuki and Merton. It seemed a miracle, even if "the mere thought of New York gives me stomach spasms," as he confided in his journal. Back at his old student stomping grounds, Columbia University, he could hear gunshots from his dorm room as he wrote of these "inevitable and understandable…forces." Muggings were not uncommon, he was told, and during his visit a man was murdered in the elevator of a building just a few blocks away.[27]

That same month Dorothy Day sorrowfully documented the murders and rapes in the elevators of nearby public housing projects, writing of "the unemployed youth hungry for movement, hungry to satisfy their curiosity about the world around them." Where were the teen recreation programs? Instead the federal government was offering the city ninety million dollars for an expressway that would rip through lower Manhattan, from her east side neighborhood to her old Greenwich Village haunts on the west side. "There is money for arms and for traffic," she wrote, "but not for the poor and unemployed—nothing for youth!" And she decried the "fear almost deliberately stirred up by the press, which makes whites fear Negroes and the rich the poor, and one neighborhood another." But unlike Merton—unlike most people—Day always brought the responsibility back to herself. "I write these things because I believe that each one of us participates" in adding to the tension, and she presented the reader with two stark choices: "an atmostphere…of fear or of the love which casts out fear."[28]

Day and Merton did cast out fear that tense June as they sensitively evoked Manhattan street life. She lovingly described the passing parade beneath her window, from an old woman lugging her laundry to "young women in stretch pants, pink pants, purple pants, green pants, orange pants." Uptown in his room on the thirteenth floor, Merton was "watching sunrise after sunrise over Harlem" while he prayerfully meditated amid "cries of life and joy coming out of purgatory...drums, bongos...dogs barking." Not that Merton lived in solidarity with the poor; the thirteenth-floor perspective was apt. He would dine downtown at a French restaurant on his last day of the trip—a fine meal, with wine, finished off with Benedictine liqueur—far from the world of the Catholic Worker in spirit, if not location.

Still, Dorothy Day would have appreciated the main point Merton gleaned from his visit with the Zen master: that regardless of one's spiritual tradition, what mattered was love. This encounter would spark Merton's book *Zen and the Birds of Appetite,* including an article that had first appeared in the *Catholic Worker,* "Zen in Japanese Art."[29] The experience crystalized for Merton the importance of silence and solitude. The following year he would move into his hermitage for good.[30]

Despite his remote location and ahead of most Washington policy experts, the monk anticipated that in 1965 the Johnson administration would send Marines into the Dominican Republic—a harbinger of U.S. combat forces in South Vietnam. And virtually alone in his monastic community, Merton reacted with skepticism when the abbot announced in August 1964 that North Vietnamese patrol boats had waged unprovoked attacks on two U.S. ships in the Gulf of Tonkin off the coast of North Vietnam. Noting the dark theories being floated by his religious superior about Red China's supposed interest in the whole affair, Merton watched helplessly as these reported "attacks" prompted near unanimous congressional authorization of U.S. military action in Vietnam. Eventually the administration's claims of two unprovoked attacks would be shown to be largely groundless.[31]

Sensing a growing catastrophe, Merton felt virtually helpless. Other than Day, what prominent Catholic was out on the stump decrying these government policies as contrary to Church teaching? And what Catholic publication, other than the *Catholic Worker,* was making this teaching clear? Day and Merton were the most prominent sponsors of the lone Catholic group explicitly focused on peace, Pax USA. Pax co-founder Eileen Egan was a good friend of Day's, while Merton supported the group from its beginnings, in 1962. "We know you will be with us in the Holy Spirit," Egan assured him.

In the meantime, Catholic Worker Jim Forest broached with Merton the idea of forming a Catholic Peace Fellowship. The monk worried that it might overlap unduly with Pax but decided that was not likely, given that CPF would be strictly pacifist and would counsel young men on avoiding the draft on conscience grounds, while Pax included members who adhered to the Just War theory and focused on trying to influence the typical American, including the typical bishop. Soon the young CPFers were barnstorming high schools and colleges to inform students that Catholics could be conscientious objectors—this, at the very time when an Americanized Vietnam War seemed increasingly likely. Both Catholic peace organizations had a role to play, Merton noted to Egan, as he lauded the efforts of her group to change the minds of Cold War Catholics. Pax offered thoughtful, diplomatic outreach/ breadth; CPF offered more passionate commitment / depth.[32]

In the summer of 1964 plans for the CPF crystalized when far-flung Catholic peace activists finally had a chance to meet up at the peace conference in Prague hosted by the International Fellowship of Reconciliation (IFOR): Jim Forest from New York City; Dan Berrigan, in the midst of his European travels; Jim Douglass from Rome; and Hermene Evans from Chicago. Evans had been the first Catholic to join Fellowship of Reconciliation, and she now apprised Merton of the Prague activities. (She also had co-sponsored Day's trip to Rome with Mothers for Peace.) "Walking the streets of Prague, they determined to found the Catholic Peace Fellowship within the Fellowship of Reconciliation," recalled Tom Cornell, who became the CPF co-director with Jim Forest.[33]

Cornell also noted, "Without Tom Merton the CPF would not have been possible. Who was Jim Forest? Who was Tom Cornell?" The monk prevailed upon some of his prominent New York friends to provide CPF with their contacts for the infant organization's fundraising letter. As Cornell put it, "Without his moral authority and without the financial support that that elicited, CPF would not have come into existence."[34] In October 1964 the Catholic Peace Fellowship newsletter first appeared. The masthead featured as sponsors Merton, Day, and some of their spiritual cohorts, from Merton friend (and Day admirer) Robert Lax to Bede Griffiths, the English Benedictine monk known for his Indian ashram. On his recent American lecture tour he had visited Merton at Day's suggestion. She had appeared alongside Griffiths at a forum and had touted his conversion memoir in the *Catholic Worker*. In her diary she reflected that Dom Bede's loving approach to Hindu piety echoed the Little Way of St. Thérèse, which urges us to do everything with love. Merton wrote at that time in his journal of the visiting Benedictine monk's "impressive" Zen-influenced liturgy. For his part, Griffiths considered his visit to Gethsemani the highlight of his U.S. visit.[35]

The founding of the Catholic Peace Fellowship prompted Merton to offer a retreat on "The Spiritual Roots of Protest," as he called it. The monk needed to host the event, otherwise he could not participate, given the travel restrictions imposed by his abbot. Holding the event at his abbey, however, meant that women could not attend, as the Gethsemani guest house lacked sleeping facilities for women. Thus one of the original CPF supporters, Hermene Evans, was excluded, as was CPF sponsor and, arguably, godmother, Dorothy Day. Her absence from the planning and execution of the retreat may help explain the fact that 1964 was the only year during the 1960s that she and Merton did not correspond. Female participants probably could have stayed just down the road, with Merton's friends the Sisters of Loretto, but the question of women's attendance was not even raised in this era when men held virtually all the official leadership roles in society, from politics to business to the arts to religion—and, yes, even in radical social movements. Still, Merton was ahead of his time in the sense that the following month, at his invitation, Mother Mary Luke Tobin, the mother superior of the Sisters of Loretto, lectured to the monks on her impressions as an official observer of the Second Vatican Council. "Mother Luke"—as Dorothy Day called her—would give a presentation about these historic events at a Catholic Worker meeting some years later.[36]

The thirteen men who participated in Merton's retreat were something of a "who's who of radical Christian leadership," in the words of Berrigan protégé Fr. John Dear. Virtually all were affiliated either with the Catholic Worker or the Fellowship of Reconciliation. And serving as a bridge between the two groups were the Catholic Peace Fellowship folks, with their links to both the Catholic Worker and FOR.

Such a gathering was "unheard of…would not have been allowed in any parish" as of 1964, Dear notes. And inviting Protestant pacifists to speak? No diocese would do such a thing. This trailblazing event—in a remote Kentucky monastery, of all places—included the most legendary Protestant pacifist of all: A. J. Muste. Almost eighty, this unassuming man with thick glasses and trademark fedora had been active in FOR since its inception in 1915. Along the way he founded several other important peace groups, participated in civil defense protests alongside Dorothy Day, helped create the prominent civil rights group Congress of Racial Equality, and forged close ties to Martin Luther King Jr. For his part, Merton would recall Muste's quiet but profound contributions to the retreat. While there is some indication that King himself was considering participating, he had to put aside all his plans to travel to Oslo to receive the Nobel Peace Prize.

On a rainy day in November 1964, the retreatants wound their way from the Louisville airport through the Kentucky hills to Gethsemani Abbey, where they were greeted by a stone arch that, appropriately enough, bore the inscription

Pax Intrantibus, "peace to all who enter." Their Trappist host welcomed them warmly and handed out a mimeographed list of themes he had worked out in consultation with Berrigan and FOR leader John Heidbrink (who was unable to attend, even though he had been the first person to raise the peace retreat idea with Merton). At each session a person would give an informal presentation and then lead the discussion, starting with Merton.

Atop his handout Merton had typed "jhs," the Greek abbreviation for Christ: a small, subtle indicator of the Way that guided all these peacemakers. At the same time, he reminded everyone that the Inquisition was not defunct; Christian peace protestors often faced attacks from within their own religious denominations. Nonetheless, they were called to bear witness to societal evils. "In a world in which total war at times seems inevitable….What we are asking," Merton noted, "is not the formulation of a program but a deepening of roots…in the ground of all being, in God….Standing in the presence of His word, knowing we are judged by it."[37]

The monk then posed a challenge regarding their own motives: "*By what right* do we presume that we are called to protest, to judge, and to witness?" Jim Forest had never considered that question, and the twenty-four-year-old Catholic Peace Fellowship leader carefully recorded Merton's elucidation: "The protestor has to remember that no one is converted by rage, self-righteousness, contempt, or hatred." Sometimes confrontation is necessary in the face of evil acts, said Merton, but any such demonstration must be rooted in love: "Until we love our enemies, we're not yet Christians."

Merton was drawing on the notes he had taken from the writings of that other Trappist-turned-hermit, Charles de Foucauld, who in the Syrian desert of the early twentieth century wrote, "One is good not because of what one says or one does but because of what one is…the extent to which our acts are acts of Jesus working in us and through us." As exemplars of such radical love, Merton cited the nonviolent resisters to racial segregation in Birmingham, Alabama, who refused to hate the police chief who used attack dogs against them. Forest's Catholic Worker lodestar Dorothy Day also famously emphasized loving one's opponents, in the spirit of the Jesus Caritas Fraternity of Charles de Foucauld, of which she was a member. Indeed, she led the way in linking activism to a deep prayer life, including retreats. Now Merton's retreat underscored the deep connection between loving God/neighbor and fighting injustice. Drawing from a life of meditation on spiritual sources, this contemplative tapped a hidden spring from which authentic protest, rooted in love, could flow.

And anticipating a danger we especially face today, Merton asked, how do we harness technology without having it harness us? Day herself regularly sounded the alarm on this issue (as in her article lauding Suzuki), but as of 1964 this problem was not at the forefront of most people's minds, and at the retreat Merton's prescient challenge was left hanging in the air. The next day Berrigan presented on the combination of theology and science laid out by his fellow Jesuit, Pierre Teilhard de Chardin, but as Merton later described it to his novices, "Of course Dan was lively...talking about Teilhard de Chardin....'There's going to be a wonderful new civilization, and it's all going to be ducky'" (followed by laughter from the class). For his part, the Jesuit found himself bowled over by the simple but radical notion of the next presenter, Mennonite theologian John Yoder: that everything centers on Christ.

What matters, Yoder said, is protest that bears witness to God made manifest in every person through the incarnation, rather than protest that calibrated the results of every action. Catholic Peace Fellowship co-founder Tom Cornell, of the Catholic Worker, was not moved by many of the presentations, but he recalled that Yoder's "theology of the cross was so clear, so beautifully put....How are we going to save ourselves from blowing ourselves up, except by forgiveness? And being willing to accept suffering." Yoder's reflections on the challenge that Christ the peacemaker poses for Christians went to the heart of the matter. And it was Yoder who recorded in his notes that as the retreat was drawing to a close, Merton invoked Foucauld's Little Brothers as emblematic of simply staying where you reside and doing your peace work there, in place. The reminder that we do not have to go chasing after publicized events in pursuit of social justice brings to mind Dorothy Day saying that "radical" means going to the root. And, of course, the retreat was called "The Spiritual Roots of Protest."[38]

Regarding Yoder himself, however, a tragedy of Shakespearian proportions would emerge a dozen years later, with many young women coming forward to provide credible stories of sexual harassment. Reflecting on this in 2014, the *Christian Century* asked, "Do Yoder's violations of his own theological claims...disqualify him from the major role he has played in modern Christian thought?" The article concluded that "against his best efforts, John Howard Yoder cannot escape God. [Yoder's] *The Politics of Jesus* is one of the great texts of Christian discipleship. It will remain that way not because Yoder's life warrants that place in history but because God providentially uses the fallen for good."[39]

Meantime, as the retreat was concluding, Merton wrote to himself that the experience had been "remarkably lively and fruitful." Years later Berrigan would recall the meeting as having provided essential support in a world that tended to see Christian peacemakers as unrealistic, if not ridiculous: whether for their peace stance, or for their belief in the incarnation—or both. In our own time, prominent peacemaker Fr. John Dear, who has been so influenced by Berrigan, Merton, and Day, reflected that "such gatherings are needed today more than ever...where ordinary Christians could gather to share, reflect, and pray...on climate change, drones, global poverty, nuclear weapons, executions, mass incarcerations... and the spiritual roots for peacemaking." And for all their radical connotations, such concerns are in line with Catholic teaching, as Merton and Day would well recognize.[40]

CHAPTER FOUR

Lives in the Balance

AS 1965 BEGAN, Thomas Merton, Dorothy Day, and their allies shared a sense of foreboding over the growing conflict in Vietnam—with so many lives in the balance—but at that time, the general public's attention was taken up with the Great Society. People watched with amazement as President Johnson persuaded Congress to pass a historic number of bills, each of them major, from immigration reform to Medicare to the Clean Water Act to the historic Voting Rights Act, and on and on. Then there was the Great Society's biggest component—something else altogether. Officially known as the Office of Economic Opportunity (OEO) it constituted an all-out War on Poverty through such programs as Head Start, food stamps, the Job Corps, and Community Action.

The dynamic, upbeat OEO director, Sargent Shriver, was a Kennedy in-law who had a wealthy lifestyle that contrasted with both the Catholic Worker and the Trappists, but he nonetheless considered Day and Merton spiritual heroes. Shriver himself, in his previous role as founding director of the Peace Corps, had inspired many young people to selfless service in poor regions of the world, and now he applied his idealism to fighting poverty. Trying to base his life on the Greatest Commandment, Shriver unobtrusively but faithfully attended daily Mass, casually cited Merton to aides, and as far back as the 1930s, as an undergraduate, had invited

Dorothy Day to speak at Yale. Now in 1965, amid the hectic War on Poverty planning, Shriver made time to arrange for a Mass in his family living room led by Dan Berrigan, an experience the Jesuit found simply amazing.[1]

Merton himself lauded the War on Poverty in a letter to President Johnson but focused the message on Vietnam, urging LBJ to seek a peaceful solution. Indeed, before 1965 ended, Merton would regret having voted at all, his grief about the war having completely overshadowed his admiration for the Great Society. Day, in the meantime, had been skeptical of the program from the outset. Her quasi-anarchist sensibility predisposed her to view big government programs negatively. When a reporter asked her for suggestions on ways people could support the War on Poverty, she instead cited grassroots aid projects independent of the government.

This interview, with the Atlanta diocesan newspaper, took place in Conyers, Georgia, where she was visiting her old friend Fr. Charles English at the Monastery of the Holy Ghost. The abbot invited her to speak to this Trappist community that she characterized to her readers as a spiritual "powerhouse," adding that she had been "begging prayers" from the monks, especially for the civil rights organizers she would be visiting in Alabama and Mississippi, but also for herself. To herself, however, she confided her worried prayers for her Trappist friend: "Sick in pain, a compulsive talker," sneaking the occasional drink or smoke, "'hanging on by his fingernails,' as the saying is." Even so, English's religious order had tapped him as one of the two official censors of Merton's works, which had proven fortuitous for the author.[2]

The following month Day spoke at a very different venue: The Center for the Study of Democratic Institutions (CSDI). The CSDI vice president, W. H. "Ping" Ferry, had attended Merton's peace retreat at his invitation. Merton understood the foundation world, as he had recently written letters of recommendation to the Guggenheim Foundation for his poet friends Bob Lax and Dan Berrigan. A few years earlier the monk had even looked into applying to the Ford

Foundation for a grant to commission a Louisville firm to design his hermitage. Dorothy Day, with her critical view of capitalism, would never consider applying for a grant from a corporate foundation. Still, one CSDI administrator, John Cogley, was a former Catholic Worker, while the moderator introduced her by saying, "No person qualifies better as a witness in our time than Dorothy Day."

Day opened her remarks by emphasizing personal responsibility as the main tool for resolving society's ills, prompting one of the hosts to ask if she thought that social problems would be solved by her approach. "It isn't my approach," she replied. "It's 2,000 years old; the problem is… it hasn't been tried." Ping Ferry pointedly asked if government ever has a role to play, and she conceded the point, recalling that migrants near starvation had been aided by New Deal programs. Day also may have been thinking of the Great Society practical nursing program that her own daughter was attending. As she mordantly put it in a letter to Merton at that time, "Holy Mother the State helps with its retraining program." She knew that we all make our compromises, for none of us are God. Perhaps that is why this woman who thought that the second cloak in her closet belonged to the poor did not presume to tell affluent people to give away all their possessions. Still, her radical witness to love of God and neighbor inspired elite figures such as Ping Ferry and Sargent Shriver to redouble their own efforts to help build a society in which it would be easier for people to be good.[3]

Well ahead of such sophisticated policy players, Day and Merton sensed a tragedy unfolding in Southeast Asia. In February 1965 the Johnson administration began systematic, open-ended bombing of North Vietnam in retaliation for an attack by insurgents on a Marine base in South Vietnam. Merton immediately grasped the gravity of the decision, characterizing it to Berrigan as "sickening." Indeed, by the end of 1968 the bombers of Operation Rolling Thunder would drop more bombs on little North Vietnam than were unleashed by all belligerents in World War II, with little discernable effect on the course of the war. Moreover, a bombing campaign of this magnitude required American troops to protect the airbases in South Vietnam, leading almost inescapably to direct U.S. combat.[4]

Merton was near despair that so many U.S. bishops seemed to equate this policy with the will of God—as he put it to Jim Douglass. The young theologian and former Catholic Worker had begun teaching theology near Merton's monastery, at Bellarmine College in Louisville. Not coincidentally, their commencement speaker that year was Daniel Berrigan. The two men planned to visit Merton, who was "delighted" at the prospect, even though he thought that his days of hosting visitors were at an end, now that he had taken up the life of a hermit. Still, he arranged for his guests to come directly to the hermitage without passing through the monastery's entrance. They would not be the last to do so. Merton would turn out to be a complicated hermit, with critics arguing that he was trying to have it both ways. Psychiatrist Gregory Zilboorg, who had seen Merton a couple of times, quipped that the monk wanted to have a sign in Times Square that read, "Thomas Merton—Hermit." (The Broadway-related jab is interesting, given that Zilboorg was known as the therapist to the Broadway stars.) But Merton's complicated type of solitude was, in part, a recognition that monastic life was inextricably intertwined with the larger society. And even with all his temptations toward the trendy, still, he would come to see that his fullest engagement with the world came precisely in his deepest moments of spiritual contemplation. Among the main people helping him parse all of this would be Dorothy Day.[5]

That visit to Merton's hermitage reminded Berrigan of the two disciples encountering Jesus on the road to Emmaus: not that their host was anything close to divine, but that Merton offered—embodied, even—a centeredness in which to more deeply encounter the divine. In fact, he had just finished writing a book-length meditation on "the higher and deeper fulfillment" that he felt God demands of the Christian.

This spiritual insight derived from a surprising source for a Catholic author: the ancient Chinese philosopher Chuang Tzu, whose insights prefigured Zen Buddhism. Merton had discovered that "for Chuang Tzu, as for the Gospel, to lose one's life is to save it, and to seek to save it for one's own sake is to lose it." This approach means "abandoning 'the need to win'....One may call this humility 'cosmic' because it is rooted in the true nature of things...for 'when the shoe fits, the foot is forgotten.'" Merton made clear that neither he nor this venerable Asian writer thought abnegation meant turning away from life. After all, Merton admired the abnegation of the Little Brothers and Little Sisters of Jesus, who lived among—lived as—the urban poor. And even as he wrote about detachment in *The Way of Chuang Tzu*, Merton kept up his vast, wide-ranging correspondence, including an appeal to the pope himself on Berrigan's behalf. Praising Paul VI's own peace statements, he begged his assistance for the Jesuit, who had been silenced by his Order after signing a peace petition. In contrast, *The Way of Chuang Tzu* had clear sailing with the Trappists; indeed, censor Fr. Charles English was reading the manuscript for his own spiritual edification.[6]

Meantime, Merton discovered an amazing personal synergy with someone in close connection with Dorothy Day, Canadian psychiatrist/author Karl Stern. Stern telephoned her at this time asking for her prayers and those of the Trappists: this, right when she happened to be discussing a Merton essay with her fellow Catholic Workers. Merton then informed her that the coincidence went even deeper, for at that moment he was reading Stern's latest book, *The Flight from Woman*. He noted approvingly Stern's critique of overly rationalist thinking, as when he wrote, "The hand of Wisdom, Sophia the maternal, is rejected" by too many men in favor of a cramped, ahistorical, unartistic approach to life. Merton had recently published *Hagia Sophia* in part as a recognition that he had largely ignored his own feminine side, and now, while reading *The Flight from Woman*, he wrote in his journal about "the part of the garden I never went to...the true (quiet) woman I never really came to terms [with] in the world. And because of this there remains an incompleteness that cannot be remedied." That hunger, that void, would be met the following year by the most blissful and excruciating personal experience of his monastic life.[7]

When Merton's letter to Day praising *The Flight from Woman* arrived at the Catholic Worker, Stern happened to be visiting her, and it could not have come at a better time, Day told Merton, as the *New York Times* had panned the book, even if novelist Caroline Gordon liked it. Five years later Kate Millett would lambast *The Flight of Woman*, finding Stern's male/female categories rigid, even deterministic. Such an argument would not sway Day, who had no patience with feminist theory and precious little interest in gender analysis of any sort. Besides, she influenced Stern more than he influenced her, the Jewish refugee crediting her as an important person in his early years as a Catholic.[8]

Merton's writing mattered much more to Dorothy Day. She used his latest *Catholic Worker* article, about a heroic priest, as the centerpiece of a retreat she was holding for a group of priests. Fr. Alfred Delp, SJ, was beheaded for defying the Nazis. Day herself had praised Delp in a newspaper piece a dozen years earlier, but in Merton she had one of the nation's most prominent priests showcasing this priest-martyr in compelling prose. This clerical subtext was important, given that these priests' superiors were constantly harping on the need to unquestioningly support American military engagements. Thus did Merton, despite his remote locale, support this amazing woman who regularly hosted retreats *for* priests—those symbols of authority over the laity—retreats that posited moral stances often at variance with those of the retreatants' own bishops.[9]

Merton also learned from her the difficulties of holding a spiritual retreat in their noisy, fluid Catholic Worker community; a pair of drug users had tried to set up shop, for one thing. In particular, though, she shared with him her personal problems, especially requesting his prayers for her daughter's husband, the father of her nine grandchildren, who had experienced a nervous breakdown. Merton assured her that he was happy to hear from her and that she most certainly was often in his thoughts and prayers.[10]

This was in the summer of 1965. They were gearing up for the final session of the Second Vatican Council that fall: their last chance to persuade the world's largest religion to move toward condemnation of war itself and support for the right of every man to avoid military service on the grounds of conscience.[11] This goal took on urgent new meaning that same summer when the Johnson administration began the fateful, open-ended commitment to engage U.S. troops in direct combat in Vietnam. Even though Merton had started living as a hermit nearly full time, he witnessed the change in strategy, for the military traffic was increasing in the skies above the woods where he walked in contemplation. Finding his new life full of "peace, silence, purpose, meaning," nonetheless he wrote detailed letters to various sympathetic bishops, suggesting specific modifications to the war and peace section of the proposed Vatican Council statement about the Church.[12]

Writing to Merton that she was cautiously optimistic, Day told him that she was considering joining those Americans in Rome who would be lobbying the Council fathers. Among those leading the way would be her good friend Eileen Egan of Pax USA. Day readily agreed to Egan's idea that the July–August *Catholic Worker* be entirely devoted to peace proposals for the Schema, and that a copy of the newspaper be distributed to every Council member. Egan aimed to counter the literature in favor of nuclear deterrence that these bishops had received from a Catholic organization that was trying to head off Pax's influence. As Egan explained to Merton, that issue of the *Catholic Worker* was sent to the newspaper's eighty thousand subscribers as well as to all the U.S. bishops—well, almost all of them. She refrained from alerting those prelates most strongly opposed to her organization's stances, even if she could not keep the Catholic chaplain of the U.S. armed forces, Cardinal Francis Spellman, from getting a copy. As archbishop of New York, he was on the mailing list of this newspaper that was published in his archdiocese. As she confided to Merton, "What a dreadful struggle we will have to keep whatever of strength there is in Schema XIII. Cardinal Spellman jumped the gun in condemning the right of conscience in war (right after he upheld the right of conscience in religious matters)."[13]

The *Catholic Worker* "Special Issue—War and Peace at the Vatican Council" featured "The Council and the Bomb" by Jim Douglass, while sociologist Gordon Zahn and two nationally known clerics answered the nuclear deterrence advocates. But it was Dorothy Day who spoke to the heart, taking the reader with her as she recounted her post-communion meditation that very morning. In those silent minutes praying before the Blessed Sacrament, her thoughts had traveled to the disciples "huddled together fearfully after Jesus' death, still hankering for a worldly victory....But after the Holy Spirit enlightened the apostles they...embraced the cross, laid down their own lives for their neighbors, in whom they were beginning to see Christ." And despite the "worldly" priorities of so many in the Church, "We long with all our hearts for such a statement from the Bishops, clear, uncompromising, courageous[:] 'Inasmuch as ye have done it unto one of the least of these my brethren you have done it unto me.'"[14]

Merton's own piece in the next issue of the *Catholic Worker* appeared just as the final session of the Council was opening in September 1965. Everybody in the Catholic peace movement—from the more moderate folks in Pax to the young pacifist activists in CPF—was grateful for this piece, Day assured him. Merton chose a very traditional frame, invoking a saint from the seventh century in this essay, "Saint Maximus the Confessor on Peace." To be a Christian meant to love one's enemies, wrote Maximus, who emphasized that we end up in conflict with others when we privilege our own desires. Merton noted the importance of voluntary poverty, and nobody knew better than the bishops themselves that the author and the *Catholic Worker* editors were living in voluntary poverty. Anticipating Merton and Day in the most fundamental of ways, Maximus concluded that our hearts should be centered on the Greatest Commandment. "And what is this commandment?…'This is my commandment: That you love one another.'"[15]

But if the "Saint Maximus" essay met the Council fathers where they were by invoking a saint from antiquity, Merton's other article that month offered a direct challenge to them. In "An Open Letter to the American Hierarchy," he declared, "You, the American hierarchy, will be sitting in the Council as citizens of a nation which is waging an undeclared war…the escalation of senseless warfare." He stressed that the Council members, like Christians in general, were "called to obey the Gospel of love." One can sense his deep grief, mingled with amazement, at "a nefarious fascination of those theologians who are willing to equate 'controlled use' of nuclear weapons" with self-defense. He countered that the Church must use its global platform "to disagree with 'the world' in the most forceful terms."[16]

Unlike Day, however, Merton was willing to go along with parts of the Just War position, noting that the Church has long conceded to nations the right "to defend themselves by just means against unjust attacks." Perhaps that is the reason he did not send the piece to her editors, even as, in taking this position, he resembled her good friend Eileen Egan and Pax. It was Egan, not Day, who lauded it.[17] Still, Merton and Egan were one with Day on the larger point: that the Council, in his words, should "unequivocally" condemn "the indiscriminate slaughter of *all* [his emphasis], combatant or non-combatant." Doubtless he had Day in mind when he added this challenge: "Catholics must therefore actively and intently study the new methods of non-violent resistance in order to use them in a truly Christian way."

And what did he mean by "a truly Christian way"? For Merton, as for Day, it always came down to "The Gospel message…summed up in the New Commandment of reconciliation and love," as he put it in his letter to the bishops. "What matters is for the bishops and the Council to bear witness clearly and without any confusion to the Church's belief in the power of love to transform not only individuals but society." He ended with a stark challenge to these prelates who knew the Gospel demands by heart: "Do we or do we not believe that love has this power? If we believe it, what point is there in using language of adroit compromise in order to leave the last word...not to the Gospel, but to power politics?"[18]

While sailing to Rome, Day seized the opportunity to share Merton's *Catholic Worker* essays with the thirty-some bishops on board. Then on September 15, 1965, both she and Merton wrote the feast day, "Exaltation of the Holy Cross," atop their personal entries marking the opening day of the fourth and last session of the Vatican Council. She turned down the opportunity to attend a strategy meeting with a sympathetic cardinal and a major donor in order to witness the solemn opening liturgy, noting, "The Mass was tremendous, sung. I could have wept at the Sanctus." She and Jim Douglass then stood for two more hours as the bishops processed into the sanctuary. With her arthritic knees and weak heart, how she wished she had brought along a seat!

Day found the grand Roman churches a mixed blessing, as she confided to a friend: "horribly ornate, colossal, but fascinating for historical and holy reasons...all permeated with prayer, with suffering." Back in her little room piled high with copies of the *Catholic Worker*, she began each day with prayer, then headed out to Mass. Often she worshiped alongside Douglass, Egan, or Hildegard Goss-Mayr, the European peace activist who would deeply impress Merton when she visited him later that fall. "A warm, fine, lovely person, radiating the spirit of Christ," he would record afterward, adding that she encouraged him to do more writing on peace.

As it happened, one of Merton's fellow Trappists, stationed in Rome, was often the celebrant at the daily Mass that Day and her companions attended. Then after a quick coffee and brioche, she was off to meet with various bishops and cardinals, many of them at their invitation, such as Bishop John

Wright of Pittsburgh. He was well versed in the issues, having received from Merton a prepublication draft of "An Open Letter to the American Hierarchy." Like Day and Merton, the prelate was a sponsor of the Catholic Peace Fellowship, and he cautioned his confreres against relying on the views of military analysts regarding what he called "our hellish weapons."[19]

Dorothy Day's own weapons were the weapons of the spirit, and she was being heard, but it would be in cloistered silence that she would make her most powerful statement. "Twenty Women Fast for Condemnation of Nuclear Weapons by Vatican Council" read the *New York Times* article by former Catholic Worker John Cogley. Taking "nothing but water," he wrote, the women would fast and pray during the ten days that the Council were deliberating on the war and peace section of the Schema. "The purpose of the fast," as Cogley put it, "is to supplicate...for a total condemnation by the Council of nuclear weapons and the military policy of nuclear deterrence." He also pointed out, "The one American in the group is Dorothy Day, 67."[20]

On the eve of the fast, Day met with a prelate who would prove a strong supporter of theirs at the Council. Like Merton, he was a prominent monastic: Rev. Christopher Butler, OSB, head of the English Benedictine Congregation. Dom Christopher had had a large hand in the war and peace draft then before the Council members, and he assured Day that he would tell the Council fathers that believers in Jesus did not need to rely on military might. Actually, the statement that his own committee had submitted for consideration just two weeks earlier had argued just the opposite: that nuclear deterrence was morally justified under some circumstances. Jim Douglass had changed the abbot's mind. As he subsequently noted to the young theology student, "On the question of peace you have to be very patient with us. We have to come a long way in a short time." Impressed by his meeting with Day—herself a Benedictine oblate—this leading Benedictine showed up the next day to support the twenty women as they began their prayerful fast.[21]

During the Council debate a few days later, Butler stood up and proposed that the Council delete the very sentences that he had helped draft, declaring, "We should not speak... about the legitimacy of preparations for nuclear war....The intention to wage war unjustly is itself unjust....The weapons of the gospel are not nuclear but spiritual; it wins its victories not by war but by suffering." The suffering and prayers of Day and her soulmates were never far from Butler's mind, including the knowledge that they took turns maintaining perpetual adoration in prayer before the Blessed Sacrament. He had promised Day that he would offer Mass for them, and on the difficult tenth day, the abbot gave a talk to the group, assuring them that the Holy Spirit had listened to their prayers and characterizing them as "a little Council."[22]

Day reflected on the link between her hunger and the world's hungry as she offered up the throbbing aches in her legs to the God whom she believed with all her heart was lovingly united with us through his redemptive suffering on the cross. Despite her weakened state, Day managed to append a note to the group's letter thanking Merton for sending them words of encouragement, and she promised to follow up with a proper letter. She also corrected him, however, on one point: her actions had no connection whatsoever to Women Strike for Peace.

Back home she reported in her newspaper column, "Everyone said our visits and our fast and vigil (we each kept an hour before the Blessed Sacrament each day besides daily Mass) did much good." Indeed, Pope Paul VI echoed the women's plea in his historic declaration at the United Nations: "No more war! Never again war! It is peace, peace, that must guide the destinies of peoples!" Merton, for his part, wrote to the pope on behalf of all American Catholics working for peace to thank him and to share with the pontiff the equally bold declaration Merton had addressed to the Council fathers.[23]

But Merton had no illusions that getting the Council to condemn nuclear war would be easy. Although the American delegation was leaning in that direction, many of its most prominent members thought such a stance amounted to appeasement. The point man for the deterrence camp, Archbishop Philip Hannon, argued that "recent developments in nuclear production...could be used tactically against nuclear targets without targeting entire cities and their civilian populations. These were called 'Davy Crockett rockets'—small, bazooka-launched tactical nuclear missiles....(Try explaining a 'Davy Crockett rocket' in Latin!)." He also made the point that many European prelates supported nuclear deterrence because during World War II their cities had been brutally attacked by Nazi—and in some cases Communist—aggressors. They viewed this tactic "as absolutely essential for keeping the peace," he added. Hannon was successful in having deleted from the Schema a sentence condemning as immoral any and all possession of nuclear weapons, but the draft did not embrace deterrence itself, instead only listing it as an option that "many regard" as a viable tactic "at this time."[24]

The bishops ratified the peace planks in December 1965, on the last day of the last session of the Second Vatican Council. "The happy news on the radio this morning is that the Vatican Council has passed with an overwhelmingly majority vote, the Schema on the Church in the Modern World, included in which is an unequivocal condemnation of nuclear warfare," a jubilant Dorothy Day told her readers. "It was a statement for which we had been working and praying." Merton put it more acerbically, albeit to only himself: "The strong statement against total war unmitigated in spite of the efforts of Cardinal Spellman and Archbishop Hannan." The Council also provided qualified but unprecedented endorsement of the conscientious-objection option for Catholics liable for the draft. As the Vietnam War escalated, Merton would provide letters of support for Catholics seeking exemption from combat on religious grounds, as sponsored by the Catholic Peace Fellowship. But in the meantime, Merton's reaction to a tragedy in November 1965 nearly destroyed his relationship with CPF—and with Dorothy Day herself.[25]

CHAPTER FIVE

A Harsh and Dreadful Love

WHEN DOROTHY DAY returned from Rome in October 1965, she was greeted at the pier by a *New York Times* reporter—and no wonder. The previous week a crush of journalists had met Catholic Worker David Miller as he descended the platform after burning his draft card: the first person to defy the new law making such an act a federal crime. Now the leader of the Catholic Worker made clear her support for Miller—and also for Tom Cornell when, just days later, this Catholic Peace Fellowship codirector and longtime Catholic Worker announced at a big antiwar strategy session that he planned to do the same thing. After that meeting, Day found herself lying awake late at night. As she often did when dealing with social conflicts, she thought of her own failures to love, and now she resolved to try to go to confession every week.[1]

That same night, although far from the action, Thomas Merton also brooded over the escalating events, writing in his journal, "People are burning draft cards...and there are ugly signs of hostility and pressure against the Peace Movement, especially the Catholic Peace Fellowship and the Berrigans." Even if he did not know that David Miller had been a student of Dan Berrigan's, Merton had his finger on the pulse of the times. More than Day, he worried that these dramatic protests would anger the general public and only serve to reinforce the Cold War attitudes that so dominated the average person's thinking. As he struggled to make sense of the whirlwind of controversy with Dorothy Day at its center, the monk would find all too apt the title of his latest book project, *Conjectures of a Guilty Bystander*.[2]

The bond between Merton and Day would be tested almost beyond measure, but their love of God and neighbor would see them through. Indeed, this episode reveals that when tensions arise between colleagues in a time of great national crisis, those tensions do not have the last word for those who strive to root themselves in the great commandment of love.

November 1965 began ominously. Merton couldn't help noting that on November 2, when Quaker Norman Morrison immolated himself just outside the Pentagon, the Church commemorated All Souls Day/the Day of the Dead. That morning Morrison had read of American aircraft strafing a South Vietnamese village in response to reports of a Viet Cong incursion in the area. A grief-stricken French missionary told *Paris-Match*, "I have seen my faithful burned up in napalm, I have seen the bodies of women and children blown to bits. I have seen all my villages razed....They must settle their accounts with God." Morrison made his horrific stance directly under the window of the war's architect, Secretary of Defense Robert McNamara. Years later McNamara himself would reflect that this action constituted "an outcry against the killing that was destroying the lives of so many Vietnamese and American youth."[3]

In a letter accompanying a news clipping of the dreadful event, Jim Douglass wrote to Merton, "Dear Tom: The apocalyptic signs deepen." The account featured a photograph of Morrison's sweet infant daughter Emily; he had been holding her when he ignited himself, although she ended up on the grass unharmed. Douglass expressed the fear that sensational media coverage of the immolation would lead to more such "desperate" actions. He also worried that reporters were aggrandizing draft card burnings, and he cited Catholic Worker Chris Kearns telling *Commonweal* that fifty such protests were planned in the coming weeks and saying, "We never felt so much power." With the nascent antiwar movement increasingly energized, even as the general public supported the growing American military involvement in Vietnam, Douglass told Merton, "We need your vision." The young theologian and former Catholic Worker, who was teaching in nearby Louisville, urged Merton to write something for the *Catholic Worker* to provide a much-needed perspective for a peace movement. "Perhaps there had to be such a sign, but what if a lot of really pathological characters now do the same thing?" Merton wrote in his journal of the Morrison tragedy, adding, "Meanwhile Catholic Workers are all burning their draft cards." Putting down his pen, he walked out to the porch of his hermitage just before dawn and found himself recalling the prophet Ezekiel's futile struggle to avoid violence.[4]

His worried words would prove prophetic—at least on the surface. Soon thereafter Catholic Worker Roger LaPorte witnessed the draft card burning by Tom Cornell and four other men, including another Catholic Worker, before a large crowd that included a few hecklers shouting, "Burn yourselves, not your draft cards!" Three days later LaPorte burned himself alive. But the notion of a link between the two kinds of protests is complicated by the fact that LaPorte seemed to have been mostly influenced by Norman Morrison's suicide. He carried out his own self-immolation exactly one week later and, like Morrison, at a major political site: in LaPorte's case, in front of the United Nations. And according to Tom Cornell, LaPorte had expressed skepticism about draft card burning as a tactic. On hearing about plans for the protest in which Cornell would participate, "LaPorte was adamant, saying that this was the wrong thing to do because we were talking about force," Cornell recalled.

> And I said, "Yes, we are talking about force, but it's soul force, a spiritual force, it's not a coercive force,

> and it doesn't compromise anyone's integrity; it doesn't insult anyone." And besides, there's a time-honored tradition of burning documents. William Lloyd Garrison burned a copy of the Constitution of the United States in the protest against slavery. In 1947 Dwight Macdonald led a burning of draft cards in Union Square, hundreds. But let me tell you, Roger said that he would not come to our demonstration.

LaPorte did end up witnessing the event, but he stood off to the side, evidently not wanting to be photographed as part of the crowd applauding the action.[5]

Unlike Merton, Dorothy Day had no qualms about supporting the burning of draft cards, for she addressed the crowd of one thousand supporters who witnessed the event in New York City's Union Square. Standing before the microphone, her plain knit cap only adding to the understated dignity of this white-haired figure, Day spoke quietly but firmly as she declared her "solidarity of purpose with these young men," noting that she herself was breaking the law by encouraging the action. Betraying none of the anxiety she felt in this, her first-ever address at an outdoor rally, she took courage from the thought that she need not compose great words, let alone try and be God. She could simply channel the divine message of love. "The word of God is the new commandment he gave us—to love our enemies, to overcome evil with good, to love others as he loved us…not to take the lives of men, women, and children, young and old, by bombs and napalm and all the other instruments of war. Instead he spoke of the instruments of peace…to feed the hungry, shelter the homeless, to save lives, not to destroy them, these precious lives for whom he willingly sacrificed his own."[6]

Three days later, in a front-page story, the *New York Times* reported, "Man, 22, Immolates Himself in Antiwar Protest at UN." "Oh God, it was awful. All of a sudden you open the paper, and there he is—ashes. And it was somebody that I knew," recalled poet Ned O'Gorman, who reviewed books for the *Catholic Worker* (including a number by Merton.) Earlier in the evening LaPorte had helped serve a meal at the Catholic Worker and then "probably walked the streets all night coming to a decision," his friend Robert Steed told the *Times*. Steed and LaPorte had shared an interest not only in the Catholic Worker but also in Merton's writings and monastic life. He "had only recently left a monastery upstate and was seeking to find his own soul among the young Catholic Workers," wrote Daniel Berrigan, SJ, who knew him slightly.[7]

Day, as a veteran journalist, immediately recognized that the press would sensationalize this tragedy, and she was sick with worry that any such irresponsible publicity might trigger copycat suicides. Sure enough, *Time*'s account would lead off by noting that the LaPorte immolation took place "one week to the day after Quaker Norman Morrison burned himself to death outside the Pentagon." A few days later another young Catholic Worker, grief-stricken by the carnage in South Vietnam, indicated that he was considering the same kind of dramatically violent gesture. "We sat on the fire escape," said Cornell, "and I figured, 'I'm not going to talk theology.'...I said, 'Don't do this to us. You're going to destroy the Catholic Worker movement.'"[8]

But although she was determined to keep the media at bay until she could release a statement, the grief-stricken sixty-eight-year-old with a heart condition found the thought of manning the door herself a painful prospect. (And "manning" is the right term: women were unwelcome as public representatives—and as reporters, for that matter.) She assigned the Catholic Peace Fellowship codirectors, Tom Cornell and Jim Forest, to deal with the parade of journalists. As Cornell put it to Merton, "Roger's burning himself shocked me deeply. I was completely incapable of seeing anything calmly or straight for hours, and Dorothy asked me to speak to the tv and press for her." Years later Cornell called it "a terrible responsibility. I knew that the reputation of the Catholic Worker was on the line."

At the end of this awful, exhausting day, Cornell and Forest were about to close up when Cornell took one last call, which happened to be from Montreal. "The caller, a broadcaster, said, 'That's funny, the lights just went out.' And I said, 'Gee, that's funny, the lights just went out here.'... And we looked out, and the only lights were headlights from cars; all the skyscrapers—dark!" That night, Day wrote in her diary of the twin shocks of this "strange and terrible day." "POWER FAILURE SNARLS NORTHEAST; 800,000 ARE CAUGHT IN SUBWAYS HERE," read the *New York Times* headline just above the Roger LaPorte story. The piece on LaPorte reported, in the words of spokesman Jim Forest, that the Catholic Worker community was "deeply shocked, perplexed and grieved," and that LaPorte "never told us what he planned. If he had, we would have discouraged him."

But despite everything, Day refused to condemn this act that was considered a mortal sin by the Church that meant the world to her. In an essay with the telling title "Suicide or Sacrifice," the Catholic Worker leader lovingly described Roger LaPorte as a "victim soul." She did not cite the fact that the young man was reported to have made a heartfelt deathbed confession to the hospital chaplain. Rather than analyze the implications of Church teaching, she preferred to focus on the Greatest Commandment. "All of us around the Catholic Worker know that Roger's intent was to love God and to love his brother," she wrote. That was her main point, but she also could not help writing, "There will undoubtedly be much...condemnation of this sad and terrible act."[9]

Condemnation, indeed: some Catholic periodicals went so far as to blame her for this tragedy that wounded her ailing heart beyond measure, and she felt physically threatened by the crowd she addressed at the NYU Catholic center. But as so often is the case in life, the most wounding criticism came from a friend—even worse, a prominent one. "DEEPLY SHOCKED AND CONCERNED ABOUT DEVELOPMENTS IN PEACE MOVEMENT. WILL THESE DO GRAVE HARM TO CAUSE OF PEACE," Merton telegraphed Dorothy Day, and he sent a cable to Jim Forest asking to be removed as a sponsor of the Catholic Peace Fellowship. "He acted impulsively," recalled Br. Patrick Hart, the monk who would serve as his secretary. "He could get quickly swayed by things," and Br. Patrick speculated that this was in contrast to Dorothy Day: that she likely was more deliberate in making her decisions, as "she was dealing with a lot of tough characters," and that, in this respect, she resembled Gethsemani's abbot, who often served as a brake on Merton's less carefully considered enthusiasms.[10]

In this instance the abbot, as a strong supporter of American Cold War policies, was happy to approve Merton sending those condemnatory telegrams to his peace activist friends. To himself he noted that the immolation came on the heels of draft card burnings by Catholic Workers, and this anxiety was palpable in his letter to Jim Forest. While acknowledging that the Catholic Peace Fellowship "is not encouraging people to burn themselves up," Merton worried that the organization was associated with a peace movement that had some "pathological" elements. And while he made clear that he knew that Catholic Worker/Catholic Peace Fellowship folks were shocked by LaPorte's suicide, Merton implicitly questioned the depth of the Catholic peace activists' commitment to nonviolence, comparing them unfavorably to Gandhi, Martin Luther King Jr., and a Catholic nonviolent community in France. Merton wrote that as a hermit who never would be able to attend any CPF strategy sessions and was in no position to counsel any young men against this horrific type of protest, he could not represent the organization in any meaningful way. Thus he felt obliged to end his sponsorship of CPF. Failing to acknowledge that this organization was leading the way in draft counseling for Catholics—and yet again decrying the immolation—Merton petulantly urged CPF to focus on disseminating information on avoiding the draft, else the bishops would think the peace movement was some kind of seedbed for ritual suicide.

The reference to the bishops serves as a reminder that Merton never lost sight of the effect that protests might have on the hierarchy and the general public. Moreover, he had to consider the likely reaction of his religious superiors, who might slam shut the door that had opened a crack regarding his publishing on peace issues—this, even as he himself worried that the rumors of his supposedly leaving the monastery were fed by people who linked him to the protests. Nonetheless, he pledged to keep helping CPF and implied that the best way was through his vocation of prayer—a view that Day, in fact, shared.[11]

Jim Forest responded with four single-spaced pages systematically addressing the monk's charges and stating that, while Merton's stance wouldn't make or break the CPF or the Catholic Worker, his opinion carried enormous weight in the Catholic peace movement. Dorothy Day considered Merton's response a betrayal. Now she had to answer the criticism leveled by this famous author and cleric, and she had to do so under the most impossible of circumstances: amid the reporters with their hectoring questions and the demands of her community living in radical solidarity with the poor and now with the blackout. People were milling about the Catholic Worker under the light of a makeshift "macabre candelabra," as Cornell described it: candles attached to a set of bedsprings that had been denuded of mattress padding by someone who had used it for fuel. One newspaper called the resulting contraption "the flaming torch."[12]

On top of everything else, Dan Berrigan was being shipped off to South America by his Jesuit provincial, who was incensed by the words Berrigan had offered at a memorial service held at the Catholic Worker community.[13] As they were reported to him, the Jesuit superior considered those remarks a countenancing of suicide and a violation of his explicit order that Berrigan not comment on the tragedy. Demonstrators protesting his fate also suspected that his prominence as an antiwar figure was a (the?) reason for the transfer. Just a few weeks earlier, the new group, Clergy Concerned about the War in Vietnam, had made a splash with its inaugural press release, and over three hundred clergy signed its statement critical of

U.S. policy, with Berrigan the lone Catholic priest among the coalition's four founders. Meantime, as Day left Sunday Mass she read in the parish bulletin the announcement of a "hip hip hooray" rally in support of U.S. policy.[14]

Grief consumed Dorothy Day. "Her face was really a mask of sorrow," recalled her friend and fellow peace activist Eileen Egan. "She felt that whatever influence she had, it was rapidly fading. Those were very difficult times. You know, you can only take so much."

Her heart aching both emotionally and physically, Day wrote to Merton, "Excuse me for writing your name wrong on the envelope....We are so full of distractions these days." With a bitterness that made Merton's seem mild by comparison, she wrote, "I am only hoping that your reaction, as evidenced by your telegram, that is, holding us responsible, is not general, but I am afraid it may be." Although Merton had acknowledged that the CPF and Catholic Worker were opposed to suicide protests, Day ignored this point, as she was in no mood to parse his statements. She felt besieged, confiding to Merton violent threats to her, personally—this, even as, with a touch of defiance, she noted that her movement had been protesting against war for three decades, adding that she was glad that antiwar protests were on the rise in light of the horrors being inflicted on Vietnamese civilians—and even some U.S. troops—by American weapons.

But even amid her grief and resentment over his telegrams, she still considered herself united with Merton in the thing that counted: love of God and neighbor. "Of course, as members of one Body we are all responsible for each other," she wrote, and she begged his special prayers for a nephew who "suffers terribly" over his severely disabled three-year-old, but who was finding spiritual nourishment in *The Seven Storey Mountain*, even though neither he nor his wife professed belief in God. And even though his wife ridiculed Merton's writing, Day sensed that the husband was drawing closer to the Church. Begging his prayers, she even closed by noting, "We all love you dearly."[15]

Merton did ask his novices to pray for Day and her cohorts, and doubtless they also were in his intentions as he participated in one of the abbey's first concelebrated Masses, which he found to be a wonderful spiritual experience. He also noted much love in Day and her cohorts' response to the LaPorte tragedy. His most important response would be to Dorothy Day, and he set that letter aside for a couple of days for further reflection. In the meantime, he apologized to both Berrigan and Forest—to the latter, point by point: for the impulsive, emotional telegram; for implying that the CPF and the Catholic Worker were part of a peace movement that was somehow pathological; for projecting on them his own fears that the Trappists might somehow label him an extremist. To both men he praised the Catholic Workers who burned their draft cards and did not share with them his very real questions about the tactic. In his journal he mused that even though he considered those burning their draft cards to be people of integrity, he thought the tactic was easily misunderstood by the public. And if he thanked Berrigan for his words linking LaPorte's witness in some ways to Christ's, Merton also confided to old friend Catherine De Hueck Doherty that he saw LaPorte not as a martyr so much as "a kind of sign of judgment, in his well-intentioned confusion." Merton added that Catholic peace people needed to be careful not to overvalue publicity. Three years later these issues would come to a head when Berrigan himself made headlines as a lead member of those burning draft board files.[16]

So where did Merton stand on draft card burning? Two days after writing to Forest and Berrigan, he provided the answer—or so it seemed. The monk published a statement critical of draft card burning, but in this case, he had the general public in mind. Although Jim Douglass was imploring him to write something for the *Catholic Worker*, Merton rejected that idea, explaining that his telegrams had caused some ill feeling. Besides, why ask Day to publicize a statement that contradicted her on the draft card burning tactic, when his viewpoint might shift over time, while hers likely would not?

Instead it appeared in the *Louisville Courier-Journal*. The newspaper had been planning to profile him in an article for its Sunday magazine, and this prompted Merton to confidentially tell the reporter that he was having a dispute over tactics with some of the Catholics who had burned draft cards, so he thought it best to provide a statement to accompany the article. "If a pacifist is one who believes that all war is always wrong and always has been wrong, then I am not a pacifist," he wrote, going on to call modern warfare "an avoidable tragedy…the number one problem of our time." And even as he defended the right of Americans to burn their draft cards, he also stated, "I do not advocate the burning of draft cards."[17]

The next day Merton sent Day a tortuous explanation of this statement. He didn't want to write one at all, he told her, because he was unable to observe the tactic, implying that this was the reason that he did not send such a piece to the *Catholic Worker*. Why, then, did he publish such a piece in Louisville's leading newspaper? He gave her a vague explanation, but they both knew that he did not publish the item in her newspaper mainly because they disagreed about the tactic.

Above all, he wrote to apologize for his "ill-considered telegram" and to thank her for her "warm, wise" response. Aware that she, for all her radical activism, admired his monastic vocation tremendously, he confided that he should steer clear of any advisory role in CPF but, rather, support them through a life devoted to prayer. Begging her own prayers, as always, he assured Day that he was with her in spirit as she faced opposition—threats even. More than ever they needed each other's loving support, and he showed that support in a conclusion that absolutely shines: "May the Lord send his angel to be very close to you in these times and may He bless you and all whom you love and serve."[18]

"I hasten to write to thank you from my heart for your most reassuring letter," Day responded, assuring him that she did "agree with it in many ways." And even though she could not resist immediately reiterating her support for the draft card burners, she yet again emphasized that his vocation was "infinitely more important than anything else." Day underscored that point by noting that two years earlier she had begged his prayers for someone who turned away from drugs at the very time that the monk started including the woman in the intentions he offered to God. "I am sure you are holding us up in your fruitful solitude," she noted.[19]

In the end Merton agreed to remain a Catholic Peace Fellowship sponsor, and the directors agreed to publish his statement making clear that, while he supported CPF's objectives, as a hermit he was not able to opine on strategy. But also wanting to stress his bond to Day's peacemaking, he sent the Catholic Worker community his new book, an edited collection of Gandhi's writings, adding that he had read with much benefit the *Catholic Worker* essay about the draft card tactic. True, sometimes an issue of the newspaper failed to reach him or got buried in his piles of books and letters and manuscript projects, but none of that mattered. What mattered was that the Catholic Worker witness to love of God and neighbor was central to him. He even noted that, back when he was a student at Columbia University, he most likely would have volunteered with the Catholic Worker if her community had been located in upper Manhattan, rather than on the Lower East Side, and if a similar movement, the Harlem Friendship House, had not sprung up near his campus. "If there were no Catholic Worker and such forms of witness, I would never have joined the Catholic Church," he declared.[20]

Merton may not have known it, but Catherine De Hueck Doherty had founded Friendship House with the encouragement of her first New York friend, Dorothy Day. To De Hueck Doherty herself, Merton confided in that he and Dorothy Day had reconciled after more than a month of "struggle." Yes, Merton and Day resumed their spiritual friendship, but she would harbor lingering resentment over that LaPorte telegram for the rest of her life. Even years after Merton himself had passed away, Day sometimes would sputter with exasperation when his name was mentioned, and ten years after his passing she would write to herself, "remembering how…Roger LaPorte immolated himself at the UN plaza and how TM wrote to urge me not to urge our young men to do this! Hard to forgive him this stupidity." On the other hand, at the very moment that she was writing those words, Day was in the middle of reading yet another of Merton's books. No wonder that diary entry went on to say that some Catholic Workers who admired Merton were visiting him at that time, and that the Trappists were always dear to her community. She cited Trappist Charles (Jack) English, her old Catholic Worker friend and Merton admirer, and how English's monastery kept taking him back into the fold despite his struggles with alcoholism. Tellingly, in her diary entry the next day, she told herself that she needed to curb her criticisms and "cultivate holy indifference." No one knew better than Dorothy Day that her steadfast nature meant that she could harbor a grudge. Publicly, in the meantime, she was clear: Thomas Merton's vision was important.[21]

Even as that tragic November finally gave way to Christmastide, Merton feared that 1966 would bring its own terrible challenges, from a growing cataclysm in Vietnam to increasing personal physical ailments. He also ruminated on his "huge flaws" that he could not lessen, save for the mercy of God. That infinite, divine love prompted him to give thanks for his life of solitude and sparked his determination to pray ever more devotedly for the cause of peace, while Christmas greetings from various Catholic Workers prompted him to reflect that they really were "authentic Christians."

For her part, Dorothy Day, who often said, "Love in practice is a harsh and dreadful thing, compared with love in dreams" (quoting Dostoevsky), powerfully echoed Merton's message of hope in the face of nearly impossible challenges, both external and internal. "Peace needs to begin with our own hearts…from the ground up, from the poverty of the stable," she wrote in her Christmas message. "And since a thousand years are as one day, and Christianity is but two days old, let us take heart and start now."[22]

JOHN ORRIS/*THE NEW YORK TIMES*/REDUX

DOROTHY DAY IN THE CATHOLIC WORKER OFFICE, NEW YORK CITY. ON HER DESK IS THE OCTOBER 1961 *CATHOLIC WORKER* FEATURING THOMAS MERTON'S ARTICLE "THE ROOT OF WAR."

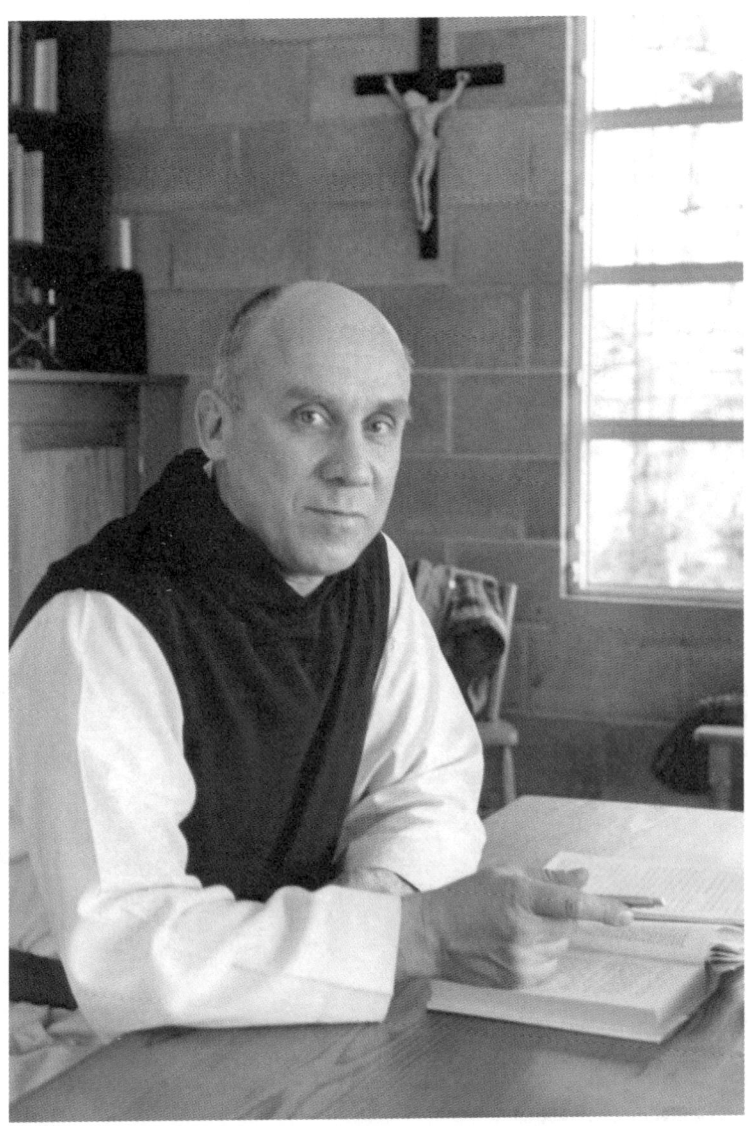

Photograph of Thomas Merton by John Howard Griffin. Used with permission of the Griffin Estate and the Thomas Merton Center at Bellarmine University.

Thomas Merton in his hermitage, 1963

Photograph by Jim Forest. Used with permission.

Daniel Berrigan listening to Thomas Merton at his retreat, "The Spiritual Roots of Protest," Gethsemani Abbey guesthouse, November 1964

Photograph by Diana Davies, courtesy of the Department of Special Collections and University Archives, Marquette University Libraries.

Dorothy Day speaking at the November 6, 1965, demonstration in New York City at which draft cards were burned by five men, two of them Catholic Workers

One of the meditative photographs taken by Thomas Merton on the monastery grounds near his hermitage

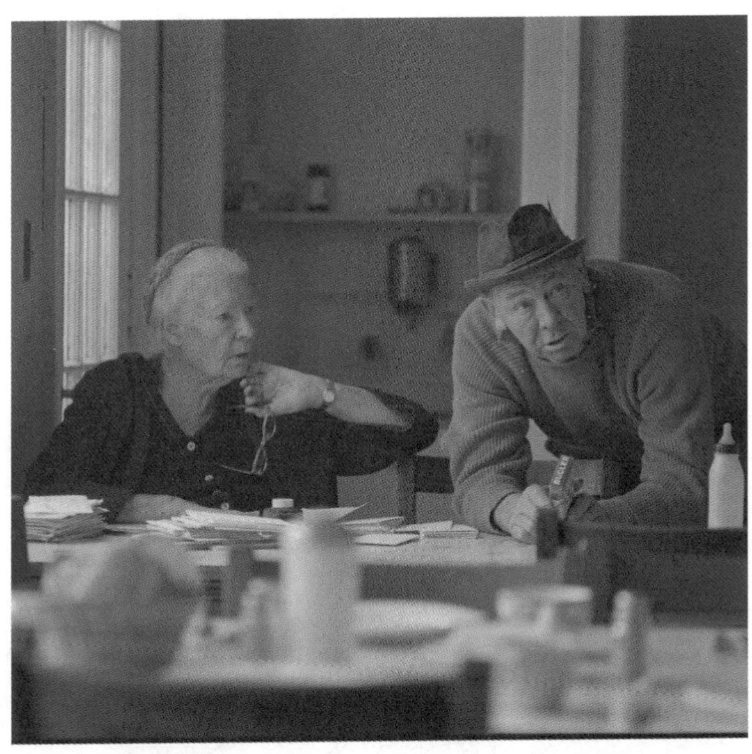

Photograph by Bob Fitch, used with permission of the Bob Fitch Photography Archive, Department of Special Collections, Stanford University Libraries.

Dorothy Day conferring with longtime Catholic Worker John Filliger while going through the mail at the Catholic Worker farm in Tivoli, New York

Dorothy Day and Thomas Merton as rendered by artist David Levine, © Matthew and Eve Levine

Above and opposite: Doubtless the only *New York Review of Books* caricatures that featured haloes of sorts

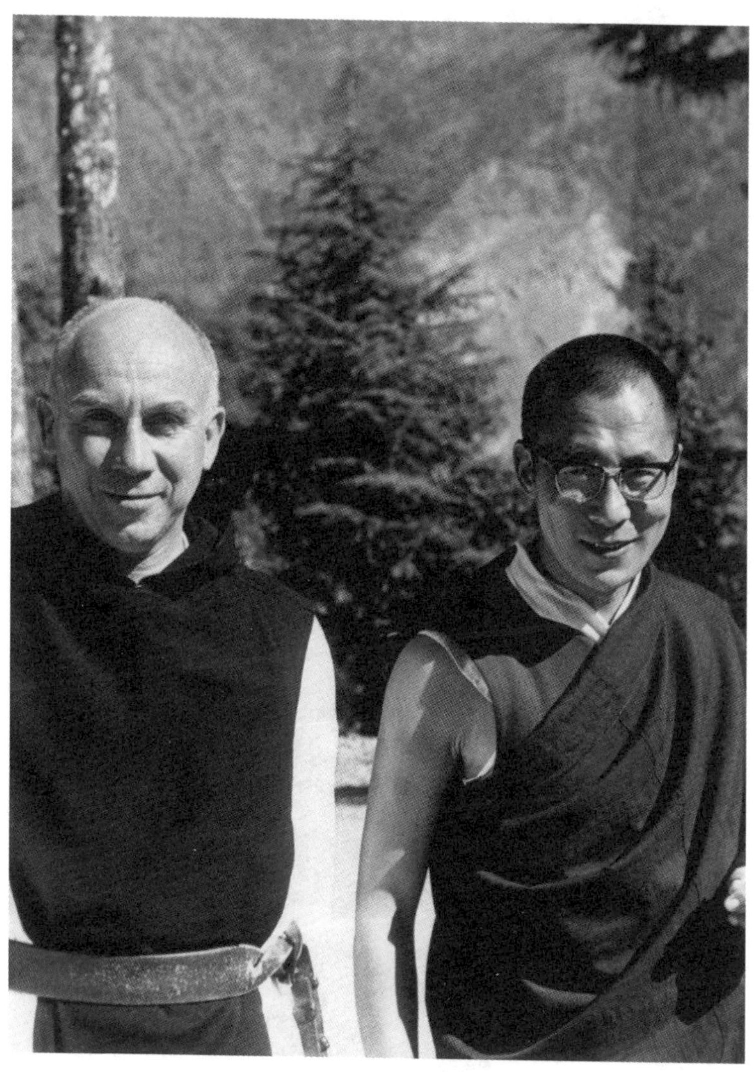

USED WITH PERMISSION OF THE MERTON LEGACY TRUST AND THE THOMAS MERTON CENTER AT BELLARMINE UNIVERSITY.

TWO MONKS: THOMAS MERTON AND THE DALAI LAMA IN 1968, JUST A FEW WEEKS BEFORE MERTON'S SUDDEN DEATH.

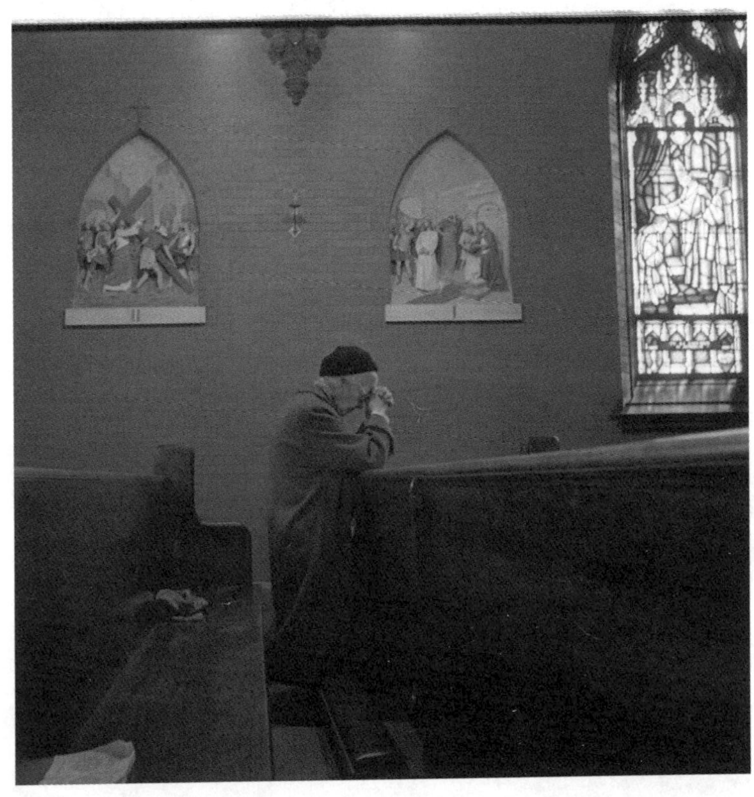

Photograph by Bob Fitch, used with permission of the Bob Fitch Photography Archive, Department of Special Collections, Stanford University Libraries.

Dorothy Day at weekday Mass in 1973. Although her health already was failing, she would live another seven years.

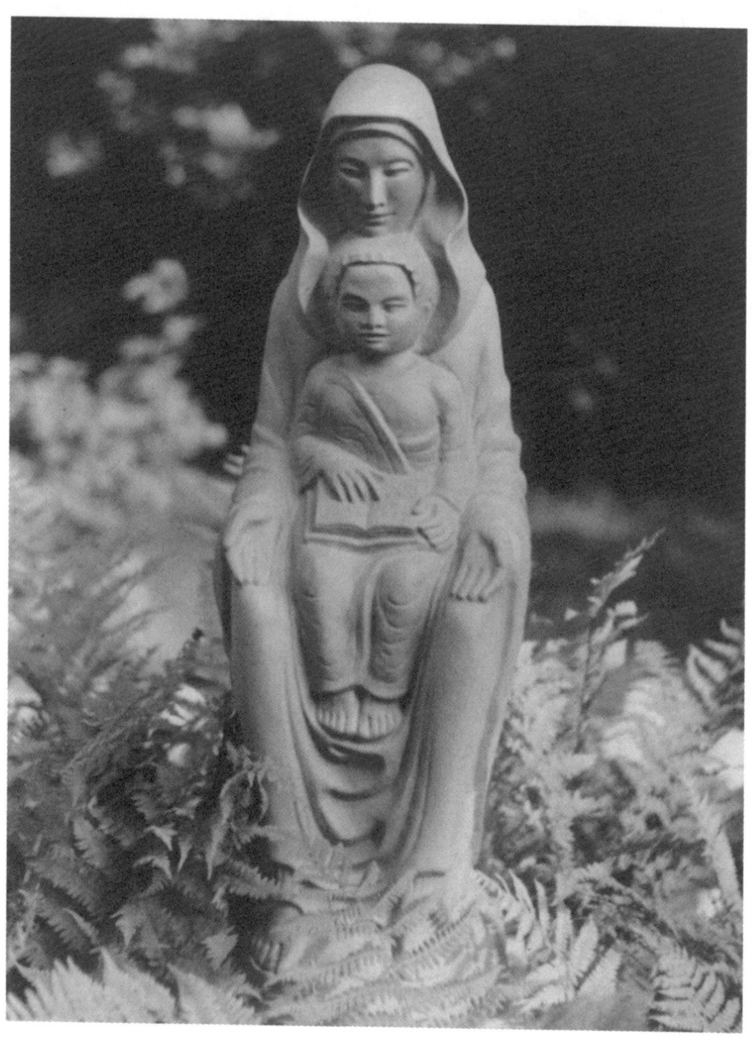

"Seat of Wisdom," by Catholic Worker artist Ade Bethune. One copy of this statue graces the woods of the Trappist monastery in upstate New York founded by the Kentucky monastery of Thomas Merton. Merton's epic poem *Hagia Sophia* features Holy Wisdom bestowing on us the power of the least as incarnated in her child.

CHAPTER SIX

One Tremendous Love

"THE SIXTIES WRECKED everybody's lives," reflected John Dear, protégé of Day and of Merton's friend Dan Berrigan. When his Jesuit superior ordered him to South America, Catholic peace activists protested, picketing St. Patrick's Cathedral and taking out a full-page advertisement in the *New York Times* charging Church authorities with punishing him for his antiwar activities as cofounder of Clergy Concerned about the War in Vietnam. The two most prominent Catholic peace figures, however, did not sign that statement, with Merton even suggesting to Day that the Jesuit's relocation might be a purifying experience for him. To Berrigan himself, the monk expressed a twinge of envy, citing Latin America as the sphere where all the creative insights were emerging. Still, in an observation as prescient as it was sympathetic, Merton wrote that Berrigan was likely to face many trials in the coming years because of his activism.[1]

For his part, Jim Forest wrote to Merton in near despair over the dissension within the peace movement. Identifying with Forest's angst, Merton replied, "Your stresses and strains, mine, Dan's, all of them, are all part of this same syndrome": tensions arising from attempting to take on society's grave injustices. Drawing on his life of prayerful meditation, however, he provided advice that resonates in any time of great crisis: "Do not depend on the hope of results," he wrote. "As you get used to this idea, you start more and more to concentrate...on the value, the rightness, the truth of the work itself." The CPF would not end the war or even turn most Catholics against it, Merton noted. The organization would make a difference, but it would be God who would measure those results. For our part, we needed to serve as conduits of God's love.[2]

One of the fruits of this approach would be a deepening of personal relationships, Merton noted, and in this vein, he offered Forest a bit of avuncular advice: take a break. He suspected that the young man was close to burnout; it turned out that he was under a personal cloud as well, for his marriage was falling apart. Indeed, as public controversies escalated, many people's lives became upended. "Thomas Merton recently pointed out that these times in the new era of world history, when the whole world is in agony, there is one gigantic struggle," Day noted in her diary, even if her personal frustrations—and, perhaps, lingering resentment over Merton's response to the LaPorte suicide—prompted her to add in irritation, "Constant interruptions—visitors, telephone, and members of the household made me lose forever what Thomas Merton was getting at."[3]

With the flowering of the counterculture, the precarious Catholic Worker community life was becoming even more chaotic, particularly at their farm at Tivoli, near arty Bard College. It got to the point that Day even considered suspending Friday night meetings there, even though they were a Catholic Worker institution dating from the start of the movement. These "roundtable discussions for the clarification of thought," as Peter Maurin had christened them, were conducted in many of their houses, but at the farm now too often led to partying.[4]

But these were the least of her problems, with Day particularly begging Merton's prayers "for me, myself." Her son-in-law, David Hennessy, was living with another woman, while her daughter Tamar was struggling to finish her courses so that she could become a practical nurse and support her nine children.[5] On top of everything else, she had stopped going to church, and this wounded her mother to the core. Dorothy Day had embraced this faith with joy as she walked the beach on Staten Island, pregnant with Tamar: a miracle, she felt, after having had an abortion. Raising her in the Church would keep Tamar from growing up spiritually rootless, Day thought, but now the light of her life had deserted the spiritual home that she herself so cherished.

"I consider the loss of faith the greatest of disasters—the greatest unhappiness," she put it to her readers, and to herself she wrote, "Theories. Why people leave Church now...Tamar for instance." She grieved over the failure of Catholics—herself as well as the hierarchy—to radiate for others the great gifts of their faith, from the Mass to the sacraments to the saints, and even the graces that came from fasting and other seemingly burdensome practices. She reflected that Tamar herself was mostly silent about her reasons for leaving the Church. One of Tamar's daughters, Kate Hennessy, recalled her mother responding, more often than not "with the straight thin line of her lips and vague flick of the fingers as if to toss it aside." Or she would simply say, with a note of resignation, "I didn't know why I was leaving the Church—I just had to do it. The Church's teachings on sex and birth control destroy men. Women are strong enough, but the men aren't."[6]

But Tamar's bitterness turned out to be even more tragic than Kate could have guessed. "I had thought that having nine children had destroyed my father and that leaving them had destroyed him all over again," the daughter wrote, "but as I came to discover, the seeds of his destruction began long before his marriage, and the clues were to be found in his early diaries." These writings by a young David Hennessy reveal a passionate relationship with a man. After the other man married and moved away, the diary entries of Day's future son-in-law become increasingly dark, short, erratic, and interlarded with references to Muscatel, Benedictine, and shots of whiskey.[7]

There is no indication that Tamar ever shared her husband's tormented backstory with her mother. How would Dorothy Day have responded? She would have bombarded Jesus and his Blessed Mother with prayers—that much we know—and she would have regarded David, with his heavy cross, as united in a special way with her crucified God. But she had heeded Church teaching even though it had meant walking away from the love of her life, the father of her child, who rejected religion and the institution of marriage, so she likely would have continued to adhere to her religion's dictum that same-sex acts were sinful, even at the risk that such a stance would drive a wedge between herself and Tamar.

And if that had happened, if Day had been alienated from the person she loved more than life itself, where would be the promise implicit in the Greatest Commandment: love of God and neighbor as one, tremendous love? Dorothy Day would have thrown that challenge back up to God and would have prayed for an increase of love on her part, with this crisis serving to remind her yet again that she was not God and also reminding her that she, Tamar, David, and everybody else were children of that selfsame God who became one of us, especially the "least": the poor, the weak—and, yes, the ostracized, the vilified, the despised. Not that this would have salved her aching heart, only that she would have been kept from suicidal despair by the belief that she was united in suffering with the broken of this world as especially cherished by her suffering savior.

Of course, all of this played out at a time when not only the Catholic Church but also the U.S. government and the American Psychiatric Association labeled homosexuality a "disorder." Thus, although at least one of their mutual friends, Dan Berrigan, was moderator of a gay student group at Cornell in the 1960s, Day and Merton largely steered clear of the topic, and when they did address it, they reflected the prevailing ethos. Even here, however, they tried to do so in a spirit that reflected their firm belief that what really mattered was that every person is a beloved child of God.

In one of his few published references to homosexuality, Merton wrote that the media made "persistent, snide allusions attempting to link nonviolence with passivity and homosexuality," and in the sole mention of the subject in his lecture notes as novice master, he labeled it as a vice. Even more, however, that lecture emphasized the need for monks to be generous of spirit, and Merton underscored that point with a quote from an ancient monastic writer who advised those in the monastery community to "accuse no one, rejoice at no man's fall...do nothing to make a monk feel less friendly toward his companions." It was in that loving spirit that he responded to a friend who was worried about his sexual orientation. While Merton did refer to same-sex activity as a sin, he emphasized that it was no more serious than any other. As for his friend's worried query as to whether any "proved homosexual" had saved his soul, Merton replied "that the first name that occurs to me...is Oscar Wilde. The poor man suffered greatly and was certainly sincere." Merton concluded the letter on a supportive note, writing, "All I can say is that God will surely understand your good intentions as well as your weakness. And He is on your side. So have courage and don't give up. And don't waste energy hating yourself. You need that energy for better purposes."[8]

Merton would die in 1968, one year before the Stonewall uprising would bring gay rights to national attention and five years before the American Psychiatric Association (APA) would remove the "disordered" label.[9] In contrast, Day lived for more than a decade after Stonewall, which took place just one mile from her Catholic Worker community. In 1975, two years after the APA reversed course, she wrote a ruminative disquisition to herself about the growing public acceptance of same-sex relationships even as her Church continued its clear opposition to such sexual activity.

Awaking at dawn, full of anguish, Day turned the problem over in her head, prayed over it, then poured out her soul in her diary. "There is no record of Jesus having taken up the subject," she recalled, but then she immediately qualified that statement, writing, "Of course He differentiates between love and lust and instinctively we understand Him," adding that both St. Paul and sections of the Old Testament inveighed against same-sex relationships. As if for the record, she explained that she was writing on this subject because two women had confided to her that they were about to declare publicly their love for each other. Day felt complimented that the couple approached her, they said, as a loving Christian, but she went on to write in this entry that Christians did need to uphold moral principles, as in one of the Spiritual Works of Mercy: "admonish the sinner."

Reflecting on the question of love for someone of one's own gender, Day, although an older woman, found herself recalling the incandescence of a gangly high school classmate who nonetheless "was transfigured with intelligence.…I loved her." And now, some fifty years later, that young woman reminded Day of the storied image of Mary as Santa Sophia—Logos/Holy Wisdom and subject of a tremendous mosaic in ancient Constantinople—and of the epic poem *Hagia Sophia* by Thomas Merton. In this tortured entry she also described at length a young Polish woman she had observed walking up to Communion, who had struck her as lovely in a strong, dignified way, evoking for Day the tremendous integrity and depth of Mary herself. She recounted this glowing experience in an article for the *Marianist*, but at that point they stopped communicating with her. "Maybe they thought charitably that I was an unconscious lesbian and 'least said, soonest mended,' as my mother used to say."[10]

But thinking about the two women who sought her out, she mused that other people as well were likely to mistake her compassion and hospitality for approval of same-sex relations. Although a pioneer in civil rights, in labor rights, the "rights" paradigm that would convince most people to rethink their view of same-sex relations did not resonate with her in this instance. The model that mattered to her when it came to sexual relations was the sacrament of marriage. As she once put it to her readers, "We are all one. We are one flesh, in the Mystical Body, as man and woman are said to be one flesh in marriage. With such a love one would see all things new, we would begin to see people as they really are, as God sees them."[11]

Even so, when she was ruminating on "homosexuality…in the CW movement," Day wrote disparagingly, not of those in same-sex relationships, but rather of those who treated homosexual people "with horror and coldness."[12] The attitudes of such individuals had prompted Robert Steed, an editor of the *Catholic Worker* in the late 1950s, to leave the community. Previously he had left Gethsemani because "I just wasn't happy there, and I was getting to feel that my sexual orientation was getting to be more and more of a problem. There was never any sex there, but I just felt that 'I just can't cope with it anymore.'"[13]

As she was writing this long, ruminative diary entry, Day was keeping one eye on the clock. She was not about to let her anguish keep her from going to Mass; she needed to finish writing but was still buffeted by emotions. When on the edge of despair, Day, like Merton, turned to the call of love, here concluding, "One must be grateful for the state of 'in-loveness' which is a preliminary state to the beatific vision, which is indeed a consummation of all we desire." Evoking the powerful spiritual persona so beloved by Merton, she added, "It is this glimpse of Holy Wisdom, Santa Sophia, which makes celibacy possible, which transcends human love. Oh, if we could only grow in faith, hope and love, and the greatest of these virtues is love."[14]

Dorothy Day's "in-love-ness" with God and with God's people shone for Ned O'Gorman, despite a conversation with her that shocked him. Years later he recalled how one day he was talking with Dorothy Day about prayer: "She was a great believer in prayer…and *I* am a great believer in prayer." Somehow the conversation turned to him asking, "'Well, Dorothy, what about the Church's reaction to homosexuality?' 'Well,' she said—words to this effect—'if they intend to go to hell, that's their decision.' So I'm thinking to myself, deep down in the inner recesses of my being: 'Holy Moses!'" But O'Gorman went on to make the point that "I don't think she was homophobic....I think she was Dorothy"—that is, given to quick retorts that she later regretted. O'Gorman explained: "I think if you said, 'Do you mean that all these people are going to hell, Dorothy? That you're condemning all these people? What about [celebrated poet W. H.] Wystan Auden, who gave you money? Is he going to hell?'—Dorothy would *not* say, 'Yes, of course.'" For one thing, Day was aware that O'Gorman was raising his son with his male partner, and she reassured the poet that he was correct to spend money on a trip to Europe with his child. "For heaven sakes, go! There's nothing wrong with beauty," she told him, noting that she regularly retreated to her cottage on a lovely little strip of Staten Island shoreline.[15]

O'Gorman underscored Dorothy Day's complex nature by recounting this icon of voluntary poverty accompanying him to the posh Metropolitan Opera.

> I belong to this thing called the Opera Club, which is very, very grand: white tie...unbelievable. And Dorothy...goes up in the elevator—there's a private elevator to go to the Opera Club—Dorothy had on a little cashmere sweater with pearls, and a lovely blue, tailored skirt....And there's John...an old figure at the Opera Club. He...was in a permanent state of drunkenness...saw Dorothy, and I thought he would faint right there on the floor. He adored her....Like all regal sensibilities, she took it all with great calmness. You could see that she wasn't happy, but that this was one of God's people.

The poet likened her to other great spiritual figures—"People so integrated in the faith, so 'catholic' at their core"—and here he cited St. Teresa of Avila, modern mystic Simone Weil, and novelist Flannery O'Connor. "She wasn't homophobic," he reiterated. "There was a radiant intelligence about

Dorothy. Dorothy wasn't divided up into the 'radical Dorothy,' into the 'socialist Dorothy,' into the '[longtime friend] Ammon Hennacy Dorothy.' She was *Dorothy*. And it always resolved in Christ Jesus. 'The final word is love.'"[16]

"The final word is love": here O'Gorman was quoting from the "Postscript" to Day's spiritual memoir, *The Long Loneliness*. This love was reflected in O'Gorman himself founding a school in Harlem in the mid-1960s. Even though he "didn't suddenly get up one day, come back from the Stork Club, wake up with a hangover and look at Dorothy and say, 'Oh I want to change my life'"—still, the small flame already burning in his heart had been fanned by her witness. In that "Postscript" she famously wrote, "We were just sitting there talking, when lines of people began to form, saying, 'We need bread.' We could not say, 'Go, be thou filled.' If there were six loaves and a few fishes, we had to divide them. There was always bread." Clearly echoing that sentiment, O'Gorman noted, "If I want to find something to make sense out of the craziness in my life, it is 'build the Kingdom.' Every day you put another brick into the structure of the Kingdom, and shut up about it, just do it.... You listen to what people want...and you become their servant." Day visited his Harlem storefront school, admired the cheerful walls covered with children's art, sat on the front steps listening to the locals' stories, then shared news of the school with her readers. "She was wonderful," said O'Gorman.

He founded the school in order "to give order and joy to the chaos of reality by creating a peaceful environment where the senses of the children can exist," the *New Yorker* reported. It had published several of his poems, and now his little school was spotlighted in the magazine's legendary "Talk of the Town" section, which also noted that the poet had three books coming out soon. One of these collections included two pieces by Merton, who called O'Gorman the best contemporary Catholic poet. "Ned O'Gorman is doing a mysterious and complex book for Random House," he wrote to a friend. "He asked me to define seven words" in a "'revolutionary' manner, as the whole book will be in that vein. I don't know how revolutionary I was in seven words, but...the one on purity will make...some...reach for their anathemas." When *Prophetic Voices: Ideas and Words on Revolution* was published, Day reported to her readers that the book contained "extraordinary...definitions by many of my favorite writers. There are two by Thomas Merton, 'Purity' and 'Death.' Startling."[17]

At this time, 1966, she received yet another personal blow when Donald Day became the first of her siblings to pass away. "We feel it keenly," she told her readers. "Family ties are strong." Concerned about her, Tom Cornell asked Merton to pray for "Dorothy's brother in Finland, who was a correspondent for the *Chicago Tribune*," noting, "Dorothy looked very tired when I saw her." Indeed, this death brought a horrible truth back to the center of her attention. "My brother Donald...was pro-German and an anti-Semite," as she confided in her diary some years later. His experience reporting from Stalinist Russia fed his anti-Communism to the point that he came to view Hitler as a necessary bulwark against Stalin. The journalist even became a broadcaster for the Nazis in 1944. In her column noting his passing, the Catholic Worker leader obliquely referenced this painful reality, writing, "Though he tried to avoid controversy, because he disagreed with my religious and political attitudes, he found it hard not to allude to these differences." At the same time, she took care to note that "Donald never wrote without asking God to bless us all."[18]

In contrast, her beloved younger brother John Day would never invoke God, for he was a Communist for much of his life. Dorothy had virtually raised him, then lived for a few years with John and his wife, and subsequently resided near them. Indeed, her first memoir, *From Union Square to Rome*, was written partially to explain to John her newfound faith. Thus he figures in accounts of Dorothy's life, as does her dear sister Della, who also lived nearby, while Donald, the Fascist expat, rarely rated a mention.

In a sense, the ideological conflict of John Day and Donald Day echoed the ideological strains between Dorothy

Day's parents, with her mother's father having fought for the Union and her father's father having fought for the Confederacy. As for John's Communism and Donald's Fascism, perhaps a psychoanalyst might posit that Dorothy Day's combination of religiosity and radical politics was an attempt to reconcile them. Day herself was no fan of psychological explanations; she considered her politics a product of her God-given intellect and her faith an outright gift of God, plus she grew up in an age that predated the widespread use of psychology. Nonetheless she did not disparage that approach per se, and she did put in contact with a therapist, at their request, interested Catholic Workers such as Bob Steed (in his case, with Gregory Zilboorg, who had seen Merton on a couple of occasions).

Dorothy Day's third brother, Sam, rarely gets a mention from her biographers, for she steered clear of this sibling who reminded her too much of her bitter, accusatory father. But now, with the death of Donald, the whole family reimposed itself at the very center of Dorothy's physically and emotionally aching heart, even as all her siblings rejected the faith that meant everything to her.

In contrast, Merton's only sibling followed him into the Church. But John Paul Merton's story ended tragically. He perished in World War II, leaving Tom Merton with no immediate family at all, the loss of his beloved John Paul inspiring his achingly beautiful, elegiac poem "For My Brother—Missing in Action 1943." Meantime, Dorothy Day held out the hope that salvation might well come to her dear loved ones—or to anybody else. "There is no time with God," she liked to say. Nor did she know all of God's ways. "How can I intrude into the personal lives of others," she wrote, "this most interior life of faith and love, of the heaven and hell that are within us?"[19]

This reflection was published in 1965, the same year that Tamar Hennessy and her children made their break with Catholicism, as did Day's soulmate Ammon Hennacy, who then married outside the Church. In her diary she anguished over how to express her grief over this idealist turning his back on her God of love. Day did find a way to write about it—by centering on that very commandment: love. Her column "What Does Ammon Mean?" was suffused with love for this dynamic man who never wavered in his devotion to peace: "Pacifism, voluntary poverty and the works of mercy, and added to that the ability to work harder than anyone else at manual labor—he is rightly famed for these things," she explained. "We often said around the Catholic Worker that Ammon worked harder than any one, was stronger than anyone else, and though he was the oldest of our group, he seemed the youngest." Also, she noted, Ammon had many friends "because he made them see how important the witness of only one person could be." All the friends of Ammon's that she listed were female: "Alice, Dorothy, Ginny, Pat, Janey, Eileen, Vivian, Mary, Carol and Molly," for, she wrote, "It was natural that Ammon would be attracted to the young, beautiful volunteers." This "affectionate" dear friend of hers "was lonely, as celibate men are lonely, as priests are lonely," she poignantly put it. That very month, a priest, Thomas Merton, reflected on his hunger for intimacy with a woman: "an incompleteness that cannot be remedied."[20]

Meantime, this celibate woman, author of *The Long Loneliness*, expressed no such emotional emptiness on her part—for one thing the "Ammon" piece was public—but she did hint that the attraction was mutual. "We all enjoyed him and his affection," she wrote, "which he was not at all averse to showing." What she could never say was that this magnetic individual just three years her senior; this man with the classic, craggy features, vivid blue eyes, and impressive shock of salt-and-pepper hair; this idealist who devoted himself body and soul to the cause of peace—this man had recently written in his memoirs that he became a Catholic because he was in love with Dorothy Day. She showed "more integrity about what was worthwhile than any two radicals or Christians I have ever known," he wrote, and he even declared that if she had published, say, the *Mormon Worker*, he would have become a Mormon. For her part, the one loving sentiment that she could express was St. Augustine's dictum that "we should always love everyone as though he or she were the only one. If we saw people as God sees them we should indeed see the beauties of each unique soul. And if we had the love of God in us we would indeed be seeing them as God sees them. So we always felt that Ammon had much of the love of God in him, that he should be so loving to people."[21]

Still, her heart was breaking. "But how can I help but sorrow, believing as I do that our soul's life depends on our daily super-substantial bread, Jesus Christ become incarnate, taking on our flesh through the flesh of Mary?" And as his godmother, how could she not feel that she had failed him? Where were the Catholics with the inspirational integrity to match Ammon's heroes, such as David Dellinger of the War Resisters League and Clarence Jordan of the brave interracial Koinonia community in Georgia? "Realizing this, our own failures, we can only pray that God will give him further light, that another conversion, that is, a turning to God and a return to his own strong mission, will come about, and that he will begin to see the Church in perspective as founded by Christ on the Rock of Peter and enduring to this day in spite of the tares among the wheat—in spite of the scandals."

No matter how horrific the scandals might be, Dorothy Day would stay rooted in her faith, which she believed she received as a gift from a God who found her, loved her, and saved her: a God, moreover, who identifies especially with the abused, and who is with us all in the breaking of the bread, and in each act of love. Her beloved Ammon Hennacy constantly exercised such acts of love and frequently went to jail in protest of the military buildup, so in recognition of that fact and "in faithfulness to our friendship with him," the *Catholic Worker* would report the activities of his Utah-based Joe Hill House and St. Joseph's Refuge. "But at the same time," she noted pointedly, "we ask for prayers for him, '*that all things work together for good to them that love God*.'"[22]

A few months later Day reflected, if only to herself, that she had managed to keep at bay any attraction she might have to a member of the opposite sex because of an even greater urge: the urge to love God, a love that brought the promise of eternal life. "But do I love Him?" Answering her own question, she reflected that the crucial test was "am I willing to sacrifice present happiness and present love" for love of God? "I have done it once," she noted: presumably a reference to having given up the love of her life, Forster Batterham, the father of her child. But the struggle never ended. Day and Batterham continued to call and visit each other. And did the total devotion she gave to the weekly Metropolitan Opera radio broadcasts stem from having soaked up such performances, from the top balcony, with her soulmate so many years earlier? Through it all she found consolation in the thought that love of God and neighbor "casts out fear." Amazingly, she even nursed her old lover's partner in the woman's last days, and she asked to be baptized shortly before leaving this world.

Not that Day considered herself particularly holy: far from it, for in the next breath she was reminding herself not to fall prey to sanctimony, writing, "We must not judge, but always try to love." Just three weeks later, in reflecting on his own spiritual journey, Merton echoed Day's emphasis on love: "What matters is to *love*"—in his case, "to be in one place in silence."[23]

But Day would have been distressed if she had known that a few months later, in the soft Kentucky spring, Merton would embrace the very kind of romantic love that she had forsworn years before. So many people were leaving the priesthood that when a priest visited the Catholic Worker without wearing his clerical collar, she found herself worried that he was leaving the way of life that brought her the Way, the Truth, and the Life in sacramental form—and Merton was no ordinary priest. As she constantly reminded him, he was blessed with an extraordinary gift—yes, as a spiritual writer of unsurpassed talent but, to her mind, even more as a monk devoted to God Alone: through the Liturgy of the Hours, as a hermit in communion with God's creation, and above all at the altar, in the incarnational act of consecration and communion.

Thus, it is not surprising that he would not mention to her his romantic involvement with the student nurse who treated him after his back operation in late March 1966. Still, a friend of hers, Dan Berrigan, would be one of a handful of folks who would facilitate Merton's communication with his newfound love, serve as a sounding board, and subsequently destroy all of the letters the monk sent to him that referred to the affair.[24] Berrigan's assistance to Merton came even as the Jesuit himself was pledged to celibacy and, indeed, kept buttoned up any sexual attractions of his own. That enduring human dilemma—whether to privilege loving fealty to first principles or embrace one's love for another—would be laid bare for Merton in this, the most agonizing challenge of his monastic life.

Margie Smith, the young nurse who attended Merton in the hospital, had been influenced by his writings, and now this author who evoked the divine so accessibly, this man who had turned away from the life of a sophisticated New York intellectual to devote himself to God—this famous, charming monk—was beholding her as beautiful, even beholding her with love. But he was decades older and famously a vowed celibate, and she had a serious boyfriend back home. These differences could serve as a brake on any budding romance. Or so they thought. As these two people found themselves ever more drawn to each other, it became clear that the implausibility of the pairing in fact could itself serve as a subterfuge.

Not that Dorothy Day did not understand the passion that drew Margie and Tom to each other. As she ruminated to herself, ostensibly about her mother's feelings: "Did every now and then that wave of sexuality wash over her that brought with it an exquisite and shattering joy at the beauty of a face, a character, or even at the pure masculinity of a friend or acquaintance, the exchange of a glance, a touch?" But as she wrote to Ammon Hennacy when he joined the

Catholic Worker two decades later, "I think older women must be pretty careful....I have a great love for you of comradeship but sex does not enter into it....There is no playing around with sex"—even as she also made clear that she could not wait to see him again and catch up. This was in 1949, when she was fifty-one, Merton's age when he met Margie Smith. With fifty the classic age of the male midlife crisis, his personal secretary, Br. Patrick Hart, has speculated that just such a phenomenon was at play. Indeed, in falling for his nurse, in effect he was falling for virtually the only woman closely interacting with him at that time. Still, this incandescent experience gave him a deeper understanding of the Incarnate God: truly human, truly one of us, and, thus, with all our drives and urges.[25]

"How terribly lonely I was for M. the first days after I left the hospital," Merton wrote in his journal a few months later.

> The letter I left asking her to write. My anxiety to hear from her. The impact of her first letter where I saw she loved me really (as I had suspected in the hospital)...also I realized how, when I began to call her on the phone...there was a very powerful drag of passion at work in me and trying to rationalize it. Yet at the same time there was an obscure sense that she was somehow supposed to enter deeply into my life and I into hers....A sense that this kind of union was possible and desirable...there was something fabulous about those days....I have never experienced such ecstasies of erotic love.

Now, in retrospect, he saw "how imprudent and careless we were, and how in fact I was forgetting the real essence of my vowed life while desperately trying to keep the mere letter of the vows."

He even mused that, when one of their telephone conversations was overheard by a Trappist brother who then informed the abbot, this turn of events "really did get me off an impossible hook." And, he concluded, "The overall impression: awareness of my own fantastic instability, complexity, frailty, and the nearness to disaster in May and early June. Providentially, we were saved from real danger....Dom James was more right than I was willing to admit," he noted: a frank acknowledgment, given that he still thought the abbot was unfair in prohibiting any trips and was steering the Gethsemani community in the wrong direction, as with overly commercialized peddling of their food products.

But even though he regretted much about the relationship, Merton still submitted for Ned O'Gorman's anthology the "Purity" essay that he had written during the peak of the affair. Indeed, this reflection conveys an insight that this monk received from his beloved: that every one of us, whatever our calling, is called to love, and while that love may most grandly be expressed in agape—that overarching, even selfless, love of God and humanity and beauty—and while each of us, in our own way, needs to keep within limits the erotic feelings that grab us, these passions do reflect a fully human God, author of that Greatest Commandment, with its call of love. "The mark of love is its respect for reality," he noted. "Such concern is not compatible with fantasy, willfulness, or the neglect of the rights and needs of other people. In this new approach to purity, the emphasis will be not so much on law as on love....We must consider not so much what is acceptable in a social milieu as what will truly provide a creative and intimately personal solution to the questions raised in each special case...in order to celebrate the love that has been given them by God, and in so doing to praise Him!"

As he put it in his journal shortly after the relationship ended, "And in the end: respect for M. and for our love, gratitude for it...that in spite of all my hectic confusion (and her seductiveness), I owe a great deal to her love and this is a lasting reality that cannot be denied." Henceforth he would carry with him this newfound appreciation of romantic, erotic love, but although he would telephone her a few times in the future, after 1966 they would never meet again. Two years later, in 1968, he matter-of-factly recorded in his journal that "among other things, I burned M.'s letters. Incredible stupidity in 1966! I did not even glance at any one of them. High hot flames of the pine branches in the sun!" In the end he saw himself as very much called to a life of solitary prayer: for a world in crisis—and, yes, for those he loved—but all of it in the embrace of "one thing only...to be open to God's will and freedom, to His love which came to save me from all in myself that resists Him and says no to Him." He signed a pledge, witnessed by his abbot, to remain a Trappist hermit for the rest of his life.[26]

As the new year began, he summed up his calling in a letter responding to a graduate student who planned to include in his thesis a biographical section on Merton. "Like every other Christian I am still occupied with the great affair of saving my sinful soul, in which grace and 'psychology' are sometimes in rather intense conflict," he explained, adding that if some readers nonetheless inferred a holiness on his part that he did not possess, perhaps his writing was to blame. "If in giving God thanks for his mercies I have sometimes helped others to do the same in their own lives, I am glad. But I still need the prayers and the compassion of my fellow Christians."

From Dorothy Day he yet again begged prayers, that he might follow God's will despite his mistakes. Offering his own spiritual comfort to the careworn Catholic Worker leader, he agreed with her that, as the Sixties were accelerating, too many people were embracing novelty for its own sake, but he voiced the hope that, with the help of the Holy Spirit, they all might "become more humble by our mistakes. I hope so."[27] Daring to fuse love of God and neighbor in one, tremendous love, these two touchingly human spiritual sojourners would increasingly signify amid events that threatened to spin out of control.

CHAPTER SEVEN

Kairos: The Providential Hour

IN 1967, WITH nearly half a million Americans fighting in Vietnam and seemingly no end in sight, more and more of the public was questioning a war that Merton, Day, and their cohorts long had scored as immoral. "This is the Kairos. It must not be missed," Merton wrote to Jim Forest. The monk had first used this notion of "Kairos"—"the providential hour," as he called it—with reference to the civil rights movement; now he saw the national attitude about the Vietnam War reaching its own critical juncture. Merton advised Forest and his Catholic Peace Fellowship partner Tom Cornell to make it clear to American Catholics that the Church officially promoted peace. He suggested that the two young CPF directors create a handout—"objective, not preachy"—showing that nonviolence resistance was called for, considering the current dangers: from the nuclear threat to the destruction of the Vietnamese countryside by American chemicals.

Even as Merton's commitment to a life of prayerful solitude was deepening, his support of CPF was increasing. He stepped up his letters of support for young men CPF was advising who were petitioning their draft boards for exemption on conscience grounds. Moreover, despite his life of voluntary poverty he even managed to support the CPF financially. He sent them some of the donations he himself received; he gave them his signed artwork to auction off at fundraisers; he provided them with a statement of support for their campaign aid to civilian victims of the war.[1]

"Many demonstrations—thousands as compared to the few score we used to be," Dorothy Day noted in her diary. Still, she worried that everyone needed to do more. As she put it to Merton, "I am at present reading your *Conjectures of a Guilty Bystander*. We all feel that way." Tom Cornell, who was close to Day, reported to Merton that she was "thrilled and delighted" with the bold article he submitted for the *Catholic Worker*. To herself, however, the Catholic Worker leader groused that the piece, "Albert Camus and the Church," was too long and theoretical for a "worker's paper." Actually, a decade earlier Day herself had devoted a column to Camus, and she employed such abstract terms as a "metaphysical revolt," so perhaps this particular criticism stemmed from her still-lingering resentment over Merton's negative telegram to her after the suicide of Catholic Worker Roger LaPorte. At any rate, to those around her she did laud the essay, and to the monk himself Day made a point of expressing "thanks from my heart," reporting that they were inundated with requests for reprints and assuring him that they were overjoyed to publish anything he might send them.

Merton probably was not surprised that the piece struck a chord. He had noticed that many thoughtful Catholics were reading Camus, especially young people. In a description that could be applied to Merton and Day themselves, he characterized Camus as someone who "has retained a kind of moral eminence (which he often repudiated) as the conscience of a new generation."[2] With words that proved timely, and that resonate anew in our own perilous age, Merton warned that we must guard against falling prey to the official lie—or even tolerating it: "To all of us, Camus is saying, 'Not lying is more than just not dissimulating one's acts and intentions. *It is carrying them out and speaking them out in truth*'" (emphasis Merton's).

As for what to resist, he cited Camus, declaring, "There is only one problem today...and that is the problem of murder. All our disputes are vain. One thing alone matters, and that is peace." Merton linked this statement to the peace teachings recently issued by the Second Vatican Council. Prophetically, he noted that war "injures the poor to an intolerable degree," thereby channeling Martin Luther King Jr., who was proclaiming that the spending on the Vietnam War was killing any hope for the American poor to advance, even as the poor were bearing the brunt of the fighting.[3]

Meanwhile, Day told Merton that Cardinal Spellman had stepped up his already-fervent support for the Vietnam War and that she had to "cry out in grief." Her direct criticism was particularly noteworthy, given that exactly a year earlier, in December 1965, she had framed her comments in terms of her obedience to the cardinal's authority. If he ever asked her to close the Catholic Worker she would do so, she had noted, even as she thought that would never happen. But now it was December 1966, and in the meantime the Johnson administration had Americanized the war, and her cardinal was the most prominent Catholic champion of that escalation. In September 1966, the *New York Times* reported that even though Pope Paul VI supported a negotiated settlement in Vietnam, "condemnation of the war by American Catholic prelates...has been nonexistent," and it quoted Cardinal Spellman declaring, "Our country...may she always be right, but our country, right or wrong."

In her December 1966 column, Day made only a cryptic reference to obeying Spellman's authority, and the following month she published a biting criticism of his Vietnam War statements. Quoting from Isaiah, she titled the January 1967 statement "In Peace Is My Bitterness Most Bitter." The Catholic Worker leader's years of devotion to a God of peace now poured out in words that speak not only to the agonies of the Vietnam era but to our own time of endless war—and, indeed, to each of our failures to choose life over death. "It is not just Vietnam," she wrote.

> It is South Africa, it is Nigeria, the Congo, Indonesia, all of Latin America. It is not just the pictures of all the women and children who have been burnt alive in Vietnam....It is not just the words of Cardinal Spellman and Archbishop Hannan. It is the fact that whether we like it or not, we are Americans. It is indeed our country, right or wrong, as the Cardinal said....We are destroying crops, setting fire to entire villages and to the people in them. We are not performing the works of mercy but the works of war.

But in an example for anyone struggling with great bitterness in the face of national events, she worked mightily to stay rooted in love. "I can sit in the presence of the Blessed Sacrament and wrestle for that peace in the bitterness of my soul," she wrote, "a bitterness which many Catholics throughout the world feel, and I can find many things in Scripture... to change my heart from hatred to love of enemy....Picking up the Scriptures at random (as St. Francis used to do) I read about...Jesus transfigured!"

Noting that a terrified St. Peter made a fool of himself in response to that vision of Christ shining like the sun, Day reflected, "Maybe they are terrified, these princes of the church, as we are often terrified at the sight of violence, which is present every now and then in our houses of hospitality, and which is always a threat in the streets of the slums. I have often thought it is a brave thing to do, these Christmas visits of Cardinal Spellman to the American troops," she added. "But what words are those he spoke—going against even the Pope, calling for victory, total victory? Words are as strong and powerful as bombs, as napalm. How much the government counts on those words, pays for those words to exalt our own way of life, to build up fear of the enemy."

Echoing Merton's *Catholic Worker* piece "The Root of War Is Fear," she prayed, "Deliver us, Lord, from the *fear* of the enemy....Love casts out fear, but we have to get over the fear in order to get close enough to love them." And, as always, she referenced her own faults. "There is plenty to do, for each one of us," she wrote, "working on our own hearts, changing our own attitudes, in our own neighborhoods."

In addressing the agony of Catholics dealing with institutional sins of the Church, Day even anticipated the many horrific clerical abuses dating from her time but only revealed in the new millennium. "As to the Church, where else shall we go, except to the Bride of Christ, one flesh with Christ? Though she is a harlot at times, she is our Mother...of which we are every one of us members or potential members." Yes, she stayed in the sometimes-prostituted Bride of Christ: "Since there is no time with God, we are all one, all one body, Chinese, Russians, Vietnamese, and He has commanded us to love another. 'A new commandment I give, that you love others as I have loved you,' not to the defending of your life, but to the laying down of your life. A hard saying. 'Love is indeed a harsh and dreadful thing' to ask of us, of each one of us, but it is the only answer."[4]

Day explained to Merton that she wrote this piece "to cry out in grief, but also to point out the fact that we all are guilty," but she did not wallow in remorse, instead embracing the Church's practices of prayer and penance. Clearly moved, Merton lauded her for spotlighting what he called "the moral insensitivity" of Spellman and his fellow bishops—and making her argument in a Christian spirit "of love more than of reproof." In words that, like hers, still resonate, Merton observed that criticizing the bishops "does not imply that we ourselves are perfect or infallible....But what is a Church after all but a community in which truth is shared."[5]

The monk closed on an entirely different note—or so it seemed, but his idea underscored her point that fear of our enemies can lead a country to commit atrocities. He suggested that he review a book about Ishi, the last surviving member of the original California tribes. In that piece for the *Catholic Worker*, Merton declared, "We are left with a deep sense of guilt and shame" for U.S. wars against the native peoples, and he linked that policy to U.S. policy in Vietnam. Foreign policy analysts might find that analogy a stretch, given the widely divergent goals, eras, and locales, but Merton's linking of Ishi's world to that of the Vietnamese did echo Dorothy Day's own cries—and their Church's own teachings—against military campaigns that harmed "the least" in scandalously disproportionate ways.[6]

In that spirit, Merton drafted a statement in support of Dan Berrigan and his cohorts, who were trying to deliver aid to North Vietnamese civilians who were the victim of U.S. bombing campaigns. He also thanked Berrigan for the obituary of A. J. Muste, the pacifist icon who had so impressed him at his peace retreat—even if Merton would never use the "pacifist" label himself. It was Day, of course, who had long worked with Muste. When he was felled by a heart attack after experiencing chest pains, she noted this in her diary, and just four days later she experienced pains in her own chest. Day had recently spoken with Muste at the courthouse where he and some compatriots were on trial for their latest civil disobedience activities against the Vietnam War. The two pacifist elders were shepherded to the hearing by Tom Cornell, who navigated through the blizzard-blanketed city in his little Volkswagen.[7]

In the meantime, Cornell's CPF partner Jim Forest was finding himself increasingly estranged from Day, even though she had served as his model in so many ways, for she was upset with his plan to divorce and remarry. Agonizing over what to write to him, finally she presented the problem before the Blessed Sacrament in their Catholic Worker chapel. In that quiet little candlelit space, she found herself writing down a few thoughts. "First, God asks great things of us, great sacrifices," but then transforms them—transforms them more powerfully than the might of all nuclear weapons combined. "Second, He is asking us to prefer Him to all beauty and loveliness. To all other love." Her own heart-wrenching sacrifice doubtless threaded through these points. After all, she had walked away from Forster Batterham—the love of her life, the father of her precious child—out of greater love for Jesus Christ and his Church. And in the decades that followed, she had steadfastly rejected romantic overtures from men who genuinely loved her, body and soul.

She wrote to Forest that if he allowed romantic love to trump the love of God, she could not support his peace work. She had come to the wrenching conclusion that she could no longer be a sponsor of the Catholic Peace Fellowship if its lead administrator was disregarding Catholic teaching, although she did sign off by sending Forest and his fiancée her love. Despite her adamant stance, however, in the end Day did remain a CPF sponsor, and Merton made the difference.

That he himself had asked to be removed from the CPF board at one point, and that Day had objected, was an irony not lost on him. When Jim Forest wrote to Merton about the flap, he replied that he was greatly inspired by Dorothy Day but that, in this case, she should take into account the private nature of the young man's action and the fact that his resignation might endanger the future of the CPF—and, also, that the Church requires Catholics to follow their faithfully informed consciences. Although Day herself stressed the role of one's conscience in responding to Catholic teaching, to her, Merton's specific points still may have leaned too far in the direction of situational ethics. What likely swayed her was his compassionate response to Forest, which must have resonated, on some level, with this woman who had famously written, "The final word is love."[8]

In 1967 the "Summer of Love" saw the counterculture capture the attention of the nation. Even Merton was not immune. "I think it would be groovy," he wrote to Berrigan, to have trailblazing cultural figures come to the hermitage to brainstorm various lifestyles, from the hermit life to the communal life. Unlike his peace retreat two years earlier, this time women would be central players: Dorothy Day, certainly, plus such figures as feminist theologian Rosemary Radford Ruether, folk singer/peace activist Joan Baez, and Sister Corita Kent, famed for her bold silkscreen evocations of spiritual topics, including a "hot tomato" artistic reference to the Blessed Mother that drew a rebuke from Cardinal James McIntyre.[9]

Within a few years Corita Kent would leave her religious order. The women forsaking convent life significantly outnumbered the men quitting the priesthood. Day, who was so upset by this trend on the part of both priests and vowed religious, tried to model fidelity to her own community and prudent behavior, much like an abbess, even though Catholic Workers took no vows and often cycled through the experience on their way to professional and married life. Thus, even as she might well have accepted Merton's invitation, to picture her ever using terms such as *groovy* is unthinkable, even comical.

Berrigan embraced Merton's confab idea. Writing on a scrap of paper he picked up while walking on an idyllic California beach, the Jesuit also expressed the hope "with all my heart that you can come…play beachcomber, as I do." He was a guest of Merton's friend W. H. "Ping" Ferry, of the Center for the Study of Democratic Institutions in Santa Barbara, and breathlessly told Merton, "I feel reborn hanging around the Center…with freewheeling Jebs and…Corita" and other amazing nuns, "two-hour masses, an all-night session of bourbon and talk of freedom, love, change, hope, you, us, them, all of it." He added, "The whole g.d. mess, from Vietnam to [religious] superiors becomes bearable, or laughable, or both. Anyway, I am going to put my gut into praying you get out here….Man, you are in my heart like very few are! Keep me in yours." In the end nothing came of Merton's plan, which had occurred to him first thing in the morning when the rising sun and a jolt of caffeine sometimes encouraged his more impulsive thoughts. Besides, even as the media was showcasing the "flower child" phenomenon, Merton himself was questioning the more trendy and hedonistic aspects of the hippie culture.[10]

Still, he was restless, sounding plaintive in a letter to Dorothy Day as he complained that he was not allowed to join the ecumenical seven-day peace fast in Geneva, Switzerland, that had been organized by people they both admired. It would be through his gift as a writer that Merton would continue to make his spiritually rooted social justice witness. "Thomas Merton is a frequent contributor to the *Catholic Worker*. His article, 'The Vietnam War: An Overwhelming Atrocity' appeared in the March issue," the newspaper's editors would write in a note accompanying his June 1968 ecological jeremiad "The Wild Places." At a time when the environmental movement was in its infancy—and, if noted at all, was widely seen as unrealistic and a threat to American jobs—this monk deep in the Kentucky woods declared that the crime of environmental degradation was, in fact, a sin. "Catholic theology ought to take note of the ecological conscience, and do it fast," he declared. "Meanwhile, some of us are wearing the little yellow and red button with a flower on it and the words 'Celebrate Life!' We bear witness, as best we can, to these things."

But if he complained to his Catholic Worker friend of his isolation from inspiring get-togethers, he also counted on her to support him in his basic call—that is, the silent life of prayer. In this time of escalating crises, more and more people he respected were urging him to forsake the cloister for the front lines of social change. These figures ranged from theologian Rosemary Radford Ruether to the Fellowship of Reconciliation peace activist John Heidbrink to Archbishop Hélder Câmara of Brazil, famous for championing the poor. Merton knew, however, that Dorothy Day was one prominent figure who steadfastly supported his desire to remain a monk. Confiding to her that the solitary life was "no picnic," marked as it was by the "annihilation" of solitary mental games, he nonetheless emphasized that this encounter with God was a great gift of that same God. And predictably, she responded with deep gratitude for his prayers.

Even so, she was not above asking him to convey her monetary needs to his donors or to ask him to pray to St. Joseph for financial aid. Day explained that the City of New York was threatening to shut down her Catholic Worker house if it did not come up to code. Nobody knew better than Dorothy Day that this isolated man of God carried on correspondence with half the world, and, sure enough, when some admiring college students asked for Merton's photo and wanted to send him a monetary gift, he requested that instead they send their donations to the Catholic Worker.[11]

In that letter Day also asked Merton if he could spare a book by a theologian who, like them, challenged some aspects of Church authority: Romano Guardini. She had read Merton's latest book, *Conjectures of a Guilty Bystander,* which tells the reader that Guardini warned against equating faith with obedience. This theologian was no outlier, of course, having influenced Pope Benedict XVI and Pope Francis in their formative years, and Francis's own English-language biographer would note that "Guardini was a huge figure in the 1950s who influenced American Catholic luminaries such as Thomas Merton." Dorothy Day herself had long referenced this theologian, as when she wrote in the 1940s that Guardini reminds us that "we must learn to live in a state of permanent dissatisfaction with the Church." She added that he advised people, as she put it, "not to say 'I am a Christian' because we are always only on the way to *becoming* one [her emphasis]. We are en-route, on pilgrimage, and our job is to trust, to hope and to pray, and also to work 'to make that kind of a social order when it is easier for man to be good.'"[12]

For Dorothy Day in April 1967, this work meant joining Rev. Martin Luther King Jr. as he led half a million people in an anti–Vietnam War march to the United Nations plaza. Catholic Workers from across the nation took part, including one marching right next to King: labor priest Msgr. Charles Owen Rice, a founder of a Pittsburgh Catholic Worker. Merton, on the other hand, was skeptical that such demonstrations would affect military policy. But with this mercurial Trappist nothing was ever simple. His criticism of the demonstrations remained largely confined to his private jottings.[13]

That same month Eileen Egan of Pax, who had accompanied Day on the UN march, had written to Merton for advice on lobbying the National Council of Catholic Bishops. Pax was asking the NCCB to call for a change in the draft law to allow exemption from military combat for nonpacifists who nonetheless considered a specific war immoral. "Pax Group Scores Draft Law," the *Catholic Worker* reported. As it was, draft counselors had the difficult challenge of trying to find loopholes for young men who objected to the Vietnam War on conscience grounds but would have served willingly in the Second World War. Merton immediately sent Egan a detailed outline of strategies to use with the hierarchy but expressed pessimism, given that most bishops supported U.S. military involvement in Vietnam.[14]

Above all, for Merton and his circle, "the summer of love" meant love of God and love of neighbor as expressed in opposition to the war that they considered an abomination. Berrigan wrote to Merton expressing the hope that he wasn't hobbled by too many chronic ailments—whether his bursitis or skin rash or stomach problems or pinched nerve—for they were all counting on his loving counsel. For her part, Day was able to report to the monk that the Catholic Peace Fellowship and Pax both hosted "very grand" peace retreats that summer. And now, five months after her anguished personal letter to CPF director Jim Forest, she was lauding his work.

The Pax conference drew over one hundred people to the Catholic Worker farm, but just as Merton had predicted, the National Conference of Catholic Bishops made no official statement regarding the draft at its meeting a few months later. At that time Dorothy Day and Eileen Egan were in London—the London of Carnaby Street, with its Beatle-mad, bell-bottomed, paisley-bedecked flower children then in full bloom. Of course these two mature, serious-minded women were operating far from that psychedelic scene. Having come from a Vatican meeting on the laity, the two friends were attending the international Pax meeting at its British headquarters—this, even if their peace goals would have resonated with the young British mods.

As she prepared to depart from England, Day reflected on the network of impressive Catholic peace women traveling with her: a sisterhood, to use the parlance of the emerging women's movement. Egan and another savvy, multilingual peace activist, Marguerite Harris, were "indefatigable...women of the world, as well as women of the Church." For his part Merton had corresponded with Marguerite Harris and of course had long admired Eileen Egan's work, even if his cohorts in the Catholic peace movement were all men—except for Dorothy Day.[15]

At this time, the monk again made clear his great admiration for the Catholic Worker. Responding to a nun's concerns about the future of religious orders, Merton pointed to Dorothy Day as nothing less than "an example of what it means to take Christianity seriously in the twentieth century." He continued,

> In our religious life, we have managed over the years to develop a kind of system that neutralizes a really radical fervor and channels it into little substitutes for real Christian action and love....We have to start from where we are, and respond to grace as we are... be open to...each new opportunity to make our life more real and less of a systematic and mechanical routine. But we have to be patient....How much frustration and how many obstacles there are in a life like Dorothy Day's, and at times the Catholic Worker seems to get nowhere at all: yet the sincerity is there. Not one of us can pick up and live out the Sermon on the Mount literally: yet we should want to try as much as we can to live in that spirit.

Dorothy Day's peace witness prompted him to add, "There is no question that the Christian spirit is a spirit of non-violence and love."

But when he noted that most Christians who supported the war did not know the reality on the ground in Vietnam, he could not have known how tragically true this was for Dorothy Day's grandson Eric Hennessy. From rural Vermont, he signed up because his buddies were enlisting. So Day noted in her diary, even as she wrote of a fear so terrible that she could not share it with her family: that he would break down amid the horror of the carnage, much as his grandfather, Forster Batterham, had been shattered by the bloodshed he encountered in the First World War. But she never could bring herself to record, even to herself, the fact that this twenty-year-old Army Ranger would find himself patrolling, weapon poised: kill or be killed.[16]

Given the tragedies that lay ahead in 1968, Merton was prescient when he noted to himself in September 1967, "We are really on the verge of a blow-up," with danger ahead, in particular for dissenters. He identified with the "Catholic nonviolent left," he told leading Protestant theologian Martin Marty, and Merton cited as examples Dorothy Day and Joan Baez.[17] One month later, Daniel Berrigan was arrested at the huge march on the Pentagon. Upon his release, he was greeted by Washington, DC, Catholic Workers who took him to their House of Hospitality. En route they heard a radio report that Dan's brother Phil and three other people had been arrested for having poured some of their own blood on draft records. "We shed our blood upon these files," their statement read, "in what we hope is a sacrificial and constructive act" of protest against a war that was causing "the pitiful waste of American and Vietnamese blood."[18]

Merton knew this was coming. A few months earlier Dan Berrigan had written to his dear friend to advise him, in confidence, that Dan's brother Phil was talking about seizing and destroying draft files. Activists were increasingly impatient. The prominent civil rights priest Fr. James Groppi was not excluding violence as an option, while young people were increasingly using the revolutionary language of Che Guevara and Stokely Carmichael. With defenders of nonviolence increasingly being vilified by the Left, along with more traditional criticisms on the Right against civil rights activism in general, activists were increasingly looking for new, dramatic options.

At the same time, Berrigan confided to Merton that he himself entertained some qualms about the use of violent methods in a nonviolent cause, even if the destruction was minor, injured no one, and, in the case of destroying draft files, could have prevented people from going to Vietnam to kill or be killed. For his part, Merton admired the peace witness of both Berrigan brothers and conceded that perhaps Phil's destruction, with his own blood, of stolen draft files might be justified, particularly in this time of acute crisis. He even was dedicating his forthcoming book, *Faith and Violence*, to Phil, along with Jim Forest. Of the situation in Vietnam, Merton wrote, "Everything is destroyed." Here he was quoting a fellow monk, one from South Vietnam, the Buddhist Thich Nhat Hanh. His quiet spiritual depth overwhelmed Merton, prompting him to write an evocative essay called "Nhat Hanh Is My Brother."

Telegraphing the Kairos nature of this moment, Merton wrote to Berrigan, "We are all now in a position where some sort of choice of direction is called for," and he wondered how long he himself could stay out of jail. Then he again turned mentor, offering a roadmap for courageously but prudently living out such a challenge. In words applicable to any time of great crisis, he advised: size up the situation by asking well-thought-out questions of those closest to the action, but be careful not to judge the importance of a protest based on people's reactions. Instead, stay true to your principles.

He did not absolutely rule out the possibility that disciplined, limited, symbolic destruction of property might further the cause of peace, but he warned, "Ethically and evangelically we are getting toward the place where we have to be able to define our limits." He thought that the Martin Luther King Jr. approach, rooted in Gandhian nonviolence, still made the most sense. In this providential hour, too many radical wannabes were spouting talk of violent revolution without clear cause, in stark contrast to the Latin American rebels challenging longstanding dictatorial military regimes. In the United States, violent gestures might well play into the hands of local police, who would seize upon the more irresponsible chants, overreacting and violating protestors' rights, while winning favor with the average Joe in the process.[19]

But why did Berrigan count on Merton's advice when he considered his fellow Catholic activist Dorothy Day nothing less than a prophet? "She taught us things no seminary or retreat had taught," he recalled years later, noting, "It was a matter of a center, a core, a heart." In a world radically off-kilter, "The *Catholic Worker* was not the image of a church given over to Good Housekeeping. It was an anti-image.... Order in the heart, disorder in the world. The well-ordered heart can sustain, penetrate, interpret, resist, minister to, even at times heal, or at least mitigate, the whirlwind. This she lived, and, so living, taught."[20]

But Merton and Berrigan shared the same vocation: having made the solemn priestly promises of voluntary poverty, chastity, and obedience, they celebrated every single day the mysterious liturgical act called the Mass. At the same time, they shared a loathing of clerical sanctimony and rarely used the word *priest* to identify themselves. Their experiences in their respective religious communities had in common a dark side, with their peace and civil rights statements evoking censure from their superiors. In contrast, Dorothy Day experienced no such limitations. Yes, on those rare occasions that archdiocesan officials called her to account she made clear her intention to respond as an obedient daughter of the Church, but it was also true, ironically, that her marginal status as a layperson and a woman gave her near-total freedom to speak her mind. And she would go ahead and do things without asking permission so that the diocesan authorities would not be put in the position of having to decide whether to say no.

"My friend suffered and did what he could," Berrigan remarked of Merton, adding that the Trappist believed that he "ought to take his cues and style from, among others: blacks, women, homosexuals, welfare clients, Jews." Here, too, Berrigan was likely speaking for himself as well. Finally, even as all three wrote on spiritual topics, Dorothy Day was very much a journalist, while Merton and Berrigan were published poets with Ivy League connections: Merton a graduate of Columbia University, Berrigan a campus minister at Cornell.

But the next year, when he invited Merton to speak on campus, the monk declined, even though his new abbot had lifted the near-total travel ban imposed by his predecessor. When Merton traveled, he would do so to deepen his own spiritual practice. Berrigan, with his love for Merton and respect for his calling, understood this. Years later he would write, "My mind returns often to this. He stayed put." Meantime, contemplating this American monk's love for his Vietnamese "brother" monk Thich Nhat Hanh inspired Berrigan to write a lyrical passage that captured that providential hour, when everything seemed on the line. Merton's Jesuit friend found himself picturing a monk in Nhat Hahn's town, the ancient city of Hué, "dragging his altar into the streets and sitting there to protest the mad war. The tanks arrive: the monk stays put....What does the monk offer us, the future, the unborn, the jaded, fed-up resisters, the makers and drivers of tanks? Who will prevail?...Shall death be robbed of its victory, its sting? We long to know. I think the monk knows."[21]

CHAPTER EIGHT

Not Survival but Prophecy

WRITING TO BENEDICTINE theologian Jean Leclercq in 1968, Thomas Merton observed, "The vocation of the monk in the modern world...is not survival but prophecy." And even as the presidential contest began, he considered it meaningless, with the nation's problems so serious that they could not be tackled but with the grace of God. Just three days after he shared those depressing thoughts with Gordon Zahn, a colleague of Merton and Day's in the Catholic peace movement, Lyndon Johnson shocked the nation by declaring that he would not seek reelection under any circumstances. This president who had been elected by a landslide in 1964 now could not speak at any venue other than a military base without attracting protests. Then, just four days after LBJ's startling announcement, Martin Luther King Jr. was struck down by an assassin's bullet.[1]

Just one week before King was murdered, Merton received an eerily prescient letter from a friend of the famed civil rights leader. It was a mistake, wrote Atlanta Quaker June Yungblunt, for "Martin" to go to Memphis. Yungblunt and her husband had been urging him to spend a few peaceful days with Merton, and the Trappist had sent her possible dates for such a retreat. Even as King was headed to Memphis, she reflected to Merton that "he might have had the wisdom in repose to stay out of Memphis" if he had spent a few days in silent reflection at the hermitage.[2]

Instead, that week turned out to be "one of the more turbulent in my quiet life: Passion Week 1968," Merton reflected in his journal. He had experienced overwhelming relief on learning of Johnson's announced withdrawal that Sunday, only to hear on Tuesday that the president planned to be "drafted" at the Democratic National Convention in order to prevent Robert Kennedy from securing the nomination. At least that was the story Merton heard from his old friend Dan Walsh, who knew Robert and Ethel Kennedy. That such an unfounded rumor could gain traction in the Kennedy camp reflected the fact that RFK and LBJ attributed to each other the worst of motives. Then on Thursday, Merton and a British guest were returning from dinner at a nearby restaurant when the radio relayed news of Martin Luther King Jr.'s assassination. "It lay on the top of the traveling car like an animal, a beast of the apocalypse. And it finally confirmed all the apprehensions—the feeling that 1968 is a beast of a year," the anguished monk confided to his journal. He feared that southern whites would rejoice, while young African Americans in the North would rebel in anger. Indeed, the riots that immediately erupted even reached the intersection in Louisville where he had experienced the life-changing insight that we are all beloved of a God who became one with us.[3]

In this dark hour, one faint glimmer of hope appeared—from the smallest of sources. The children of King's top associate, Ralph Abernathy, asked if they could hate the man who had killed Dr. King, but before any of the grownups could respond, Dexter King, age seven, and Martin Luther King III, age ten, both said that "no, they couldn't hate the man, because their Daddy told them they were not to hate anyone"—so reported Yungblunt to Merton. She had been looking after the King children while their mother flew to Memphis to bring their father's body back to Atlanta. When the widow walked into the house upon her return, the two women embraced without uttering a word.[4]

As it happened, Merton had been working on "Freedom Songs" for an event that King was slated to attend, the National Liturgical Conference in Washington, DC, and these lyrics were to be sung by a chorus that included one of his daughters. Now that concert would serve as a memorial. "The songs were enough to break down the walls of Jericho. People wept with joy," Dorothy Day reported to Merton as soon as she returned to her room late that night. Her sad heart was brimming with gratitude for this tremendous gift, she told him, but she left unmentioned the award that the conference had bestowed on her.[5]

Day's *Catholic Worker* essay on the assassination was, as one author has put it, "a study in grim realism." She reported that King "was shot through the throat....His blood poured out." On a deeper level, however, her grief-stricken column relayed hope—not optimism, mind you, but hope—the same Christ-centered social justice passion that the slain preacher himself embodied. Situating him among her beloved communion of saints, Dorothy Day noted that his blood was "shed for whites and blacks alike. The next day was Good Friday, the day commemorated by the entire Christian world as the day when Jesus Christ, true God and true man, shed His blood." Underscoring her hope, Day made the larger point that Dr. King's vision of a Beloved Community was made manifest in the days that followed his murder. "Love and grief were surely in the air," she wrote, "in the labor movement, and the civil rights movement and in the peace movement." Thousands joined the striking sanitation workers in Memphis that King had supported, while in Atlanta "half a million people gathered from coast to coast to walk in the funeral procession, following the farm cart and the two mules which drew the coffin of the dead leader."[6]

Many of those working in the social justice trenches now transferred a bit of their hope to Robert F. Kennedy. He had arranged for the plane that flew King's widow to Memphis, and he was the person that June Yungblunt turned to for solace on arriving at the King funeral. Struck by their sad encounter, Merton mentioned it to his novices, little knowing that Robert Kennedy himself would be assassinated just two months later.[7]

At that point the movement became unmoored. As Merton noted to the slain senator's widow, Robert Kennedy represented the last hope: the only presidential candidate with a chance of winning who, at the same time, was willing to consider a negotiated settlement in Vietnam. A few years earlier Ethel Kennedy had told Merton that her husband had placed the monk's *Seeds of Destruction* "front and center" on his bookshelf, and she had made clear that both of them appreciated his prayers, especially in the wake of President Kennedy's assassination. Now Robert Kennedy was dead as well, and Merton assured his widow that he was saying Masses for the murdered leader. "God is our only hope," he concluded, for, like Dorothy Day, he traded not in optimism but, rather, in a faith rooted in a God of love.[8]

On the other hand, Day did not know Ethel Kennedy; for the quasi-anarchist Catholic Worker leader, party politics were beside the point. Even so, the Kennedy brothers had visited the Catholic Worker as young men, while their brother-in-law, Sargent Shriver, counted Day and Merton as spiritual heroes who inspired his work as director of the Peace Corps and the War on Poverty. Day herself attended the funeral Mass for Robert Kennedy, which was held in New York City at St. Patrick's Cathedral, and she found the liturgy an "example of faith. What strength it brings," she noted to a friend. "What joy, even in the midst of tragedy."[9]

During the few weeks between the King and Kennedy assassinations, yet another shocking event took place, this one featuring Day and Merton's friend Dan Berrigan. On May 17, 1968, news cameras captured the Jesuit activist and eight other people standing before a pile of draft records they had just set afire in Catonsville, Maryland. They all were Catholics, and by way of demonstrating that not all Catholics supported the Vietnam War, these protestors purposely chose to take the Selective Service files from a building owned by a prominent Catholic organization that defended the war, the Knights of Columbus. The Catonsville Nine were very much a team, but the Jesuit Daniel and his then-Josephite priest brother Phil stood out in their clerical blacks. Praying over the smoldering pile, the two Berrigans quickly became the most controversial priests in the country. In particular, the media cited the evocative words of that man of letters, Dan Berrigan: "Our apologies, good friends, for the fracture of good order, the burning of paper instead of children."[10]

No one could have guessed that, just four days earlier, the author of those powerful words had still harbored doubts about the planned action—doubts underscored by the skepticism expressed by his cherished friend and spiritual mentor Thomas Merton. He pointed out to Berrigan that violent destruction of property in the name of nonviolence departed from the method championed by King. And now King himself had been felled by violence. While Merton had tolerated Phil's pouring of his own blood on stolen draft files, the monk feared that setting files aflame might unwittingly contribute to an atmosphere in which irresponsible people might hurl Molotov cocktails at buildings and then start planting bombs. The monk's apprehension anticipated the wanton violence of the Weather Underground in the coming decade: an extremely different kind of group, to be sure, but nonetheless one that would demonstrate Merton's fears in action, planting bombs in civilian buildings.

If Merton was pulling Dan Berrigan in one direction, Phil Berrigan was pulling him in the other. In an all-night session with his brother just four days before the raid, the Jesuit poet/activist arrived at the conclusion that setting on fire files soaked in napalm would dramatically demonstrate the horror that was being visited on men, women, and children, whose skin was being scorched by use of this gelatinous substance: part of the violent American technology that was turning South Vietnam into a gutted, ruined country. Moreover, fire would destroy far more files than would staining them with blood. In the end, 378 young men would not be called up for military service because their records were destroyed by the Catonsville Nine, while similar raids in the coming months, many by Catholic Workers, would keep countless more young men from being sent to Asia to kill or be killed. From now on, Daniel Berrigan would be known for ritual acts of destruction against government military property.[11]

That summer so many people asked Merton his opinion of the raid that he addressed the question in a circular letter. "To many their acts of protests have seemed incomprehensible, wild, extreme. Well, I think they were intentionally 'extreme,' though they remained in essence non-violent," he wrote. He explained that the demonstrators felt that they either had to stop the war or go to jail, and while he acknowledged that such a stance shocked many people, he argued that what really should shock people was that Catholics failed to call foul when a bishop labeled U.S. policy in Vietnam an act of Christian love! But although he explained the rationale for the Catonsville tactics with eloquence, Merton did not go so far as to endorse them. Instead he stated his preference for radical resistance of a more purely nonviolent nature. On a deeper level, he reflected that ignoring God was "at the root of our trouble." Sounding like Dorothy Day, he concluded, "Let us pray for one another, and try in everything to do what God asks of us." As he put it to one correspondent at that time, "Where I fit seems to me to be in the sort of niche provided by the *Catholic Worker*."[12]

In the meantime, Day's affection for the Berrigans led her initially to tell them that any criticism she might have of their protest tactics was of little account in light of the atrocities of this war that they were protesting. Soon after he was released on bail, she asked Dan to celebrate the Mass blessing the New York Catholic Worker's new residence (and to bless Tom Cornell, who was about to be imprisoned). The liturgy was held in the living area, children of the draft protestors toddling about. Afterward Dorothy Day, this tall, dignified woman, sat next to the intense priest with the warm, impish smile. "Does anyone have any questions?" she asked, and she nodded when Berrigan explained that he took part in burning the draft records because incremental actions no longer worked in the face of such rapid, immoral escalation of the war.[13]

The Catonsville action inspired several subsequent draft file burnings, however, even as the Catholic Peace Fellowship was receiving angry letters about the tactic and a death threat as well, which arrived on the same day that Robert Kennedy was assassinated. Day began to voice some quiet concern about the method. Eventually she even questioned, at least privately, the advisability of the nonviolent raids themselves. Might breaking into government facilities frighten the employees (as in fact had been the case with two Catonsville clerks)? Tom Cornell put it this way: might an inexperienced guard at some military installation find himself shooting an elderly trespassing nun and thus be saddled with that guilt for the rest of his life? Merton, for his part, would not live to observe Dan Berrigan's many subsequent civil disobedience break-ins, but the fact that Day and Merton both questioned ritual burnings in the name of nonviolence, even at a time of extreme violence in Vietnam, may help explain why subsequently Dan Berrigan would pour blood on military items—even hammer nuclear warheads—but seldom if ever would set any government property on fire after 1968.[14]

Meantime, like a stove's steady pilot light, Pax leader Eileen Egan continued her peace outreach, and nobody appreciated her persistent efforts more than Day and Merton. Pax kept urging the National Council of Catholic Bishops to endorse the peace statements of Paul VI and Vatican II, well aware that most U.S. bishops remained resolutely silent or, like many of their faithful, openly supported the Vietnam War. Merton himself faced ridicule from such Catholics, as in March 1968, when his local diocesan newspaper published letters lambasting his antiwar stance, including one irate correspondent claiming to have burned his copies of Merton's books. No wonder that same month he wrote to Egan expressing his gratitude for her work.

Merton and Day knew, better than most people, that beneath her prim hairdo and deliberate manner beat the heart of a passionate idealist. In the aftermath of World War II Egan had advocated on behalf of desperate refugees, an effort that contributed mightily to the establishment of one of the world's leading charitable organizations, Catholic Relief Services. And even if she may have done a bit of mundane, long-distance secretarial work for Merton in this era when women still were regularly asked to do such tasks, as of 1968 she was cluing him in to the counterculture. His symbol-strewn, stream-of-consciousness epic poem *Geography of the Lograire* reminded Egan of the latest album by the psychedelic folk group The Incredible String Band, and Merton eagerly accepted her offer to send him a copy of their latest record album.[15]

But of course it was Day who counted Egan as a longtime friend, with the front page of the October 1968 *Catholic Worker* featuring her provocative headline, "Are You Ready to Commit Instant Auschwitz?" This Pax article scored the U.S. bishops for failing to endorse the Council's statements, issued several years earlier, condemning nuclear war. Meantime, that summer, as in the previous six summers, the Catholic Worker farm in the Hudson River Valley hosted the Pax conference, with Egan calling Dorothy Day "the luminous center" of the annual event. Day, for her part, remarked in her diary on the wide variety of peace supporters jammed into their rural residence for the three-day Pax meeting in the summer of 1968.[16]

Egan solicited from Merton an essay that was read aloud at the event by a *Catholic Worker* editor. The monk pointed out that those in seats of power twist the word *nonviolence* to mean *weakness*, when in fact nonviolent resistance is powerful: "not pragmatic, but prophetic…the language of Kairos." Eerily anticipating his own demise at the end of that year so filled with tragic deaths, Thomas Merton concluded, "This is the day of the Lord, and whatever may happen to us, He shall overcome." As he put it to Egan, their hope had to be sober at this time of great crisis: not survival but prophecy. For her part, the Pax leader would note that this essay constituted Merton's last published essay on peace. In the meantime, she informed him that the "marvelous" piece was enthusiastically received and that he was truly with them in spirit, most especially at the two Masses said for his intentions.

For her part, Dorothy Day complained to herself that Merton's Pax essay, with its title "A Footnote from *Ulysses*," was too literary for its audience, just as she had scored his *Catholic Worker* Camus piece as overly abstract. But just as she had lauded that article in public, so now to others she praised "A Footnote from *Ulysses*," urging her readers to purchase this "magnificent" piece. More important, Egan shared with Merton the exciting news that Pax's efforts were finally starting to bear fruit: the U.S. hierarchy was considering a statement critical of nuclear war. It would take years, but in 1983 the National Conference of Catholic Bishops would make history by issuing a strong document calling all nations to pursue peace, above all.[17]

Presciently, Egan also had invited to that Pax conference someone who would soon make his mark nationally: a champion of nonviolence who represented the labor movement and the rising Latino movement: United Farm Workers (UFW) leader César Chávez. "I feel he is someone the Church has sorely needed," she wrote to Merton, "a worker who realizes that nonviolence is a practical way of achieving social ends."[18]

Chávez could not participate, however, for his union was in the midst of a major fight for recognition from California's powerful grape growers. UFW members were busy mobilizing Americans nationwide to support "La Causa" by boycotting grapes. Also, travel was difficult for the farm worker leader, who suffered from the effects of his twenty-three-day fast in March. This was nonviolence of the most radical sort: life-threatening, sacrificial action aimed not at growers so much as at his own members, some of whom had struck back when attacked by farm security personnel and local police. That Chávez finally broke the fast by receiving communion at Mass only reinforced Dorothy Day's admiration for this reflective, dedicated person who had visited her the previous year. Telling her readers that the UFW often marched behind the banner of Our Lady of Guadalupe, she noted that on entering their Catholic Worker house, "When César Chávez saw the picture of Our Lady of Guadalupe… he immediately left his seat at the table and stood before it a few moments." The Catholic Worker had been supporting farm workers for decades, and now their Houses of Hospitality were hosting boycott organizers nationwide. Famously, Day's final civil disobedience imprisonment would be in support of a UFW strike, and she would feature Chávez in her writing just two months before her death in 1980. He, in turn, would attend her funeral.[19]

Day did not mention Chávez to Merton, as he never had shown any interest in the labor movement. Thus, he never wrote, even to himself, about the controversial labor history of the company that provided the fortune for his friend and sometime publisher James Laughlin. Day, on the other hand, had characterized the company, Jones and Laughlin, as "bitter anti-union steel employers," calling the firm's actions during a 1930s labor dispute "terrorism." Still, ever since his baptism as a graduate student, Merton had found the truest Christian witness among those striving to make real the Works of Mercy by living with, and defending, the poor. He also could well have appreciated Chávez as an iconic figure of Catholic nonviolence. Indeed, this monk with wide-ranging vision had long considered Latin America the vanguard in social reform and artistic creativity. Moreover, Merton knew that Chávez was scheduled to speak at a nearby university the following year, and if he had lived, doubtless the monk would have invited the UFW leader to the hermitage.[20]

Moreover, Merton was acquainted with one of the most prominent figures supporting César Chávez: folk singer and peace activist Joan Baez. She and Thomas Merton shared a deep interest in promoting nonviolence, and he found achingly resonant her beautiful renditions of traditional love songs, which he discovered the summer that he was enraptured with Margie Smith. Baez visited Merton along with writer/activist Ira Sandperl, and as they conversed over a bottle of scotch, she even offered to arrange for Tom and Margie to rendezvous. No such meeting materialized—which, in retrospect, both the singer and the monk thought all for the best. Merton later recalled that she told him that she learned to pray by reading his work. And although she did not understand the meaning of his solitary life and urged him to spend his time giving campus talks, he was very impressed with her as a clarion voice for beauty, honesty, and peace. Baez, for her part, considered him "a man who emanates warmth and honesty": full of fun, and a bit of a rebel, but also somehow true to his monastic vocation and, at the same time, to the cause of peace.[21]

It would be thanks to Joan Baez that Dorothy Day would participate in the farm worker strike of 1973. The folk singer had invited Day to visit the Institute for the Study of Nonviolence in northern California, and these two strong UFW supporters proceeded to join the picket lines of the strike being conducted by César Chávez's union. The photograph of this old, frail woman quietly facing down the beefy, pistol-packing policemen became iconic, as did the smock she was wearing, which was signed by Joan Baez, along with Day's jail companions.[22]

Meantime, who but Dorothy Day would invoke the United Farm Workers when reporting that she received Holy Communion from the pope himself? "Of course I was happy at that Mass, feeling as I did that I was representing...all Cesar Chavez's fellow workers in California and Texas, and the little babies and small children of the agricultural workers who are at present at our farm in Tivoli in the day-care center." She sounded almost dutiful in this newspaper piece as she mentioned having been selected as one of two Americans receiving communion from Pope Paul VI at this Mass for the Conference of the Laity. The other American was astronaut

James McDivitt, "who presented the cone of his space capsule to the Holy Father."

The Conference of the Laity held workshops on "spiritual attitudes, the family, tensions between generations, cooperation between men and women, social communications, economic development and access to culture, peace and world community and migration," Day reported, adding that the sessions were marked by "amity and order." In her peace workshop, "everyone felt that large segments of the articulate laity certainly had been heard." But in all candor, she concluded that "it was...the conviction that nothing had really been settled, especially in the fields of birth control and war. (Racism was condemned unanimously.)" Among the pastors who had traveled to Rome with their parishioners, she "heard one priest say that it was surprising how many of the delegates, far more than had been expected, were against birth control. Another priest said rather coldly that it was evident that the Congress was packed with conservatives." She noted that, regarding birth control, "Practically all the priests I spoke to said that the decision was to be made by the married couples themselves, according to their conscience": an ominous observation, given that a few months later Paul VI would issue *Humanae Vitae*, the controversial encyclical upholding Church opposition to artificial contraception.[23]

With birth control, as with other sex-related issues, Day and Merton seldom voiced an opinion. While her daughter did indeed have nine children, and while Day did not oppose her Church's stance on contraception, her newspaper almost never featured an article on the topic. As she put it to archdiocesan officials as far back as the 1930s, "We are not going into the subject of birth control." The few times she mentioned the issue publicly, invariably she did so in the context of poor and/or minority women being denied adequate medical support and being peddled contraception by people who were as prejudiced as they were powerful. And, of course, she had reported that, on this issue, the typical pastor thought their parishioners should be able to decide for themselves.[24]

Merton also avoided talking about birth control. In 1964, when replying to a correspondent who reported contributing an essay to a Catholic book that supported the contraception option, Merton offered no opinion on the issue. Instead, like Day, he proffered a larger frame, in his case, nuclear war: criticizing people, especially Church officials, who refused to see the nuclear threat as a "respect for life" issue. It was within that context that he made one of his rare statements on sexual reproduction issues. In one of his 1961 Cold War Letters, the monk decried so many theologians remaining silent about the threat of nuclear mass murder while "we are so wildly exercised about the 'murder' (and the word is of course correct) of an unborn infant by abortion, or even the prevention of conception which is hardly murder." By 1967 he was more persuaded than ever that he was not called to opine on such issues. Much as his hermit life made him ill-suited for advising activists on antiwar tactics, his solitude, along with his celibacy, made him "out of touch...with what concerns married people," he mused to himself, reflecting that he should focus on his life of prayer. And out in the world, nobody encouraged that approach more consistently than Dorothy Day.

Meantime, in 1968 she mentioned in a letter to Catholic peace activist Gordon Zahn that she was no feminist, even adding that she followed the lead of Peter Maurin. In reality, even when her cofounder was alive, Dorothy Day directed this national movement, making virtually all of the major administrative decisions. In that sense she did reflect the feminist ethos, such that she was posthumously honored for National Women's History Month. Still, Day never warmed to the women's rights cause. Born in the Victorian age, scarred by her own abortion experience, and wedded to her Church, she was not about to champion reproductive rights, and she worried that feminism would complicate the civil rights and labor movements. It was Merton, the member of a male-only priesthood, who in 1968 praised Mary Daly's *The Church and the Second Sex* for, in his words, "unmasking the latent anti-feminism of so much Catholic thinking and practice."[25]

In July 1968, newspaper headlines announced *Humanae Vitae,* the encyclical that reaffirmed the Church's opposition to contraception, but for Merton the big news that month was his abbot granting him permission to attend a monastic conference in Bangkok. On this trip he also would stop in India and Sri Lanka, with tentative plans for visits to monasteries from Japan to Switzerland. In sharing this exciting development with Dorothy Day, he took pains to explain that the monks and nuns attending the Bangkok meeting were Catholic, and that he would attend the event as the peritus, or official theological representative, of his religious community.

He sent a similar, carefully worded message in a circular letter to friends: this in the face of persistent rumors that he was leaving the priesthood to marry or becoming a Zen Buddhist. Both stories were unfounded, but they were fed by his charming personality and his evident interest in Asian spiritual traditions. For her part, Day may not have shared his passion for exploring Buddhism, but she believed in appreciating goodness wherever it might be found, and one of the pieces in his new book *Zen and the Birds of Appetite* had originally appeared in the *Catholic Worker.* Meantime, this book referenced the literary figure so beloved of Dorothy Day: Dostoevsky's Staretz Zossima. Merton wrote that from this fictional character we learn "that paradise is something attainable because, after all, it is present within us and we have only to discover it there."

This lesson is simple but not easy: like love—*as* love. Our job? Humility and openness to God's grace. So said Merton in his Bangkok talk, citing both Zen master D. T. Suzuki and the ancient desert hermit St. Anthony. This Trappist with the protean mind revealed that anyone who believes in Jesus must perforce be lovingly open to the deepest beliefs of others: that a Christian appreciates the gifts provided by other faiths, not despite one's own faith, but *because* of it. After all, the Greatest Commandment of Jesus is a command to love.

In a circular letter to friends at this time, he wrote that the Tibetan Buddhists, from the Dalai Lama to the humblest monk, dedicated themselves to trying to break free of both passion and illusion, even as he went on to express his "consolation in my own faith in Christ and His indwelling presence. I hope and believe He may be present in the hearts of all of us." That loving impulse shines through the closing remarks of his Bangkok talk, which spotlighted the Zen insight that we should strive toward "a recovery of unity which is not the suppression of opposites, but a simplicity beyond opposites." For his part, the Dalai Lama would write that meeting Merton was a highlight of those years, that the Trappist "introduced me to the real meaning of the word 'Christian.'"[26]

At the conclusion of the presentation Merton quipped, "Now I will disappear," and headed off to his room for a midday rest. As reported the next day on the front page of the *New York Times*, and often recounted thereafter, he was discovered two hours later lying on the floor, the room's large, standing fan on his chest, blades rotating. Merton was pronounced dead by an abbess attending the conference who was a physician. Evidently he either suffered a heart attack while reaching for the fan—or, much more likely, was electrocuted when he turned it off, for the fan had faulty wiring that caused a severe shock if one touched any part of the metal. Also, despite all of his health complaints, Merton had never suffered from a heart condition. That the police discounted the fan problem and played up the heart attack explanation may well be a case of the officers wanting to head off any media coverage of their local conference center's physical shortcomings. At any rate, for half a century, the accounts of this famous monk's tragic death described it as accidental.[27]

Then in 2018 *The Martyrdom of Thomas Merton* appeared. This self-published book raises a number of challenging questions. For one thing, the authors write that none of the witness statements mentioned electrocution as the likely cause of death. But as to its thesis that elements of the CIA killed Merton: the authors cite no documents from the agency pinpointing such a plot. Of course, by its nature the CIA is secretive. It is also the case, however, that Dorothy Day would seem the more likely target—a public figure regularly called a Communist, who criticized capitalism, was arrested for defying civil defense laws, gave speeches in support of draft card burnings, and whose FBI file was ten times larger than Merton's.[28]

A review of *The Martyrdom of Thomas Merton* published in the International Thomas Merton Society's *Merton Seasonal* concluded that the authors failed to provide convincing evidence for their case. In contrast, the reviewer for the *Catholic Worker* wrote that this "edifying" book presented "new evidence [that] suggests that Thomas Merton was murdered while bravely championing peace at the height of the U.S. war in Vietnam." Despite their sharply divergent readings, both reviewers indicate that the jury is still out on the "martyrdom" book's conclusion. Indeed, with regard to human events, conclusions are often contingent—this, even as the straightforward, conventional explanation more often than not turns out to be the one that prevails. At any rate, more than half a century after his passing, Thomas Merton clearly continues to signify. And reflecting his enduring importance to Dorothy Day's acolytes, the *Catholic Worker* was the first periodical of any significance to review this book.[29]

Day herself, on hearing the news of his sudden death, thought that Merton likely experienced a fatal heart attack, perhaps because she suffered from chronic, serious heart problems and because, as she told her readers, "A year ago Thomas Merton was sending out his Advent-Christmas letter and telling of the death of three close friends by heart attacks. 'Both were about my age,' he wrote. 'So if I suddenly follow their example I will be the last one to be surprised.'"

Day pointed out that the *New York Times* obituary called Merton "a writer of singular grace about the City of God and an essayist of penetrating originality on the City of Men." She described her community's shock at the news, explaining that this "friend of the Catholic Worker" had contributed innumerable articles to their newspaper while also publishing many widely read books. Calling her sad tribute "Thomas Merton, Trappist," Day was determined to counter the persistent rumors that he was somehow quitting his religious order. Not mentioning that he had been scoping out possible alternative hermitage sites and meeting with Buddhists, Day emphasized the man who many times had told her, and had written to the end, that his faith constituted the center of his life. And surely she would have found it more than a tragic coincidence that the date of this Trappist's death, December 10, marked the anniversary of his entrance into the monastery (in 1941).

She always sought to close on a note of hope, and here—writing of yet another shocking death at the close of a year marked by so many—the Catholic Worker found words of solace from the very person they were mourning. Exactly a year earlier, in his Christmas 1967 circular letter to his friends, Merton had written, "The times are difficult. They call for courage and faith. Faith is in the end a lonely virtue.... If we are just looking for a little consolation we may be disappointed. Let us pray for one another, love one another in truth, in the sobriety of earnest Christian hope, for hope, says Paul, does not deceive." Refusing to despair, and despite their own faults, Dorothy Day and Thomas Merton gave enduring witness to facing grave crises with faith, hope, and, above all, love.[30]

Coda

THE FINAL WORD IS LOVE

IN JULY 1976 DOROTHY DAY wrote to herself that she needed to pray to Merton "for aid now, and patience, and 'diligence' in my work"—this after seeing a film of the talk he gave on the day of his death. Now, eight years after Merton's passing, Day herself had entered the final stage of life. Nearing eighty, and long plagued by heart ailments along with arthritis, she was felled by a serious heart attack in September 1976 after giving a talk to eight thousand people at a Eucharistic congress in Philadelphia. One also could say, however, that that event broke her heart.[1]

Ever since she turned seventy-five, in 1972, Dorothy Day had been finding herself increasingly celebrated. It was as if people were waking up to the fact that this bold spiritual figure and social justice champion was still around but would not be for much longer. The *New York Times*, in its birthday profile, called her "the most influential lay person in the history of American Catholicism"—perhaps destined to be declared a saint. That same year Notre Dame bestowed its highest award on her, the Laetare Medal. Actually, she had tried to duck the prize, and the university knew better than to offer her an honorary degree, as she refused to accept one from any institution that sponsored an ROTC program. No wonder Bill Moyers titled his PBS profile *Dorothy Day: Still a Rebel*.[2]

When she spoke at the 1976 Eucharistic Congress in Philadelphia, Dorothy Day was joined by two soulmates: her old friend Eileen Egan of Pax and Mother Teresa. Egan had arranged for the two women to meet when Day visited India along with the Pax leader in 1970, and she recalled that Mother Teresa greeted Dorothy Day by placing on her a garland of flowers. Meantime, Egan had suggested to Merton that he look up Mother Teresa when he visited Calcutta, where she and the members of her religious order took in the destitute dying and treated them like "another Christ." Merton's Asian journal makes no mention of her, but he doubtless was familiar with her work well ahead of most Americans, for *Jubilee*, the magazine published by his friends, had featured her on its cover several times by 1960.[3]

The three women's conference session was called "Women and the Eucharist." At this time the women's movement was in high gear—with state after state approving the Equal Rights Amendment (even if it would barely fall short of the three-fourths of state legislatures needed for ratification)—but if "Women and the Eucharist" was a nod to women's rights, any such reference went unmentioned by the conference planners in this institution officially run by men. For their part, Day and her two cohorts did not call themselves feminists. They only referenced the issue of women's rights by their leadership example.

As they made their way to the session, Day confided to Egan that she was sick at heart. The congress included a Mass in honor of the U.S. military, and, like the women's session, was scheduled for August 6, which happened to be the anniversary of the nuclear attack on Hiroshima. The Catholic Worker leader felt obligated to decry that military theme, even though she considered the Mass more important than life itself, containing within it that most precious of gifts: the Eucharist—and even as the congress, of course, was dedicated to the Eucharist.

As she mounted the platform, "Dorothy's tall frame was slightly stooped and her blue checked cotton dress hung loosely upon it," Egan recalled. In all their long friendship, the Pax leader had never seen her friend speak from a prepared text, but now Dorothy Day carefully placed her speech on the lectern. Even so, she felt unprepared and silently invoked the biblical words, "Fear not." Her remarks, which she titled "Bread for the Hungry," opened with a devoted evocation of the Eucharist. Day shared with her listeners her deep, abiding "love and gratitude to the Church" as nothing less than "a mother who taught me the crowning love of the life of the Spirit." But love in action can be a harsh and dreadful thing, and now she plunged ahead, noting that this mother "also taught me that 'before we bring our gifts of service, of gratitude, to the altar—if our brother have anything against us, we must hesitate to approach the altar to receive the Eucharist.'"

Speaking with an anguish made even more dramatic by her careful, understated manner, Day said, "And here we are on August 6th." Acknowledging other holocausts, notably the Turkish attacks on the Armenians and the Nazi persecution of Jews, "God's chosen people," she then sounded like a prophet. "It is a fearful thought that unless we do penance, we will perish," she firmly stated, reminding her listeners that, at that very moment, military leaders were processing into the cathedral nearby. Out in front a few Catholic Workers, having fasted and prayed, were among those handing out leaflets objecting to the liturgy's theme, and she called for "fasting, as a personal act of penance, for the sin of our country, which we love." Asking why that religious service could not have been held on a different date, "I plead," she said, "that we regard the military Mass, and all the Masses today, as an act of penance, begging God to forgive us." That her audience broke into resounding applause only partly salved Day's wounded heart, which suffered an actual physical attack a few weeks later.[4]

"I had a mild heart attack in September," she told her readers, "pains in my chest and arms and a gasping of fresh air. It is certainly frightening not to be able to breathe." Hinting that she had entered the last stage of life, she added, "Hereafter if I travel it will be for pleasure," and she indicated that henceforth, others should answer most of the Catholic Worker correspondence. What would happen to this movement so closely associated with Dorothy Day, after she passed away? The question hung in the air. In the meantime, "I will always write," she noted. Indeed, her final diary entry came just nine days before her death.

The Catholic Worker leader spent her final years in Maryhouse, their new House of Hospitality for women. This longtime dream of hers became a reality mainly thanks to a former colleague of Merton's, Fr. John Eudes Bamberger. He had entered the Trappists inspired by *The Seven Storey Mountain* and had helped Merton counsel his novices before being tapped to head the Abbey of Our Lady of the Genesee in upstate New York. Abbot John Eudes had invited Day to be the first woman ever to speak within their monastic enclosure, and his community was so taken with her witness that they turned over to her a bequest they had received so that she could purchase an old music school and convert it into a home for destitute women.[5] These Trappists have a statue by Catholic Worker artist Ade Bethune; not coincidentally, she was the lay affiliate of a monastery, as a Benedictine oblate—just like her old friend Dorothy Day.[6]

Bamberger expressed the hope that Day would "grow strong daily, and that before long you can do some quiet visiting where you will not have to speak," affectionately hinting that perhaps such a trip might be "to a certain Trappist monastery in upstate New York." For her part, Day noted in her diary that the abbot visited them and pronounced himself delighted with this new home that could hold fifty residents: fifty, that is, if you placed mattresses side-by-side on the floor (though, as always, Day had her own room). And it was to Maryhouse that people came to pay their respects after the Catholic Worker leader passed away on November 29, 1980.[7]

That impoverished neighborhood on the Lower East Side would gentrify beyond anything Day and Merton ever

could have imagined. Nonetheless the dispossessed still find their way to the Maryhouse door, just as they come to the more than two hundred Catholic Worker houses across the country and beyond. Catholic Workers and their allies continue to protest at military installations, often facing jail time in the process, while Day and Merton's friend Dan Berrigan became the nation's most famous Jesuit.[8]

Berrigan protégé Fr. John Dear noted that when Pope Francis praised Day and Merton to Congress and the world, "I almost passed out—fainted—it was daring. Dan was still alive, and I was with him maybe a week after that, and he just smiled and chuckled. You can't even imagine that such a thing would happen. But for him to hear the pope invoke his two friends...." Less than a year later, the president of the Pontifical Council for Justice and Peace, Cardinal Peter Turkson, invited several Catholic peacemakers to advise the pope on his peace message draft. Most of them were, in effect, spiritual grandchildren of Day and Merton, from John Dear to the leaders of Eileen Egan's Pax group, now known as Pax Christi. Much of their wording made its way into the historic 2017 address by Pope Francis, "Nonviolence—A Style of Politics for Peace." For the first time in its two-thousand-year history, the Roman Catholic Church officially named nonviolence as the preferred solution to world conflicts.[9]

But even as Francis took this major step, its effect was clouded by the persistent issue of Church scandals and cover-ups on a scale that Day and Merton never could have anticipated. Still, their model of honest, clear-eyed faithfulness, even in the darkest times, speaks volumes. When one of their mutual friends, Catholic sociologist and peace activist Gordon Zahn, expressed near despair over the bishops blessing American military adventures, Day consoled him with words that resonate anew in our troubled times: "I never expect much of the bishops," she wrote. "In all history, popes and bishops and father abbots seem to have been blind and power loving and greedy." But reaffirming the faith that meant everything to her, she then declared, "It is the saints who keep appearing all through history that keep things going": their inspiring witness, along with "the bread of life" as constantly made manifest in the Eucharist. "Please Gordon, struggle on...be faithful," she urged, assuring him of her love and her prayers. Reflecting on Day's and Merton's legacies, peace activist John Dear put it this way, "For me, their greatest thing is...that they kept at it until the day they died. They never gave up. They were rocks, they were so faithful. They were like St. Francis; they were giants of the Church, against every adversary possible, and that is a powerful thing."[10] In light of Dorothy Day's prayerful devotion to the Works of Mercy, the U.S. bishops themselves are promoting her sainthood cause. Bishop Robert Barron, famed for explaining Catholicism in the mass media, put it this way: "She was a person who had made Jesus in all of his concreteness the center of her life. Her 'conservative' piety is expressive of this continual act of centering, and her 'liberal' social commitment is her living out of the unambiguous message and style of Jesus." And while her canonization is by no means assured—some prospective saints end up stalled midway in the process—Day and Merton tell us that most saints are hidden among us and that, in fact, we all are called to be saints.[11]

The pope's praise notwithstanding, there is no indication whatsoever that the bishops have any interest in considering Thomas Merton for sainthood. At the same time, he seems well on his way to becoming part of the canon of major spiritual writers like John Henry Newman, Gerard Manley Hopkins, and Thérèse of Lisieux: unfamiliar to the average journalist, perhaps, but individuals who change people's lives. Most of Merton's books remain in print, and "a 'classic' is a book that remains in print," as his Columbia University professor, Mark Van Doren, famously quipped. This prize-winning literary figure noted, on Merton's passing, that he "will be missed as few persons of his time will be....I for one have never known a mind more brilliant, more beautiful, more serious, more playful"—indeed, one marked by an "immeasurable...capacity for love." Even now, more than a half century after his death, previously unpublished Merton writings regularly appear, and invariably they are appreciatively reviewed in the *Catholic Worker*.[12]

Moreover, just as Merton had predicted, the monastic spirit is blossoming in new ways, even as traditional religious vocations are declining. Laypeople are hearing the call to formally affiliate with a monastery, joining up in far greater numbers than when Dorothy Day herself professed as a Benedictine oblate. Many of these monastic communities also find their retreats overbooked, with people from every walk of life seeking "contemplation in a world of action," as Merton called it.[13] The Center for Action and Contemplation, founded in 1986 by Merton/Day acolyte Richard Rohr, OFM, has gained fame thanks to his popular retreats, publications, and presentations. Like Merton in his last years, Rohr is rooted in Catholic spirituality but draws insights from other traditions as well. This theological dance has drawn criticism from some conservatives, but Bishop Barron, a media figure popular with traditional Catholics, argues that Merton did not reject Church doctrine so much as reveal that it bids us appreciate whatever is of God, wherever it may be found.[14] For their part, a trio of Trappists profoundly influenced by Merton—Thomas Keating, William Meninger, and Basil Pennington—worked to bring contemplative practices to ordinary folks. Over the past half century such meditation groups have spread across the nation and beyond, and now they serve as points of light in our dark time.[15]

Once a week our group sits in a circle, in the darkness, around a candle. In the stillness, if we find a thought grabbing our attention, we just take a deep breath or repeat to ourselves our special word and go on—go on in the great silence. This period of reflection is followed by a brief Scripture reading, and on one December night the passage was read by Els, a university administrator, her lilting, Dutch-inflected voice beginning with the words, "There were shepherds abiding in the fields, keeping watch over their flocks by night, and the angel of the Lord came upon them." Such elemental words, going back to childhood, and yet such a strange image. I found myself wondering, yet again, how those of us in the circle who were Catholic could believe in the incarnation or resurrection when we consider the creation story symbolic, with the world certainly not formed in the space of a week!

But as I mulled this over in my mind, Els broke through my internal chatter, quietly inviting us to comment on anything in the reading that might have touched our hearts. Jane spoke of this baby, of the Savior coming as such a weak thing, of us not having to look to kings and powers for our solace. Her reflection trumped my vexing thoughts. She may be known as the mother of many and grandma of many more—you might not notice her on the street, with her conventional sweater and hairdo—but as our meditation leader she has a grace about her, grace born of years of loving devotion to others and to this spiritual practice. And Merton, as a celibate, surely would treasure the ways her love draws on her deep parenting experiences, especially at this particular moment. Our holiday season had been darkened by the recent massacre at the elementary school in Newtown, Connecticut, just an hour away from where we gathered. "Those babies," Jane called them.

As we moved to the close of our session, the pastor, Fr. Byrne, appeared. He participated whenever he could—just another spiritual pilgrim. He greeted us with that warm, strong, life-affirming voice of his, but the chemotherapy had laid him low, so that he entered the room bent over, precarious. He would have to give up the pastorate soon, he told us, and he made the point that our prayers had brought many graces to the parish. "Keep up the practice, if you can," he said. "We promise," I replied. As we held hands in our circle, we asked God's blessings on all the world, my left hand in that of Steve the psychotherapist, my right in the warm, trembling hand of Fr. Byrne, that veteran of so many prayers—and so many actions, as a longtime member of Pax Christi.[16]

Only as we were breaking up did I notice that a longtime member had returned to us after a prolonged absence:

Thelma, originally from the Dominican Republic. She had been kept at home much of the time caring for her chronically ill husband, but here she was, looking well, in her bright lipstick and even brighter smile. I suspect a pollster would find many of her policy views at odds with mine, but that mattered not as we embraced and bonded anew. Communion: that's what it is, a rare kind of communion, born of this simple but profound spiritual practice.

I was reminded of an insight shared by the poet James Autry with PBS journalist Bill Moyers:

> People ask me now, "How are you doing?" and I say, "Considering everything there is to complain about, I have no complaints." So it was partly that, and partly my own need to bring some sort of calmness in my life....I would walk in the morning. I'd come back and be all agitated about the war or the politics. And I thought, "You know, this isn't supposed to be healthy I don't think." So it evolved into a gratitude walk and where I try to just make it like a meditation.

Driving home, reflecting on all of this, I choked up, then found myself singing, "There were shepherds abiding in the fields, keeping watch over their flocks by night," from Handel's transporting *Messiah*. Amid our doubts, and amid so much darkness, there is the promise of light and life.

If Thomas Merton reveals to us the meditative—the mystical, even—alive in our wounded world, Dorothy Day reminds us that our loving actions signify in mysterious ways beyond all telling. We do things "by little and by little," and God does the rest, she wrote, referencing St. Paul. This insight came to the rescue when a friend and I were fighting off despair. We had run into each other at our local farmers market, the stalls abounding in colorful produce, the Hudson River Palisades majestic in the background on that glorious autumn day, but we found ourselves sharing our grief over the pedophilia cover-ups in the Catholic Church. "It's as bad as the time of the Borgias," I said to him. "It's worse than the Borgias," Tom replied, citing additional major scandals, starting with the venal influence of big money on our body politic, threatening our democratic system itself. Grasping for hope—and knowing that Tom had read Richard Rohr, who so admires Merton and Day—I quoted Day as saying that we work "by little and by little." This, in turn, prompted him to mention some tiny points of light: people working to preserve precious water resources in places such as Bangladesh.[17]

Even though they have much more pressing survival concerns than do we suburbanites, Bangladeshis also have more impetus to address climate issues, for they suffer much more from rising tides. "Millions have been made homeless," Tom told me, but they are responding, he said, with great courage: part of a worldwide network of more than three hundred Waterkeeper groups, with this alliance first begun in 1966 by a few fishing folk living along the Hudson, upset at the pollution of this great river that they loved, and that their families had loved for generations.

Today, with humanity itself at risk, we will not be saved by starry-eyed optimism or clever cynicism. We will not even be saved by calculating the effects of our good deeds. "Everything is compassion," Merton reflected on beholding the Polonnaruwa Buddhas of Sri Lanka. This love shone through his last circular letter to his friends. As he headed out on that fateful journey, Merton wrote, "I shall continue to feel bound to all of you in silence and prayer." And in words that resonate anew in our own time of crisis, he concluded, "Our real journey in life is interior: it is a matter of growth, deepening, and of an ever greater surrender to the creative action of love and grace in our hearts. Never was it more necessary for us to respond to that action." Or, as Dorothy Day put it, "The final word is love." In this famous postscript to *The Long Loneliness,* she observed, "We cannot love God unless we love each other, and to love we must know each other. We know Him in the breaking of bread, and we know each other in the breaking of bread…even with a crust, where there is companionship. We have all known the long loneliness, and we know that love comes with community."[18]

Thomas Merton and Dorothy Day call us to bear witness to love as embodied in the divine, and in that spark of the divine in every person, but especially present in the destitute, the ostracized, the attacked (whether by hatred or by war). Today, as we face crises seemingly unprecedented in their magnitude, may we respond with a bravery rooted in love—despite everything, and because everything is at stake.

Notes

PROLOGUE

1. Dorothy Day, "On Pilgrimage—December 1948," *Catholic Worker*, accessed March 8, 2017, http://www.catholicworker.org/dorothyday/articles/262.html.

2. "Dorothy Day," *Christopher Closeup*, 1971, accessed March 8, 2018, https://www.avemariapress.com/resources/22/2800/; Dorothy Day, *On Pilgrimage: The Sixties* (New York: Curtis Books, 1972), 212.

3. Dorothy Day was referring to the poem "The Hound of Heaven," by Francis Thompson, which she first heard in the back of a dive bar frequented by Greenwich Village artists and radicals, as recited by Eugene O'Neill, who had drifted away from the Catholic faith even as she was being drawn toward it. Dorothy Day, *The Long Loneliness* (New York: Harper and Row, 1952; HarperCollins, 1980), 84; Dorothy Day, *The Duty of Delight: The Diaries of Dorothy Day*, ed. Robert Ellsberg (Milwaukee: Marquette University Press, 2008), 110.

4. Thomas Merton, *The Sign of Jonas* (New York: Harcourt, Brace and Co., 1953), 361–62.

5. Jim Forest, *All Is Grace: A Biography of Dorothy Day* (Maryknoll, NY: Orbis Books, 2011), 138; "Thomas Merton's Correspondence: List of Those in Correspondence with Merton," Merton.org, accessed February 8, 2017, http://www.merton.org/Research/Correspondence/.

6. Thomas Merton, *The Hidden Ground of Love: The Letters of Thomas Merton on Religious Experience and Social Concerns*, ed.

William H. Shannon (New York: Farrar, Straus and Giroux, 1985), 136–37.

7. Anna L. Pycior, "Inspired" (n.p., 1995), in author's possession; Robert Coles, *Dorothy Day: A Radical Devotion* (Reading, MA: Perseus Books, 1987), preface.

8. In confirming that he suggested the Day/Merton topic to Pope Francis, Cardinal Dolan made clear that, actually, many prelates made suggestions for that papal speech. But Dolan is the likely source, given (a) that he was the only cardinal who publicly showcased Merton and Day prior to the pope spotlighting them and (b) Dolan's prominence as cardinal archbishop of New York and, at that time, president of the USCCB. "Transcript: Pope Francis's Speech to Congress," *Washington Post*, accessed February 17, 2018, https://www.washingtonpost.com/local/social-issues/transcript-pope-franciss-speech-to-congress/2015/09/24/6d7d7ac8-62bf-11e5-8e9e-dce8a2a2a679_story.html?utm_term=.bb8555ad51a6; Cardinal Timothy Dolan to author, April 18, 2016; Julie Leininger Pycior, "Catholic Nuns, the Vatican and Straight but Crooked Lines," *Huffington Post*, October 5, 2012, http://www.huffingtonpost.com/julie-leininger-pycior/the-nuns-the-vatican-and-straight-but-crooked-lines_b_1929725.html.

9. Catholics of a certain age can recite the definition of a sacrament from memory. Pycior, "Catholic Nuns, the Vatican, and Straight but Crooked Lines"; "The Sacraments," *Baltimore Catechism*, accessed July 24, 2017, http://www.catholicity.com/baltimore-catechism/lesson23.html.

10. Dorothy Day, "In Peace Is My Bitterness Most Bitter," *Catholic Worker*, January 1967, accessed March 8, 2017, http://www.catholicworker.org/dorothyday/articles/250.html; Merton, *The Hidden Ground of Love*, 152.

11. Sharon Otterman, "In Hero of the Catholic Left, a Conservative Cardinal Sees a Saint," *New York Times*, November 29, 2012, http://www.nytimes.com/2012/11/27/nyregion/sainthood-for-dorothy-day-has-unexpected-champion-in-cardinal-timothy-dolan.html; Hannah Rosin, "Vatican to Weigh Sainthood for Reformer Dorothy Day," *Washington Post*, March 17, 2000, http://www.washingtonpost.com/wp-srv/WPcap/2000-03/17/074r-031700-idx.html.

12. International Thomas Merton Society, "Merton and Catechism Letter Campaign," accessed January 31, 2017, http://www

.merton.org/letter/; Timothy Dolan, *Called to Be Holy* (Huntington, IN: Our Sunday Visitor Press, 2005), 111.

13. Julie Leininger Pycior to Timothy Dolan, April 17, 2012, and Timothy Dolan to author, April 30, 2012; "Moral Conscience," *The Catechism of the Catholic Church*, accessed January 31, 2017, http://www.vatican.va/archive/ccc_css/archive/catechism/p3s1c1a6.htm.

14. Marie Rohde, "Milwaukee Documents Show That Dolan Asked to Transfer Funds," *National Catholic Reporter*, July 2, 2013, https://www.ncronline.org/news/accountability/milwaukee-documents-show-dolan-asked-transfer-funds; Laurie Goodstein, "Dolan Sought to Protect Church Assets, Files Show," *New York Times*, July 1, 2013, https://www.nytimes.com/2013/07/02/us/dolan-sought-vatican-permission-to-shield-assets.html.

15. Transcript, "Cardinal Timothy Michael Dolan Commencement Speech, May 12, 2012," e-mail attachment, Peter McHugh to author, April 4, 2016; Gerald F. Cavanagh, SJ, to author, February 10, 2019.

16. Sharon Otterman, "As Church Shifts, a Cardinal Welcomes Gays; They Embrace a 'Miracle,'" *New York Times*, June 13, 2017, https://www.nytimes.com/2017/06/13/nyregion/catholic-church-gays-mass-newark-cathedral.html; Michael O'Laughlin, "Cardinal Tobin Says It's All about Listening," *America*, October 18, 2016, https://www.americamagazine.org/faith/2016/10/18/cardinal-joseph-tobin-says-its-all-about-listening; Thomas Merton, *Love and Living*, ed. Naomi Burton Stone and Patrick Hart (New York: Harcourt Brace, Jovanovich, 1985), 34; Joseph W. Tobin, endorsement on the back cover of James Martin, *Building a Bridge: How the Catholic Church and the LGBT Community Can Enter into a Relationship of Respect, Compassion, and Sensitivity* (New York: Harper One, 2017); Dorothy Day, "Why Do the Members of Christ Tear One Another?," *Catholic Worker*, February 1942, accessed October 23, 2017, http://www.catholicworker.org/dorothyday/articles/390.html.

17. Dorothy Day, "On Pilgrimage—February 1948," *Catholic Worker*; Thomas Merton, *Conjectures of a Guilty Bystander* (New York: Doubleday, 1966), 311; Matthew Schmitz, "Who Is the Philosopher Who Holds So Much Influence over Pope Francis?," *Washington Post*, June 25, 2015, https://www.washingtonpost.com/news/acts-of-faith/wp/2015/06/25/who-is-the-philosopher

-who-holds-so-much-influence-over-pope-francis/?utm_term=.db42c79d3246; Tracy Rowland, "Benedict's Intellectual Mentors and Students," *Crisis*, February 19, 2013, http://www.crisismagazine.com/2013/benedicts-intellectual-mentors-and-students; Benedict XVI, address to Romano Guardini congress, October 29, 2010, accessed July 21, 2017, https://w2.vatican.va/content/benedict-xvi/en/speeches/2010/october/documents/hf_ben-xvi_spe_20101029_fondazione-guardini.html; Austen Ivereigh, *The Great Reformer: Francis and the Making of a Radical Pope* (New York: Henry Holt, 2014), 197–98.

18. Both Merton and Day regularly lauded St. Francis. In 1966, for example, Day structured her autumn letter to her readers around his spirituality, while Merton, for his part, wrote to a diocesan editor that Francis was his favorite saint. Dorothy Day, *All the Way to Heaven: The Selected Letters of Dorothy Day*, ed. Robert Ellsberg (Milwaukee: Marquette University Press, 2008), 451–52; Thomas Merton, *Witness to Freedom: Letters in Times of Crisis*, ed. William H. Shannon (New York: Farrar, Straus and Giroux, 1994), 164; Dorothy Day, "Fall Appeal," *Catholic Worker*, October–November 1966, accessed July 23, 2019, https://www.catholicworker.org/dorothyday/articles/844.html.

19. Children's Hospital of Philadelphia, "Fetal Surgery Continues to Advance," CHOP News, June 22, 2011, http://www.chop.edu/news/fetal-surgery-continues-advance; Pam Belluck, "Premature Babies May Survive at 22 Weeks, if Treated, Study Finds," *New York Times*, May 6, 2015, https://www.nytimes.com/2015/05/07/health/premature-babies-22-weeks-viability-study.html; Planned Parenthood, "Abortion," accessed March 8, 2017, https://www.plannedparenthood.org/learn/abortion; Joshua A. Krisch, "When Racism Was a Science: 'Haunted Files: The Eugenics Record Office' Recreates a Dark Time in a Laboratory's Past," *New York Times*, October 3, 2014, https://www.nytimes.com/2014/10/14/science/haunted-files-the-eugenics-record-office-recreates-a-dark-time-in-a-laboratorys-past.html?mtrref=duckduckgo.com&gwh=DDFD323BD248903F771BC970A88E0E61&gwt=pay&assetType=nyt_now.

CHAPTER ONE

1. William H. Shannon, ed., "The Correspondence of Dorothy Day and Thomas Merton," in *American Catholic Pacifism: The Influence of Dorothy Day and the Catholic Worker Movement*, ed. Anne Klejment and Nancy L. Roberts (Westport, CT: Praeger, 1996), 101; Robert Giroux, "Thomas Merton's Durable Mountain," *New York Times Book Review*, October 11, 1998; Thomas C. Cornell, interview with author, Peter Maurin Catholic Worker Farm, Marlboro, New York, August 21, 1997.

2. Robert Steed, interview with author, March 26, 2012, Hobart, New York; Robert Steed, "Street Photographer," *The Catholic Worker*, October–November 2000.

3. Steed interview; John Stanley, interview with author, March 4, 2012, New York City; Robert Steed, "John Stanley, 1921–2016," *Catholic Worker*, October–November 2016; "Merton's Correspondence with Stanley, John," accessed November 25, 2018, http://merton.org/Research/Correspondence/y1.aspx?id=1906.

4. Day had published a shorter, more episodic spiritual memoir in the late 1930s. Dorothy Day, *From Union Square to Rome* (Silver Spring, MD: Preservation of the Faith Press, 1938); Day, *The Long Loneliness* (New York: Harper and Row, 1952; HarperCollins, 1980), copyright page; Jim Forest, *The Root of War Is Fear: Thomas Merton's Advice to Peacemakers* (Maryknoll, NY: Orbis Books, 2016), 19–20; Dorothy Day, *The Duty of Delight: The Diaries of Dorothy Day*, ed. Robert Ellsberg (Milwaukee: Marquette University Press, 2008), 250; Dwight MacDonald, "Profiles: The Foolish Things of the World," *New Yorker*, October 4, 1952, and October 11, 1952.

5. Dorothy Day, "On Pilgrimage—July–August 1957," *Catholic Worker*, accessed April 25, 2019, https://www.catholicworker.org/dorothyday/articles/724.html; Dorothy Day, *All the Way to Heaven: Selected Letters of Dorothy Day*, ed. Robert Ellsberg (Maryknoll, NY: Orbis Books, 2010), 254–55; Shannon, "The Correspondence of Dorothy Day and Thomas Merton," editor's prefatory note, 99–100.

6. Thomas Merton, *A Search for Solitude: Pursuing the Monk's True Life*, ed. Lawrence Cunningham (San Francisco: HarperSanFrancisco, 1996), 181–83.

7. Day, *The Long Loneliness*, 165–73.

8. Thomas Merton, "CHEE$E, by Joyce Killer-Diller: A Christmas Card for Brother Cellarer," accessed August 1, 2018, http://merton.org/Research/Manuscripts/manu.aspx?id=3611; Forest, *The Root of War Is Fear*, 24; Thomas Merton, *The Hidden Ground of Love: The Letters of Thomas Merton on Religious Experience and Social Concerns*, ed. William H. Shannon (New York: Farrar, Straus and Giroux, 1985), 136.

9. Forest, *The Root of War Is Fear*, 22, 24; Merton, *The Hidden Ground of Love*, 136; Day, "On Pilgrimage—July–August 1957"; Dorothy Day, "We Mourn Death of Gandhi, Nonviolent Revolutionary," *Catholic Worker*, February 1948, accessed August 21, 2018, https://www.catholicworker.org/dorothyday/articles/463.pdf; author interview with Jim Forest, Hastings-on-Hudson, New York, April 17, 1997; Robert Lax, taped response to author's written questions, recorded April 20, 1999, Patmos, Greece; Robert Lax, Christmas poem, *Jubilee*, vol. 9, no. 8 (December 1961).

10. Merton, *The Hidden Ground of Love*, 137; *Catholic Worker*, July–August 1960, 1, 6; Shannon, "The Correspondence of Dorothy Day and Thomas Merton," 103, 106; Dorothy Day, "On Pilgrimage—January 1959," *Catholic Worker*, accessed November 25, 2018, http://www.catholicworker.org/dorothyday/articles/178.html.

11. Merton, *The Hidden Ground of Love*, 201–3, 308–9.

12. Shannon, "The Correspondence of Dorothy Day and Thomas Merton," 103.

13. Peter Maurin's birthplace, Outlet, is located about 150 miles west of St. Antonin-Noble-Val, where Merton spent a few years as a boy. Brigid O'Shea Merriman, *Searching for Christ: The Spirituality of Dorothy Day* (Notre Dame, IN: University of Notre Dame Press, 1994), 74; Certificate, "Final Oblation of Secular Oblates of Saint Benedict," for Dorothy Benedicta Day, April 26, 1955, St. Procopius Abbey, accessed August 8, 2018, https://www.procopius.org/dorothy-day-s-oblation; Jim Forest, "Biography of Peter Maurin," accessed August 8, 2018, http://www.catholicworker.org/petermaurin/pm-biography.html; Merton, *The Seven Storey Mountain*, 45–51.

14. Merriman, *Searching for Christ*, 86–87, 92–100, 109; Frederick Dunne to "Dear friends," April 15, 1936, and Frederick Dunne to Dorothy Day, January 4, 1939, February 3, 1939, September 5, 1939, August 11, 1941, April 3, 1945, December 16, 1946, all in "Abbots of Monasteries, 1934–1984," D-1, Dorothy Day–Catholic Worker Collection, Marquette University Archives (hereafter "DD-CW"); Day, *The Long Loneliness*, 49; Dorothy Day, "On Pilgrimage—November 1953," *Catholic Worker*, accessed August 8, 2018, http://www.catholicworker.org/dorothyday/articles/657.html.

15. Merton had written two antiwar pieces earlier that year, but both had addressed historical topics. Thomas Merton, *Original Child Bomb: Points for Meditation to Be Scratched on the Side of a Cave* (New York: New Directions, 1962). Forest, *The Root of War Is Fear*, 25–31; Thomas Merton, *Turning toward the World: The Pivotal Years; The Journals of Thomas Merton, Volume Four, 1960–1963*, ed. Victor A. Kramer (San Francisco: HarperSanFrancisco, 1997), 172–75.

16. In a 1960 radio interview, Dorothy Day put *Catholic Worker* circulation at sixty-five thousand. Dorothy Day, interview by Eugene Boyle, "Pacifism and the Catholic Church," May 3, 1960, Pacifica Radio Archives, accessed January 13, 2019, https://soundcloud.com/pacificaradioarchives/from-the-vault-489-dorothy-day; Anne Klejment, "War Resistance and Property Destruction: The Catonsville Nine Draft Board Raid and Catholic Worker Pacifism," Box 5, Zarrella Collection, TMC; Shannon, "The Correspondence of Dorothy Day and Thomas Merton," 105.

17. Shannon, "The Correspondence of Dorothy Day and Thomas Merton," 105; Forest, *The Root of War Is Fear*, 25–31; Thomas Merton, *New Seeds of Contemplation* (New York: New Directions, 1962), 119–22; "Share Your Shelter? Not on Your Life," *Catholic Advocate* (Religious News Service), September 28, 1961, https://thecatholicnewsarchive.org/?a=d&d=ca19610928-01.2.41&srpos=6&e=-------en-20--1-byDA-txt-txIN-%22l.+c.+mchugh%22------.

18. Dorothy Day, "On Pilgrimage—December 1961," *Catholic Worker*, accessed September 13, 2018, http://www.catholicworker.org/dorothyday/articles/788.html; Merton, *The Hidden Ground of Love*, 140–43.

19. "Share Your Shelter? Not on Your Life"; CBS NEWS, "Fallout Shelter Gun Debate," accessed September 3, 2018, https://www.youtube.com/watch?v=vW5TyPrvw2U.

20. Merton, *Turning toward the World*, 175–76; Thomas Merton, "The Vision of Peace: Some Reflections on the Monastic Way of Life," *Jubilee* (September 1961).

21. William H. Shannon, "Introduction" and Cold War letters correspondents, in Thomas Merton, *Cold War Letters* (Maryknoll, NY: Orbis Books, 2006), v–ix, 26–29, 42–44, 194–202; Merton, *The Hidden Ground of Love*, 443–44, 448; Merton's correspondence with Ethel (Skakel) Kennedy, accessed April 7, 2020, http://merton.org/Research/Correspondence/y1.aspx?id=1052.

22. Thomas Merton, *The School of Charity: The Letters of Thomas Merton on Religious Renewal and Spiritual Direction*, ed. Patrick Hart (New York: Harper Collins, 1990), 141–43; William H. Shannon, headnotes to Thomas Merton, *A Passion for Peace* (New York: Crossroad, 1995), 55, 65.

23. Patricia Burton, introduction to Thomas Merton, *Peace in a Post-Christian Era* (Maryknoll, NY: Orbis Books, 2007), xxv–lvi; Huston Smith, interview by Phil Cousineau, 2012, Berkeley, CA, accessed April 26, 2019, https://www.youtube.com/watch?v=nzE3-NOcPNE.

24. Forest, *The Root of War Is Fear*, 34–36; Merton, *Turning toward the World*, 172–74, 178; Shannon, "The Correspondence of Dorothy Day and Thomas Merton," 105; Merton, *The Hidden Ground of Love*, 259–60.

25. Kurt Hemmer, ed., *Encyclopedia of Beat Literature* (New York: Infobase Publishing, 2010), 282–83; Day, *All the Way to Heaven*, 283–87, 289–90, and note by editor Robert Ellsberg, 286; Merton, *The Hidden Ground of Love*, 143–45; Dorothy Day to Jack (Fr. Charles) English, June 3, 1962, D-1, "Personal Correspondence, 1923–1980," DD-CW; Day, *The Duty of Delight*, 322–23 and note by editor Robert Ellsberg, 323.

26. Dorothy Day, "On Pilgrimage in Cuba—Part One," *Catholic Worker*, September 1962, http://www.catholicworker.org/dorothyday/articles/793.html; Dorothy Day, "On Pilgrimage in Cuba—Part Two," *Catholic Worker*, October 1962, http://www.catholicworker.org/dorothyday/articles/795.html; Dorothy Day, "On Pilgrimage in Cuba—Part Three," *Catholic Worker*, November 1962, http://www.catholicworker.org/dorothyday/articles/796.html; "On Pilgrimage in Cuba—Part Four," *Catholic Worker*, December 1962, https://www.catholicworker.org/dorothyday/articles/798.pdf, all accessed September 20, 2018; Merton, *Turning*

toward the World, 273, 276–77; Merton, *The Hidden Ground of Love*, 76.

CHAPTER TWO

1. William H. Shannon, ed., "The Correspondence of Dorothy Day and Thomas Merton," in *American Catholic Pacifism: The Influence of Dorothy Day and the Catholic Worker Movement*, ed. Anne Klejment and Nancy L. Roberts (Westport, CT: Praeger, 1996), 111; Thomas Merton, *The Wisdom of the Desert* (New York: New Directions, 1960), "Author's Note"; Dorothy Day, "On Pilgrimage—September 1970," *Catholic Worker*, accessed May 5, 2014, http://www.catholicworker.org/dorothyday/articles/503.html.

2. Thomas Merton, *The Hidden Ground of Love*, ed. William H. Shannon (New York: Farrar, Straus and Giroux, 1985), 137, 147; Shannon, "The Correspondence of Dorothy Day and Thomas Merton," 111; Dorothy Day, "Spring Appeal," *Catholic Worker*, April 1957, accessed April 10, 2014, http://www.catholicworker.org/dorothyday/articles/720.html; Thomas Merton correspondence with "Young People at the Catholic Worker (Elin, Bob K., et al.)," November 3, 1962, see http://www.merton.org/research/Correspondence/y1.aspx?id=4043 (accessed January 13, 2020); Thomas Merton, "There Has to Be a Jail for Ladies," in *Emblems of a Season of Fury* (New York: New Directions, 1963), 30–33; Thomas Merton to Robert Steed, March 25, 1962, accessed September 16, 2018, https://personalist.livejournal.com/10249.html; Sidney H. Griffith, introduction to Thomas Merton, *Pre-Benedictine Monasticism*, ed. Patrick O'Connell, Initiation into the Monastic Tradition 2 (Collegeville, MN: Cistercian Publications, 2007), lix.

3. Thomas Merton, *Dancing in the Waters of Life: Seeking Peace in the Hermitage; The Journals of Thomas Merton, Volume Five, 1963–1965*, ed. Robert Daggy (San Francisco: HarperSanFrancisco, 1997), 15–16; Dorothy Day, diary entry, September 10, 1962, DD-CW; Julie Leininger Pycior, "'We Are All Called to Be Saints': Dorothy Day, Thomas Merton, and Friendship House," *The Merton Annual* 13 (2001): 38.

4. Shannon, "The Correspondence of Dorothy Day and Thomas Merton," 111; Dorothy Day, "On Pilgrimage—November

1946," *Catholic Worker*, 1, 7, 8, accessed January 13, 2020, https://www.catholicworker.org/dorothyday/articles/226.html; Merton, *The Hidden Ground of Love*, 147; Hebrews 7:17, accessed July 30, 2019, https://biblehub.com/hebrews/7-17.htm.

5. Shannon, "The Correspondence of Dorothy Day and Thomas Merton," 111; Thomas Merton, *Turning toward the World: The Pivotal Years, The Journals of Thomas Merton, Volume Four, 1960–1963*, ed. Victor A. Kramer (San Francisco: HarperSanFrancisco, 1997), 289–90.

6. Griffith, introduction to Merton, *Pre-Benedictine Monasticism*, lix; author interview with Father James Conner, OCSO, Chicago, June 11, 2011; author interview with Brother Patrick Hart, OCSO, Gethsemani, Kentucky, July 4, 1999.

7. In mentioning the diverse composition of the peace delegation, Dorothy Day noted a lovely delegate from Hiroshima, adding that the contingent was racially integrated with two African Americans: a young woman who worked with at-risk teens in New Jersey and a civil rights activist from Mississippi. Virginia Naeve, "Proposal: Pilgrimage to Rome for an Audience with Pope John about Peace Issues," Martin Luther King Center Archives; Dorothy Day, "On Pilgrimage—June 1963," *Catholic Worker*, 1, 2, 6, 8, accessed January 13, 2020, https://www.catholicworker.org/dorothyday/articles/804.pdf; Merton, *The Hidden Ground of Love*, 274, 276; Shannon, "The Correspondence of Dorothy Day and Thomas Merton," 111; Merton, *Turning toward the World*, 314, 315; Benedict Moore (Thomas Merton), "Dutch Non-Violent Resistance to Hitler," *Catholic Worker*, July–August 1963, 1; Paul Elie, *The Life You Save May Be Your Own: An American Pilgrimage* (New York: Farrar, Straus and Giroux, 2003), 332–34.

8. Jim and Sally Douglass to Dorothy Day, March 15, 1963, October 4, 1963, Series D-1, DD-CW; Dorothy Day, "On Pilgrimage—June 1963"; Dorothy Day to Jim Forest, March 12, 1963, Box 2, D-5, DD-CW.

9. Jim and Sally Douglass to Dorothy Day, June 30, 1962, March 15, 1963, October 4, 1963, Series D-1, DD-CW; Day, "On Pilgrimage—June 1963"; Thomas Merton to Herbert Burke, December 11, 1962, and Hildegard Goss-Mayr to Thomas Merton, October 31, 1962, Thomas Merton Center, Bellarmine University, Louisville, Kentucky (hereafter "TMC"); Thomas Merton, *Witness to Freedom: Letters in Times of Crisis*, ed. William H. Shannon (New

York: Farrar, Straus and Giroux, 1994), 96; note by William H. Shannon, ed., in Merton, *The Hidden Ground of Love*, 326; Jim Forest, *Living with Wisdom: A Life of Thomas Merton* (Maryknoll, NY: Orbis Books, 2008), 163.

10. Jim Forest, *All Is Grace: A Biography of Dorothy Day* (Maryknoll, NY: Orbis Books, 2010), 231.

11. Merton expressed his pleasure at Cardinal Bea's initiatives in a letter to an activist priest. Forest, *All Is Grace*, 230–31; Dorothy Day, "On Pilgrimage—June 1963"; Thomas Merton to David Kirk, April 2, 1963, in Thomas Merton, *Witness to Freedom*, 307; *Daily American* [Rome], April 15, 1963, DD-CW; Douglass to Day, May 30, 1963, DD-CW; Elie, *The Life You Save May Be Your Own*, 348.

12. Snyder and Merton shared an interest in lay Catholic communities devoted to the poor, but the two were not close; Fr. Urban did not approve of the Vatican Council reforms, let alone the nascent Catholic peace movement. William Miller, *Dorothy Day: A Biography* (New York: Harper and Row, 1972), 473; Day, "On Pilgrimage—June 1963"; "Father Urban John Francis Snyder," accessed June 6, 2013, http://www.dailycatholic.org/aug2ttt.htm; "Casper, Alice Kathryn," accessed July 19, 2012, http://merton.org/Research/Correspondence/y1.aspx?id=303; Hart interview.

13. Dorothy Day, "On Pilgrimage—June 1963"; Dorothy Day, "On Pilgrimage—October 1963," *Catholic Worker*, accessed January 13, 2020, https://www.catholicworker.org/dorothyday/articles/808.html; Gerard Rainer Horn, *The Spirit of Vatican II: Western European Progressive Catholicism in the Long 1960s* (New York: Oxford University Press, 2015), 44–45.

14. Merton, *Turning toward the World*, 325; 331–32, 340–41; Dorothy Day, *The Duty of Delight: The Diaries of Dorothy Day*, ed. Robert Ellsberg (Milwaukee: Marquette University Press, 2008), 340; Dorothy Day, "On Pilgrimage—June 1963"; Dorothy Day, "On Pilgrimage—July–August 1963," *Catholic Worker*, accessed October 28, 2018, http://www.catholicworker.org/dorothyday/articles/805.html; "Vatican Told Bishops to Cover Up Sex Abuse," *Guardian*, August 17, 2003, accessed October 29, 2018, https://www.theguardian.com/world/2003/aug/17/religion.childprotection; Thomas Merton's correspondence with Paul VI (Giovanni Montini), accessed July 27, 2019, http://www.merton.org/Research/Correspondence/y1.aspx?id=1572.

15. *Catholic Worker*, July–August 1963, 1, 2, 7; Pycior, "We Are All Called to Be Saints," 30–35; Dorothy Day, "Day by Day," *Catholic Worker*, March 1934, accessed November 25, 2018, http://www.catholicworker.org/dorothyday/articles/311.html.

16. *Catholic Worker*, July–August 1963, 1, 2, 7; Emma C. Edmunds, "Danville Civil Rights Demonstrations of 1963," *The Encyclopedia of Virginia*, ed. Brendan Wolfe, accessed July 20, 2012, http://www.EncyclopediaVirginia.org/Danville_Civil_Rights_Demonstrations_of_1963; *Danville Bee*, July 10, 1963, 1.

17. Thomas Merton to Therese Lentfoehr, SDS, February 19, 1963, Box 3, Thomas Merton Collection, Columbia University; Thomas Merton, "Black Revolution"; Merton, *Dancing in the Waters of Life*, July 23, 1964, 130; Thomas Merton, *Passion for Peace: The Social Essays*, ed. William H. Shannon (New York: Crossroad, 1997), 154; Day, "On Pilgrimage—June 1963."

18. Merton, *Dancing in the Waters of Life*, 44, 286, 298; Thomas Merton, *Conjectures of a Guilty Bystander* (New York: Doubleday Image, 1968), 282; author interview with Tom Cornell, August 21, 1997, Peter Maurin Catholic Worker Farm, Marlboro, New York; author interview with Jim Forest, April 17, 1997, and June 12, 2008, Hastings-on-Hudson, New York.

19. Daniel Berrigan to Thomas Merton, June 14, 1963, TMC; David D. Cooper, ed., *Thomas Merton and James Laughlin: Selected Letters* (New York: W.W. Norton, 1997), 227; Merton, *Emblems of a Season of Fury*, 33–34.

20. Berrigan to Merton, June 14, 1963; Merton, *Dancing in the Waters of Life*, October 2, 1963, 20–21; Merton, *The Hidden Ground of Love*, 76–79; Thomas Merton, *The Road to Joy: Letters to New and Old Friends*, ed. Robert E. Daggy (New York: Farrar, Straus and Giroux, 1989), 246; Day, "On Pilgrimage—June 1963"; Merton, *Turning toward the World*, 6; Merton, *Dancing in the Waters of Life*, 13, 14; Tony Walsh to Thomas Merton, February 1, 1962, and August 21, 1962, TMC.

21. Merton, *Dancing in the Waters of Life*, 13, 14.

22. Merton, *Turning toward the World*, 330–33; Dorothy Day to Jack (Fr. Charles) English, January 19, 1963, Series D-1, DD-CW; Dorothy Day, *All the Way to Heaven: The Selected Letters of Dorothy Day*, ed. Robert Ellsberg (Milwaukee: Marquette University Press, 2010), 291–92, 294–95; Thomas Merton to Edward R. Sammis, June 18, 1963, TMC; Thomas Merton, "A Letter from Thomas

Merton," back cover of Dorothy Day, *Loaves and Fishes* (New York: Harper and Row, 1963); Cornell interview.

23. Dorothy Day, *Loaves and Fishes*, xiii, 10, 67, 80–82, 84, 88, 89, 96, 101, 131–33, 136–38, 168–71, 176, 190–92, 203, 210, 214, 216, back cover; Thomas Merton to Edward R. Sammis, June 18, 1963, TMC; Merton, *Turning toward the World*, 332–33.

24. Robert Lax moved to Greece in 1962, eventually settling on the island of Patmos, where he lived in solitude for thirty years, and where, according to tradition, John the Evangelist spent his last years. Lax himself spent his last years with his relatives in Olean, New York (which Merton had visited on summer breaks while he and Lax were students at Columbia University). Robert Lax, tape recorded answers to written questions submitted by the author, May 1999; Margaret Garvey and Michael Quigley, eds., *The Dorothy Day Book* (New York: Templegate, 1982), 102; William Packard, review of *The Circle of the Sun*, by Robert Lax, *Catholic Worker*, October 1962, accessed July 27, 2019, https://thecatholicnewsarchive.org/?a=d&d=CW19621001-01.2.12&srpos=23&e=-------en-20-CW-21-byDA-txt-txIN-lax------; Rory McCormick (pseudonym), "Christian Pacifism in Today's World" and Robert Kaye, review of *New Poems*, by Robert Lax, both in the *Catholic Worker*, February 1963, accessed July 27, 2019, https://thecatholicnewsarchive.org/?a=d&d=CW19630201-01.2.11&srpos=5&e=-------en-20-CW-1-byDA-txt-txIN-%22robert+lax%22------; "Robert Lax," The Poetry Foundation, accessed July 27, 2019, https://www.poetryfoundation.org/poets/robert-lax.

25. One of the other *Loaves and Fishes* photographers, Vivian Cherry, was a friend of Robert Steed (who had been a Catholic Worker and, before that, a Trappist but who became disenchanted with both communities and with the Catholic Church in general). Robert Steed, interview with author, March 10, 2012, Hobart, New York; Brooklyn Museum, "Exhibitions: Vivian Cherry, Working Street Photographer, 1940s to 1960s," accessed January 15, 2020, https://www.brooklynmuseum.org/opencollection/exhibitions/2663; Lax interview.

26. Pycior, "We Are All Called to Be Saints," 27–62; Dorothy Day, "Retreat," August 1959, accessed July 27, 2019, https://www.catholicworker.org/dorothyday/articles/755.html.

27. Merton came to Foucauld through the French scholar of Islam Louis Massignon, whose life was radically changed by the

witness of Foucauld, and after his untimely death, the desert hermit's writings were published by Massignon, who also was largely responsible for making Foucauld's vision of the Little Brothers and Little Sisters of Jesus a reality. Herbert Mason, "Merton and Massignon in Correspondence," accessed August 5, 2019, http://herbertwmason.com/images/MM3.pdf; Thomas Merton, *Learning to Love* (San Francisco: HarperCollins, 1997), 137; Day, *All the Way to Heaven*, 334; "Welcome: Jesus Caritas Fraternity," accessed July 30, 2019, http://www.fraternitejesuscaritas.org/fjc/index.php; Merton, *The Hidden Ground of Love*, 75; Gordon Oyer, *Pursuing the Spiritual Roots of Protest: Merton, Berrigan, Yoder, and Muste at the Gethsemani Abbey Peacemakers Retreat* (Eugene, OR: Wipf and Stock, 2014), 74, 84–85.

28. Day, *Loaves and Fishes*, 210, 214, 216, back cover.

CHAPTER THREE

1. Dorothy Day, "On Pilgrimage—September 1963," *Catholic Worker*, accessed April 29, 2019, https://www.catholicworker.org/dorothyday/articles/806.html; Thomas Merton, *Dancing in the Waters of Life: Seeking Peace in the Hermitage, The Journals of Thomas Merton, Volume Five, 1963–1965*, ed. Robert Daggy (San Francisco: HarperSanFrancisco, 1997), 12, 18.

2. Day, "On Pilgrimage—September 1963"; Dorothy Day, *All the Way to Heaven: The Selected Letters of Dorothy Day*, ed. Robert Ellsberg (Milwaukee: Marquette University Press, 2010), 384; Dorothy Day, diary entry, February 8, 1963, D-4, Dorothy Day–Catholic Worker Collection, Marquette University (hereafter "DD-CW").

3. Day, "On Pilgrimage—September 1963"; Dorothy Day, "On Pilgrimage—November 1963," *Catholic Worker*, accessed November 3, 2018, http://www.catholicworker.org/dorothyday/articles/809.html; Day, *All the Way to Heaven*, 376; Thomas Merton, *Turning toward the World: The Pivotal Years, The Journals of Thomas Merton, Volume Four, 1960–1963*, ed. Victor A. Kramer (San Francisco: HarperSanFrancisco, 1997), 348.

4. Adolph Eichmann was found guilty of war crimes in December 1961 and hanged in June 1962. Dorothy Day, "On

Pilgrimage—September 1963"; Thomas Merton, *Emblems of a Season of Fury* (New York: New Directions, 1963), 30–32, 36–37, 43–47; David D. Cooper, ed., *Thomas Merton and James Laughlin: Selected Letters* (New York: W.W. Norton, 1997), 230; Poetry Foundation, "Thomas Merton," accessed January 15, 2020, https://www.poetryfoundation.org/poets/thomas-merton; "Eichmann Trial," *Holocaust Encyclopedia*, United States Holocaust Museum, accessed November 1, 2018, https://encyclopedia.ushmm.org/content/en/article/eichmann-trial.

5. Merton noted to himself that, of all the people to whom he sent copies of *Emblems of a Season of Fury*, one of the few who wrote to thank him was Dorothy Day. *Emblems of a Season of Fury*, 51–53, 61–69; Thomas Merton, *Darkness before Dawn: New and Selected Poems*, ed. Lynn Szabo (New York: New Directions, 2005), 71; Thomas Merton, *A Thomas Merton Reader*, ed. Thomas McDonnell (New York: Image Books, 1974), 511; photograph of *Seat of Wisdom* statue by Ade Bethune, c. 1960, Box 23, John Stokes Collection, University of Dayton; *Seat of Wisdom* statue by Ade Bethune, Abbey of Our Lady of the Genesee, photograph by author.

6. Dorothy Day, "On Pilgrimage—March 1966," *Catholic Worker*, accessed December 30, 2017, http://www.catholicworker.org/dorothyday/articles/249.html.

7. Day, "On Pilgrimage—March 1966."

8. Although Merton mostly compiled *Seasons of Celebration* in 1963, it was not published until 1965. Thomas Merton, "Liturgical Renewal: An Open Approach," in *Seasons of Celebration* (New York: Farrar, Straus and Giroux, 1965).

9. Merton, *Dancing in the Waters of Life*, 49.

10. Merton, *Dancing in the Waters of Life*, 44–45, 49, 339; Day, "On Pilgrimage—March 1966."

11. Merton, *Dancing in the Waters of Life*, 32.

12. Tom Cornell and his wife Monica Durkin Cornell are the founding leaders of Peter Maurin Catholic Worker Farm, the Cornell's children are affiliated with the Catholic Worker, and Monica Cornell grew up in a family that joined the Catholic Worker soon after its founding. Jim Forest, *All Is Grace: A Biography of Dorothy Day* (Maryknoll, NY: Orbis Books, 2019), 243; Edward Rice, *The Man in the Sycamore Tree: The Good Times and Hard Life of Thomas Merton* (New York: Doubleday, 1970), 82. Thomas C. Cornell and

Monica Ribar Cornell, interview with author, May 7, 2006, Peter Maurin Catholic Worker Farm, Marlboro, New York.

13. The Trappists who would become hermits included Merton's own abbot, even though he had been reluctant to allow Merton to pursue this solitary life. Merton, *Dancing in the Waters of Life*, 36–39; Merton, *The Hidden Ground of Love*, 149; Dorothy Day, "On Pilgrimage—December 1963," *Catholic Worker*, accessed January 15, 2020, https://www.catholicworker.org/dorothyday/articles/810.pdf; Daniel Berrigan to Thomas Merton, n.d. (December 1963), Box 136, Daniel and Philip Berrigan Collection, Cornell University; Dorothy Day, *Loaves and Fishes: The Story of the Catholic Worker Movement* (New York: Harper and Row, 1963), 136.

14. English was rushed to the hospital by a monk, John Eudes Bamberger, who would himself become a friend of Day's some years later and in fact would arrange the funding for the last great project of her life. John Eudes Bamberger to Thomas Merton, November 15, 1963, Thomas Merton Center, Bellarmine University, Louisville, Kentucky (hereafter "TMC"); Thomas Merton, *The Hidden Ground of Love: The Letters of Thomas Merton on Religious Experience and Social Concerns*, ed. William H. Shannon (New York: Farrar, Straus and Giroux, 1985), 148; Merton, *Dancing in the Waters of Life*, 35, 42; William H. Shannon, ed., "The Correspondence of Dorothy Day and Thomas Merton," in *American Catholic Pacifism: The Influence of Dorothy Day and the Catholic Worker Movement*, ed. Anne Klejment and Nancy L. Roberts (Westport, CT: Praeger, 1996), 112; Dorothy Day, diary entry, January 24, 1964, Box 1, D-4, DD-CW; Alice Zarrella to Dorothy Day, January 14, 1964, Box 5, Zarrella Collection, TMC.

15. Shannon, "The Correspondence of Dorothy Day and Thomas Merton," 112.

16. Dorothy Day, diary entry, February 26, 1964, Box 1, D-4, DD-CW; Charles (Jack) English to Dorothy Day, 1964, "Jack English," D-1, DD-CW.

17. The Jesuit college in Syracuse is LeMoyne College. Jim Forest, *At Play in the Lions' Den: A Biography and Memoir of Daniel Berrigan* (Maryknoll, NY: Orbis Books, 2017), 61; Jim Douglass to Dorothy Day, February 13, 1964, D-1, DD-CW; Daniel Berrigan, *To Dwell in Peace* (Eugene, OR: Wipf and Stock, 2007), 141–43; Gordon Oyer, *Pursuing the Spiritual Roots of Protest: Merton, Berri-*

gan, Yoder, and Muste at the Gethsemani Abbey Peacemakers Retreat (Eugene, OR: Wipf and Stock, 2014), 13.

18. Daniel Berrigan to Thomas Merton, February 11, 1964; March 5, 1964; June 2, 1964, Box 136, Daniel and Philip Berrigan Collection, Cornell University; Merton, *The Hidden Ground of Love*, 80–83; Michael Mott, *The Seven Mountains of Thomas Merton* (Boston: Houghton Mifflin, 1984), 400–401; Thomas Merton, *The School of Charity: The Letters of Thomas Merton on Religious Renewal and Spiritual Direction*, ed. Patrick Hart (New York: HarperCollins, 1990), 227–28; Merton, *Dancing in the Waters of Life*, 126–27.

19. George Monteiro, "The Literary Uses of a Proverb," *Folklore Enterprises* 87, no. 2 (1976): 216–18; Day, *All the Way to Heaven*, 187–89; Jim Forest, e-mail to author, October 6, 2012.

20. Thomas Merton, *The Road to Joy: Letters of Thomas Merton to New and Old Friends*, ed. Robert E. Daggy (New York: Farrar, Straus and Giroux, 1989), 248; Berrigan, *To Dwell in Peace*, 144.

21. Merton, *The Hidden Ground of Love*, 167–69.

22. Dorothy Day, "The Case of Cardinal McIntyre," *Catholic Worker*, July–August 1964, accessed January 16, 2018, http://www.catholicworker.org/dorothyday/articles/196.html; Shannon, "The Correspondence of Dorothy Day and Thomas Merton," 115.

23. Day, "The Case of Cardinal McIntyre."

24. Dorothy Day, "On Pilgrimage—September 1964," *Catholic Worker*, accessed January 22, 2018, http://www.catholicworker.org/dorothyday/articles/818.html; Day, "The Case of Cardinal McIntyre."

25. Paul Elie, *The Life You Save May Be Your Own: An American Pilgrimage* (New York: Farrar, Straus and Giroux, 2004), 317; Merton, *Dancing in the Waters of Life*, 108–9; William H. Shannon, editor's note, in Merton, *The Hidden Ground of Love*, 560–61.

26. Dorothy Day, "On Pilgrimage—September 1970," *Catholic Worker*, accessed January 17, 2020, https://www.catholicworker.org/dorothyday/articles/503.html; Dorothy Day, "On Pilgrimage—November 1957," *Catholic Worker*, accessed January 17, 2020, https://www.catholicworker.org/dorothyday/articles/731.pdf; Merton, *Turning toward the World*, 233–34.

27. Merton, *Dancing in the Waters of Life*, 114, 130.

28. Dorothy Day, "On Pilgrimage—June 1964," *Catholic Worker*, accessed January 17, 2020, https://www.catholicworker.org/dorothyday/articles/816.pdf.

29. Day, "On Pilgrimage—June 1964"; Thomas Merton, "D. T. Suzuki: The Man and His Work" and "Zen in Japanese Art," in *Zen and the Birds of Appetite* (New York: New Directions, 1968).

30. Merton, *Dancing in the Waters of Life*, 133; Merton, *The Hidden Ground of Love*, 84.

31. Like Dorothy Day, Merton was among the few Americans who as of 1964 subscribed to the muckraking newsletter *I. F. Stone's Weekly*, which raised challenging questions about American Cold War policy. "Izzy" Stone would become a friend of Day/Merton friend Dan Berrigan. Merton, *The Hidden Ground of Love*, 80–81; Merton, *Dancing in the Waters of Life*, 133; U.S. Naval Institute, "The Truth about Tonkin," accessed May 14, 2019, https://www.usni.org/magazines/naval-history-magazine/2008/february/truth-about-tonkin.

32. Catholic Relief Services, "About Eileen Egan," accessed January 11, 2018, https://www.crs.org/about/careers/egan-journalism-fellowship/about-eileen-egan; "Gordon Zahn Papers," University of Notre Dame Archives, accessed January 11, 2018, http://archives.nd.edu/findaids/ead/xml/zhn.xml; Merton, *The Road to Joy*, 322–23; Eileen Egan to Thomas Merton, June 12, 1962, and Merton to Egan, April 25, 1962, both in Thomas Merton Correspondence with Eileen Egan, TMC; Eileen Egan, *Peace Be with You: Justified Warfare or the Way of Nonviolence* (Maryknoll, NY: Orbis Books, 1999), 170, 213–14, 287; Jim Forest, *The Root of War Is Fear: Thomas Merton's Advice to Peacemakers* (Maryknoll, NY: Orbis Books, 2016), 98–111; Catholic Peace Fellowship, "Jim Forest, Bob Cunnane, and Tom Cornell on Merton's 1964 Peacemaking Retreat," accessed January 13, 2018, http://www.catholicpeacefellowship.org/wp/wordpress/about-cpf/histories/jim-forest-bob-cunnane-and-tom-cornell-on-mertons-1964-peacemaking-retreat-on-the-spiritual-roots-of-protest/; "Antonia S. Malone: Eileen Egan, Pacifist, Helped Start Pax Christi," *National Catholic Reporter*, October 20, 2000, accessed January 11, 2018, http://natcath.org/NCR_Online/archives2/2000d/102000/102000h.htm; Eric Martin, "The Long Formation of Daniel Berrigan," in *Crossings and Dwellings: Restored Jesuits, Women Religious, American Experience, 1814–2014*, ed. Kyle Roberts and Stephen Schloesser (Leiden, Netherlands: Brill, 2017), 531.

33. William H. Shannon, editor's note, in Merton, *The Hidden Ground of Love*, 401–2; Jim Forest, "Learning to Be Peacemakers,"

accessed August 16, 2012, http://www.jimandnancyforest.com/2007/04/03/peacemakers/; James H. Forest and Thomas C. Cornell, "Catholic Peace Fellowship—Histories," accessed January 5, 2018, http://www.catholicpeacefellowship.org/wp/wordpress/about-cpf/histories/; Catholic Peace Fellowship, "Jim Forest, Bob Cunnane, and Tom Cornell on Merton's 1964 Peacemaking Retreat," accessed January 13, 2018, http://www.catholicpeacefellowship.org/wp/wordpress/about-cpf/histories/jim-forest-bob-cunnane-and-tom-cornell-on-mertons-1964-peacemaking-retreat-on-the-spiritual-roots-of-protest/; Jim Forest to Thomas Merton, September 10, 1964, Merton Correspondence with Jim Forest, TMC; Jim Forest, interview with author, April 17, 1997, and June 12, 2008, Hastings-on-Hudson, New York.

34. Tom Cornell, interview with author, August 21, 1997, and May 7, 2006, Peter Maurin Farm, Marlborough, New York.

35. "Catholic Peace Fellowship Officers and Sponsors," *Catholic Peace Fellowship Bulletin*, June 1965, digital archives, University of Notre Dame Archives, accessed April 30, 2019, http://archives.nd.edu/CPF/CPF_1965-06.pdf; Forest, *At Play in the Lions' Den*, 65–66; Thomas C. Cornell, "Catholic Peace Fellowship," *National Catholic Reporter*, April 25, 1975, accessed January 11, 2018, http://www.catholicpeacefellowship.org/wp/wordpress/; Dorothy Day, diary entries, April 10, 1960, and July 20, 1961, Series D-4, DD-CW; Dorothy Day, "On Pilgrimage—March 1960," *Catholic Worker*, accessed April 30, 2019, https://www.catholicworker.org/dorothyday/articles/762.html; Dorothy Day, "On Pilgrimage—September 1963"; Dorothy Day, "On Pilgrimage—November 1963"; Merton, *Turning toward the World*, 199, 200.

36. "Merton's Correspondence with Day, Dorothy," accessed December 29, 2017, http://www.merton.org/Research/Correspondence/y1.aspx?id=460; Gordon Oyer, *Pursuing the Spiritual Roots of Protest* (Eugene, OR: Cascade Books, 2014), 9, 34–41, 95; Merton, *The School of Charity*, 227–28, 250–51, 255; Merton, *Dancing in the Waters of Life*, 178; Forest, *At Play in the Lions' Den*, 61, 66; Thomas Merton, *Witness to Freedom: Letters in Times of Crisis*, ed. William H. Shannon (New York: Farrar, Straus and Giroux, 1994), 104; Mary Luke Tobin, *Hope Is an Open Door* (Nashville: Abingdon Press, 1981), 92–93; Merton, *The Hidden Ground of Love*, 83–85, 93; "Friday Night Meetings," *Catholic Worker*, May 1976;

Kathleen Desutter Jordan, "Sr. Mary Luke Tobin, RIP," *Catholic Worker*, December 2006.

37. Most of the retreatants did arrive together, but a few arrived later. John Dear, *Thomas Merton, Peacemaker* (Maryknoll, NY: Orbis Books, 2015), chap. 13; Oyer, *Pursuing the Spiritual Roots of Protest*, 9, 13, 101, 129–33, 138, 148–61, 234; Dorothy Day, "On Pilgrimage—December 1957," *Catholic Worker*, accessed January 21, 2018, http://www.catholicworker.org/dorothyday/articles/733.html.

38. Forest, *The Root of War Is Fear*, 68–70; 113–21; Oyer, *Pursuing the Spiritual Roots of Protest*, 9, 13, 74, 84, 95, 148–61, 178–79; 243–44; Day, *All the Way to Heaven*, 334.

39. David Cramer, Jenny Howell, Paul Martens, and Jonathan Tran, "Theology and Misconduct: The Case of John Howard Yoder," *Christian Century*, August 4, 2014, accessed January 18, 2018, https://www.christiancentury.org/article/2014-07/theology-and-misconduct.

40. The radical implication of staying in place would be made clear by a group in Merton's religious order. In the 1990s a community of Trappists would remain in their Algerian monastery, in solidarity with their neighbors, unto death. Their witness would be made famous in the acclaimed film *Of Gods and Men*. Carol Glatz, "Monks Killed in Algeria, Depicted in 'Of Gods and Men,' Will Soon Be Beatified," *America*, January 4, 2018, https://www.americamagazine.org/faith/2018/01/04/monks-killed-algeria-depicted-gods-and-men-will-soon-be-beatified; Dear, *Thomas Merton, Peacemaker*, chap. 13; Merton, *The Hidden Ground of Love*, 648–54; author's notes, John Dear, presentation at the Corpus Christi chapter of the International Thomas Merton Society, New York City, January 28, 2016.

CHAPTER FOUR

1. *Catholic Worker*, April 1964, accessed January 25, 2018, http://www.catholicworker.org/dorothyday/articles/189.pdf; Julie Leininger Pycior, "Sargent Shriver," *American National Biography*, accessed July 31, 2019, https://doi.org/10.1093/anb/9780198606697.article.1501362; Bill Moyers, foreword, in Scott Stoessel, *Sarge: The Life and Times of Sargent Shriver* (Washington, DC:

Smithsonian Books, 2004); Daniel Berrigan to Jim Forest, September 1965, Box 90, Daniel Berrigan Collection, Cornell University.

2. Dorothy Day, "On Pilgrimage—February 1965," *Catholic Worker*, accessed January 22, 2018, http://www.catholicworker.org/dorothyday/articles/822.html; Dorothy Day, *The Duty of Delight: The Diaries of Dorothy Day*, ed. Robert Ellsberg (Milwaukee: Marquette University Press, 2008), 356; Thomas Merton to Lyndon Baines Johnson, February 20, 1965, Thomas Merton Center, Bellarmine University, Louisville, KY (hereafter "TMC"); Thomas Merton, *Seeds of Destruction* (New York: Farrar, Straus and Giroux, 1964), copyright page; Thomas Merton, *Seasons of Celebration* (New York: Farrar, Straus and Giroux, 1965), copyright page; Thomas Merton, *The Way of Chuang Tzu* (New York: New Directions, 1965), copyright page; Merton, *Dancing in the Waters of Life: Seeking Peace in the Hermitage, The Journals of Thomas Merton*, vol. 5, 1963–1965, ed. Robert Daggy (San Francisco: HarperSanFrancisco, 1997), 271.

3. Building a society in which it is easier for people to be good was a saying attributed by Dorothy Day to Peter Maurin. Thomas Merton, *The Hidden Ground of Love* (New York: Farrar, Straus and Giroux, 1985), 168, 201, and explanatory note by editor William H. Shannon, 75–76; James Arthur Ward, *Ferrytale: The Career of W. H. "Ping" Ferry* (Palo Alto, CA: Stanford University Press, 2001), 61; Thomas Merton to Robert Lax, June 20, 1960, "Guide to the Center for the Study of Democratic Institutions," Special Collections, University of California, Santa Barbara, accessed January 26, 2018, http://www.oac.cdlib.org/findaid/ark:/13030/tf3s2006vg/; Dorothy Day, "On Pilgrimage—September 1963," *Catholic Worker*, accessed January 31, 2018, http://dorothyday.catholicworker.org/articles/806.html; Edward B. Fiske, "John Cogley Dies at 60; Expert on Catholicism," *New York Times*, March 30, 1976; Dorothy Day, "On Pilgrimage—December 1955," *Catholic Worker*, accessed January 12, 2019, http://www.catholicworker.org/dorothyday/articles/696.html; CSDI Audio, "Witness," March 16, 1965, Digital Collection, University of California, Santa Barbara, accessed January 26, 2018, http://digital.library.ucsb.edu/items/show/5387; John Cogley, "Twenty Women Fast for Condemnation of Nuclear Weapons at Vatican Council," *New York Times*, October 6, 1965.

4. President Richard Nixon's bombing campaign, "Operation Linebacker," would result in even more bombing attacks on

North Vietnam. Jim Forest, *The Root of War Is Fear: Thomas Merton's Advice to Peacemakers* (Maryknoll, NY: Orbis Books, 2016), 86–89; Merton, *The Hidden Ground of Love*, 86; Noam Chomsky and Howard Zinn, *The Pentagon Papers* (Boston: Beacon Press, 1971), 269–388.

5. Paul Elie, *The Life You Save May Be Your Own: An American Pilgrimage* (New York: Farrar, Straus and Giroux, 2003), 255; Garry Wills, "Shallow Calls to Shallow: On Thomas Merton, Fifty Years after His Death," *Harpers* (April 2019), https://harpers.org/archive/2019/04/on-thomas-merton-mary-gordon-review/; David Joseph Belcastro, "Praying the Questions: Merton of Times Square, the Last of the Urban Hermits," accessed August 5, 2019, http://merton.org/ITMS/Annual/20/Belcastro123-150.pdf.

6. Merton, *Dancing in the Waters of Life*, 271; Merton, *The Hidden Ground of Love*, 489–90, 613; Thomas Merton, *The Way of Chuang Tzu* (New York: New Directions, 1965), 5, 12, 26–27, 31; Edward Rice, "Thomas Merton Today," *Jubilee* 13 (March 1966): 32.

7. Also at this time Merton ruminated over his emotional relationship to his female literary agent, writing in his journal, "I guess in a way we love each other, and we are both so complicated—And so devout (or she is, anyway) that it gets funny, and is very inhibited, or rather not." Merton, *Dancing in the Waters of Life*, 259–60, 327–28; "Merton's Correspondence with Karl Stern," TMC, accessed February 16, 2018, http://www.merton.org/Research/Correspondence/y1.aspx?id=1919; Thomas Merton, *The Nonviolent Alternative*, ed. Gordon Zahn (New York: Farrar, Straus and Giroux, 1971), 172–77; Dorothy Day, *All the Way to Heaven: The Selected Letters of Dorothy Day*, ed. Robert Ellsberg (Milwaukee: Marquette University Press, 2010), 310–11; Karl Stern, *Pillar of Fire* (New York: Noonday/Farrar, Straus and Giroux, 1951), 250.

8. Day, *All the Way to Heaven*, 401; Kate Millett, *Sexual Politics* (New York: Doubleday, 1970), 330.

9. Another laywoman who served as a spiritual advisor to priests was Day/Merton soulmate Catherine De Hueck Doherty, head of Madonna House, in Combermere, Ontario (even if she, unlike Day and Merton, eschewed most controversial policy stances). Day, *All the Way to Heaven*, 310–11; Thomas Merton, "The Prison Meditations of Fr. Delp," *Jubilee* 10, no. 11 (March 1963): 32–35; Dorothy Day, "On Pilgrimage—October 1953," *Catholic Worker*, http://www.catholicworker.org/dorothyday/articles/655

.html; Robert Wild, *Catherine's Friends: Some Famous People in the Life of Catherine De Hueck Doherty* (Ottawa: Justin Press, 2011), 32, 36; Julie Leininger Pycior, "'We Are All Called to Be Saints': Dorothy Day, Thomas Merton, and Friendship House," *Merton Annual* 13 (2001): 33–34.

10. Day, *All the Way to Heaven*, 310–11; Audrey H. Cole, "The Catholic Worker Farm, Tivoli, New York, 1964–1978," *Hudson River Valley Review* 8, no. 1 (1991); Merton, *The Hidden Ground of Love*, 148.

11. In 2008 Islam would overtake Catholicism as the world's largest religion. Associated Press/WITN, "Islam Surpasses Catholicism," MuslimMatters, March 31, 2008, accessed April 30/2019, https://muslimmatters.org/2008/03/31/islam-surpasses-roman-catholicism-as-worlds-largest-religion/.

12. Merton, *Dancing in the Waters of Life*, 269–70, 283–84; Thomas Merton, *Contemplation in a World of Action* (Notre Dame, IN: University of Notre Dame Press, 1998); Thomas Merton, *The School of Charity: The Letters of Thomas Merton on Religious Renewal and Spiritual Direction*, ed. Patrick Hart (New York: Farrar, Straus and Giroux, 1990), 250–51; Merton, *The Hidden Ground of Love*, 219.

13. Eileen Egan, *Peace Be with You: Justified Warfare or the Way of Nonviolence* (Maryknoll, NY: Orbis Books, 1999), 171–73; Day, *The Duty of Delight*, 366n235, 371, 372; William H. Shannon, ed., "The Correspondence of Dorothy Day and Thomas Merton," in *American Catholic Pacifism: The Influence of Dorothy Day and the Catholic Worker Movement*, ed. Anne Klejment and Nancy L. Roberts (Westport, CT: Praeger, 1996), 113.

14. "Special Issue—War and Peace at the Vatican Council," *Catholic Worker*, July–August 1965, accessed April 30, 2019, https://thecatholicnewsarchive.org/?a=d&d=CW19650701-01&e=-------en-20-CW-21-byDA-txt-txIN-merton------; Egan, *Peace Be with You*, 171–73.

15. Thomas Merton, "St. Maximus the Confessor on Nonviolence," *Catholic Worker*, September 1965; Shannon, "The Correspondence of Dorothy Day and Thomas Merton," 113; Dorothy Day, "On Pilgrimage—October 1965," *Catholic Worker*, accessed February 18, 2018, http://www.catholicworker.org/dorothyday/articles/832.html.

16. Thomas Merton, "An Open Letter to the American Hierarchy: Schema XIII and the Modern World," *Worldview*, September 1965, February 15, 2018, accessed May 28, 2019, https://carnegiecouncil-media.storage.googleapis.com/files/v08_i009_a003.pdf.

17. Merton, *The Hidden Ground of Love*, 345, 546–47, 608–10; Merton, *Dancing in the Waters of Life*, 257–58; Eileen Egan to Thomas Merton, September 22, 1965, Thomas Merton Correspondence with Eileen Egan, TMC.

18. Merton, "An Open Letter to the American Hierarchy"; Dorothy Day, "On Pilgrimage—July/August 1965," *Catholic Worker*, accessed November 8, 2018, http://www.catholicworker.org/dorothyday/articles/828.html; Eileen Egan to Thomas Merton, September 22, 1965, TMC.

19. Day, *The Duty of Delight*, 369–71; Day, *All the Way to Heaven*, 312, 313, 314; Edward B. Fiske, "John Cogley Dies at 60; Expert on Catholicism," *New York Times*, March 30, 1976; William D. Miller, *Dorothy Day: A Biography* (New York: Harper and Row, 1982), 439; Thomas Merton to Alice Casper, January 30, 1965, May 30, 1967, TMC, "Merton's Correspondence with Casper, Alice Kathryn," accessed March 6, 2018, http://www.merton.org/Research/Correspondence/y1.aspx?id=303#19651225.

20. John Cogley, "Twenty Women Fast for Condemnation of Nuclear Weapons by Vatican Council," *New York Times*, October 7, 1965, accessed November 8, 2018, https://www.nytimes.com/1965/10/07/archives/20-women-fast-for-condemnation-of-nuclear-weapons-by-vatican.html.

21. James W. Douglass, *The Nonviolent Cross: A Theology of Revolution and Peace* (New York: Macmillan, 1966), 110–17; Day, *The Duty of Delight*, 371; Dorothy Day, "On Pilgrimage—November 1965," *Catholic Worker*, accessed May 1, 2019, https://www.catholicworker.org/dorothyday/articles/835.html.

22. Day, *The Duty of Delight*, 369–71; James W. Douglass, *The Nonviolent Cross*, 110–17; Barbara Lucas, "Peace at the Council," *Pax Bulletin*, January 1966.

23. "Pope Paul VI at the United Nations," October 4, 1965, C-SPAN, accessed May 9, 2018, https://www.c-span.org/video/?328121-1/pope-paul-vi-united-nations; Day, "On Pilgrimage—November 1965"; Thomas Merton, *Witness to Freedom: Letters in Times of Crisis*, ed. William H. Shannon (New York: Farrar, Straus

and Giroux, 1994), 95–96; Egan, *Peace Be with You*, 166; Merton, *Dancing in the Waters of Life*, 297–98; Day, *Duty of Delight*, 372; Merton, *The Hidden Ground of Love*, 472, 490.

24. The logical candidate to lead the pro-deterrence side of the debate was Cardinal Francis Spellman, the archbishop of New York and head of the U.S. Military Vicariate, but evidently the nation's most prominent prelate wanted to avoid leading an effort that was likely to prove less than successful. Merton, *The Hidden Ground of Love*, 427; "Philip Hannan, 98, Dies: New Orleans Archbishop," *New York Times*, September 30, 2011, accessed February 19, 2018, http://www.nytimes.com/2011/09/30/us/archbishop-philip-m-hannan-dies-at-98.html; Philip Hannan, Nancy Collins, Peter Finney, *The Archbishop Wore Combat Boots* (Huntington, IN: Our Sunday Visitor Press, 2010), "Appendix: Recollections of the Major Documents of Vatican II."

25. Merton, *Witness to Freedom*, 111–12; Merton, *Dancing in the Waters of Life*, 323.

CHAPTER FIVE

1. Tom Cornell had previously burned several of the draft cards he had been issued. Dorothy Day, *The Duty of Delight: The Diaries of Dorothy Day*, ed. Robert Ellsberg (Maryknoll, NY: Orbis Books, 2008), 373; Tom Cornell, interview with author, August 21, 1997, Peter Maurin Catholic Worker Farm, Marlboro, New York.

2. Thomas Merton, *Dancing in the Waters of Life: Seeking Peace in the Hermitage, The Journals of Thomas Merton*, vol. 5, 1963–1965, ed. Robert Daggy (San Francisco: HarperSanFrancisco, 1997), 309; Thomas Merton, *Conjectures of a Guilty Bystander* (New York: Doubleday, 1966).

3. "Daughter of the Flames," *Washington Post*, December 2, 1985, https://www.washingtonpost.com/archive/lifestyle/1985/12/02/daughter-of-the-flames/9cb57665-edf2-4c28-9481-9d7bbd277406/?utm_term=.42af188a233c; Robert McNamara, *In Retrospect: The Tragedy and Lessons of Vietnam* (New York: Knopf Doubleday, 2017), 216, 402.

4. Merton, *Dancing in the Waters of Life*, 313; Cornell interview; Jim Douglass to Thomas Merton, November 3, 1965, "Thomas

Merton Correspondence with James W. Douglass," Thomas Merton Center, Bellarmine University, Louisville, Kentucky (hereafter "TMC"); "Daughter of the Flames," *Washington Post*, December 2, 1985.

5. Thomas Buckley, "Man, 22, Immolates Himself in Antiwar Protest at UN," *New York Times*, November 10, 1965, https://timesmachine.nytimes.com/timesmachine/1965/11/10/issue.html?action=click&contentCollection=Archives&module=LedeAsset®ion=ArchiveBody&pgtype=article; "Pacifist Student Sets Fire to Himself at UN," *New York Herald Tribune, European Edition*, November 10, 1965, https://iht-retrospective.blogs.nytimes.com/2015/11/09/1965-pacifist-sets-fire-to-himself/; Daniel Berrigan, *No Bars to Manhood* (New York: Bantam, 1970), 12; Cornell interview.

6. Dorothy Day, "Union Square Speech," November 6, 1965, accessed March 14, 2018, http://voicesofdemocracy.umd.edu/day-union-square-speech-speech-text/; Dorothy Day, *The Duty of Delight*, 373–74; Paul Elie, *The Life You Save May Be Your Own: An American Pilgrimage* (New York: Farrar, Straus and Giroux, 2003), 377; Ned O'Gorman, interview with author, March 31, 2012, New York City; Cornell interview.

7. O'Gorman interview; Berrigan, *No Bars to Manhood*, 12; Robert Steed, interview with author, March 26, 2012, Hobart, New York; Buckley, "Man, 22, Immolates Himself in Antiwar Protest at UN."

8. "Roman Catholics: The Human Voice Means More," *Time*, November 19, 1965; Cornell interview.

9. Also sharing the *New York Times* front page with all the reports on the blackout was a piece reporting a "big victory" by Americans over a contingent of Viet Cong. O'Gorman interview; Buckley, "Man, 22, Immolates Himself in Antiwar Protest at UN," and "Power Failure Snarls Northeast," *New York Times*, November 10, 1965, accessed March 23, 2018; "Pacifist Student Sets Fire to Himself at UN," November 10, 1965; Tom Cornell to Thomas Merton, February 21, 1967, "Thomas Merton Correspondence with Tom Cornell," TMC; Day, *The Duty of Delight*, 374; Dorothy Day, "Suicide or Sacrifice," *Catholic Worker*, November 1965, http://www.catholicworker.org/dorothyday/articles/834.html; Steed interview; Eileen Egan, interview with author, May 10, 2000, New York City.

10. Thomas Merton, telegram to Dorothy Day, November 11, 1965, "Thomas Merton Correspondence with Jim Forest," folder 6, TMC; Judith Emery to author, March 11, 2018, New York City; Patrick Hart, OCSO, interview with the author, July 4, 1999, Gethsemani, Kentucky; Jim Forest to author, April 25, 2015; Thomas Merton to the editor, Catholic Peace Fellowship newsletter, September 22, 1965, Thomas Merton Collection, Nazareth College, Rochester, New York.

11. Thomas Merton, *The Hidden Ground of Love: The Letters of Thomas Merton on Religious Experience and Social Concerns*, ed. William H. Shannon (New York: Farrar, Straus and Giroux, 1985), 285–87, 290; Day, *The Duty of Delight*, 374, 409–10; Merton, *Dancing in the Waters of Life*, 314–15.

12. Jim Forest to Thomas Merton, November 16, 1965, TMC; Cornell interview; Day, *The Duty of Delight*, 374; Patrick Allitt, *Religion in America since 1945: A History* (New York: Columbia University Press, 2005), 71, 101.

13. The memorial service was held at the suggestion of Nichole D'Entremont, who wrote a touching reminiscence of her friend Roger LaPorte for the *Catholic Worker*. "Chrystie Street," Nicole D'Entremont, *Catholic Worker*, November 1965.

14. Day, *The Duty of Delight*, 374; Jane Sammon to author, December 18, 2015, Catholic Worker Maryhouse, New York City; Clergy Concerned about the War in Vietnam, press release draft (n.d., October 1965), Box 90, Berrigan Papers, Cornell University.

15. Eileen Egan, interview with author, May 10, 2000, New York City; Berrigan, *No Bars to Manhood* 12; Daniel Berrigan, *To Dwell in Peace: An Autobiography* (Eugene, OR: Wipf and Stock, 2007, previously New York: Harper and Row, 1987), 187; Jim Forest, *At Play in the Lions' Den: A Biography and Memoir of Daniel Berrigan* (Maryknoll, NY: Orbis Books, 2017), 92–93; Day, *All the Way to Heaven*, 317–18; Merton, *The Hidden Ground of Love*, 138.

16. Merton, *The Hidden Ground of Love*, 23–24, 88–89, 162, 287–90.

17. "Talks with and about Thomas Merton," by journalist/editor James Morrissey, would appear in the January 23, 1966, issue of the *Louisville Courier-Journal* Sunday magazine, and Merton would find the profile acceptable. Thomas Merton, *Witness to Freedom: Letters in Times of Crisis*, ed. William H. Shannon (New York: Farrar, Straus and Giroux, 1994), 113–14; Thomas Merton, *The Road to*

Joy: Letters to New and Old Friends, ed. Robert E. Daggy (New York: Farrar, Straus and Giroux, 1989), 71, 288; Thomas Merton, "Peace and Protest," *Continuum* (Winter 1966); Thomas Merton, *Faith and Violence: Christian Teaching and Christian Practice* (Notre Dame, IN: University of Notre Dame Press, 1968), 40–46; Thomas Merton, *The Nonviolent Alternative*, ed. Gordon C. Zahn (New York: Farrar, Straus and Giroux, 1971), 66–69.

18. Merton, *The Hidden Ground of Love*, 148–50.

19. Day, *All the Way to Heaven*, 319–20.

20. Merton, *The Hidden Ground of Love*, 150–51, 162–63.

21. Merton, *The Hidden Ground of Love*, 23–24, 88; Day, *The Duty of Delight*, 410, 616; William H. Shannon, ed., "The Correspondence of Dorothy Day and Thomas Merton," in *American Catholic Pacifism: The Influence of Dorothy Day and the Catholic Worker Movement*, ed. Anne Klejment and Nancy L. Roberts (Westport, CT: Praeger, 1996), 99–121; Jane Sammon to author, May 4, 2018, Maryhouse Catholic Worker, New York City.

22. Merton, *Dancing in the Waters of Life*, 326, 328; Dorothy Day, "Notes by the Way," *Catholic Worker*, January 1944, accessed August 2, 2019, https://www.catholicworker.org/dorothyday/articles/398.html; Dorothy Day, "On Pilgrimage—April 1965," *Catholic Worker*, accessed August 2, 2019, https://www.catholicworker.org/dorothyday/articles/825.html; Dorothy Day, "On Pilgrimage—October/November 1978," *Catholic Worker*, accessed August 2, 2019, https://www.catholicworker.org/dorothyday/articles/593.html; Dorothy Day, "On Pilgrimage—December 1965," *Catholic Worker*, accessed May 2, 2019, https://www.catholicworker.org/dorothyday/articles/248.html.

CHAPTER SIX

1. Clergy Concerned about the War in Vietnam would be best known by its later name, Clergy and Laity Concerned about the War in Vietnam. John Dear, telephone interview with author, February 17, 2017; Thomas Merton, *The Hidden Ground of Love: The Letters of Thomas Merton on Religious Experience and Social Concerns*, ed. William H. Shannon (New York: Farrar, Straus and Giroux, 1985), 22–23; "An Open Letter to the Authorities of the

Archdiocese of New York and the Jesuit Community in New York City," *New York Times*, December 12, 1965, in "Berrigan, Daniel, 1965–1977," W-6.4, Box 1, Dorothy Day–Catholic Worker Collection, Marquette University (hereafter "DD-CW"); "In This Issue," *Jubilee*, February 1966; Daniel Berrigan to Father General, June 4, 1966, Box 90, Daniel Berrigan Collection, Cornell University.

2. Merton, *The Hidden Ground of Love*, 294–97, 300–303.

3. Dorothy Day, *All the Way to Heaven: The Selected Letters of Dorothy Day*, ed. Robert Ellsberg (Milwaukee: Marquette University Press, 2010), 331–34.

4. Dorothy Day, *The Duty of Delight: The Diaries of Dorothy Day*, ed. Robert Ellsberg (Milwaukee: Marquette University Press, 2008), 379, 389–90; Dorothy Day diary entries, June 8, 1966, and September 7, 1967, Box 1, D-4, DD-CW; Deane Mary Mowrer, "A Farm with a View," *Catholic Worker*, March 1968; Audrey H. Cole, "The Catholic Worker Farm, Tivoli, New York, 1964–1978," *Hudson River Valley Review* 18, no. 1 (1991).

5. Day, *The Duty of Delight*, 379, 389–90; Dorothy Day diary entry, June 8, 1966, Box 1, D-4, DD-CW; Cole, "The Catholic Worker Farm, Tivoli, New York, 1964–1978;" *Baltimore Catechism*, "Lesson 13: On the Sacraments in General," Catholic News Agency, accessed February 13, 2020, https://www.catholicnewsagency.com/resources/catechism/baltimore-catechism/lesson-13-on-the-sacraments-in-general.

6. Day, *All the Way to Heaven*, 310–11; Dorothy Day, "Reflections during Advent—Part Four, Obedience," *Ave Maria*, December 17, 1966, accessed May 3, 2019, https://www.catholicworker.org/dorothyday/articles/562.html; Dorothy Day diary entry, September 7, 1967, Box 1, D-4, DD-CW; Kate Hennessy, *Dorothy Day: The World Will Be Saved by Beauty* (New York: Scribner, 2017), 245; Dorothy Day diary entry, September 7, 1967, Box 1, D-4, DD-CW.

7. Hennessy, *Dorothy Day: The World Will Be Saved by Beauty*, 223–26.

8. Robert Giroux, a friend of Merton's from his student days at Columbia, who happened to be gay, would publish several of Merton's books, including the best-selling autobiography that first brought him to national attention, *The Seven Storey Mountain*. Thomas Merton, "Nonviolence and Black Power," in *Faith and Violence: Christian Teaching and Christian Practice* (Notre Dame, IN: University of Notre Dame Press, 1968), 122–23 (also in Thomas

Merton, *The Nonviolent Alternative*, ed. Gordon Zahn [New York: Farrar, Straus and Giroux, 1971], 199); Thomas Merton, *Pre-Benedictine Monasticism*, ed. Patrick F. O'Connell, Initiation into the Monastic Tradition 2 (Collegeville, MN: Cistercian Publications, 2007), 86–88; Thomas Merton, *The Road to Joy: Letters to New and Old Friends*, ed. Robert E. Daggy (New York: Farrar, Straus and Giroux, 1989), 344–45; Boris Kachka, *Hothouse: The Art of Survival and the Survival of Art at America's Most Celebrated Publishing House, Farrar, Straus, and Giroux* (New York: Simon and Schuster, 2013), 91–92.

9. Jack Drescher, "De-pathologizing Homosexuality," *Behavioral Sciences* 5, no. 4 (December 2015), https://www.ncbi.nlm.nih.gov/pmc/articles/PMC4695779/.

10. Day, *The Duty of Delight*, 551–53.

11. Dorothy Day, "To Die for Love," *Catholic Worker*, September 1948, accessed June 4, 2018, http://www.catholicworker.org/dorothyday/articles/470.html.

12. Day, *The Duty of Delight*, 553.

13. Robert Steed, interview with author, March 26, 2012, Hobart, NY; Dorothy Day, "Workers of the World Unite," *Catholic Worker*, May 1958, accessed August 2, 2019, https://www.catholicworker.org/dorothyday/articles/177.html.

14. Day, *The Duty of Delight*, 553.

15. Ned O'Gorman, interview with author, March 31, 2012, New York City.

16. W. H. Auden praised Dorothy Day to the skies in the *New York Review of Books*, with the celebrated poet speculating that he paid the taxes that the Catholic Worker owed to New York City in part out of guilt that he lived so much more comfortably, and telling his readers that this community's voluntary poverty was even more challenging than the austere life of the monastery, for Catholic Workers sacrificed their privacy as well. Meantime, at his monastery, Merton had read Auden's poetry to the novices, calling the poet among the best introductions to the modern canon. W. H. Auden, "Happy Birthday, Dorothy Day," *New York Review of Books*, December 14, 1972; David D. Cooper, ed., *Thomas Merton and James Laughlin: Selected Letters* (New York: W. W. Norton, 1997), 260; O'Gorman interview.

17. "Addie Mae Collins," accessed November 18, 2018, https://insideschools.org/school/05MAXF; Dorothy Day, *The Long*

Loneliness (New York: Harper and Row, 1952), "Postscript"; O'Gorman interview; "Ned O'Gorman," *New Yorker*, December 2, 1967, 54; Merton, *The Road to Joy*, 256; Dorothy Day, "On Pilgrimage—December 1969," *Catholic Worker*, accessed June 6, 2018, http://www.catholicworker.org/dorothyday/articles/905.html.

18. Dorothy Day, "On Pilgrimage—October/November 1966," *Catholic Worker*, accessed May 5, 2019, https://www.catholicworker.org/dorothyday/articles/845.html; Tom Cornell to Thomas Merton, October 17, 1966, Thomas Merton Collection, Nazareth College, Rochester, New York; Day, *The Duty of Delight*, 359–60.

19. Della occasionally gave Dorothy items of clothing as gifts. Hennessy, *Dorothy Day: The World Will Be Saved by Beauty*, 244–46; Day, *All the Way to Heaven*, 168–69, 326; Jim Forest, *All Is Grace: A Biography of Dorothy Day* (Maryknoll, NY: Orbis Books, 2011), 196–201; Day, *The Duty of Delight*, 359–60; Merton, *Dancing in the Waters of Life*, 259; Steed interview; Thomas Merton, "For My Brother, Reported Missing In Action, 1943," accessed November 18, 2018, https://www.poemhunter.com/poem/for-my-brother-missing-in-action-1943/#content.

20. Dorothy Day, "What Does Ammon Mean?," *Catholic Worker*, June 1965, accessed November 17, 2018, https://www.catholicworker.org/dorothyday/articles/826.html; Thomas Merton, *Learning to Love* (San Francisco: HarperCollins, 1997), 50; Day, *The Long Loneliness*.

21. Day, "What Does Ammon Mean?"; Ammon Hennacy, *The Book of Ammon* (New York: Catholic Worker Books, 1965), 347.

22. Day, "What Does Ammon Mean?"

23. Hennessy, *The World Will Be Saved by Beauty*, 317; Day, *The Duty of Delight*, 375–76, 395; Thomas Merton, *Learning to Love: Exploring Solitude and Freedom, The Journals of Thomas Merton*, vol. 6, 1966–1967, ed. Christen Bochen (San Francisco: HarperCollins, 1997), 50.

24. Daniel Berrigan to Therese Lentfoehr, SDS, February 1976, Daniel and Philip Berrigan Papers, Cornell University; John Dear, telephone interview with author, February 17, 2017.

25. Hennessy, *The World Will Be Saved By Beauty*, 346; Forest, *All Is Grace*, 136; Julie Leininger Pycior, "'We Are All Called to Be Saints': Dorothy Day, Thomas Merton, and Friendship House," *Merton Annual* 13 (2000): 27–62; Br. Patrick Hart, OCSO, inter-

view with author, July 4, 1999, Gethsemani, Kentucky; "Half-Dead: Men and the 'Mid-life Crisis,'" *Scientific American*, October 3, 2011, https://blogs.scientificamerican.com/bering-in-mind/half-dead-men-and-the-mid-life-crisis/; Daniel Burke, "Book on Monk Thomas Merton's Love Affair Stirs Debate," *USA Today*, December 23, 2009, http://usatoday30.usatoday.com/news/religion/2009-12-23-Merton23_st_N.htm; Merton, *Learning to Love*, 16, 121–23; Jim Forest, *Living with Wisdom: A Life of Thomas Merton* (Maryknoll, NY: Orbis Books, 2008), 193–94; note by Sr. Therese Lentfoehr, Thomas Merton Papers, Columbia University; Dear interview.

26. Merton, *Learning to Love*, 121–23; Forest, *Living with Wisdom*, 194–203; Thomas Merton, *The Other Side of the Mountain: The End of the Journey*, ed. Patrick Hart (New York: HarperCollins, 1998), 157; Thomas Merton, "Death" and "Purity," in *Prophetic Voices*, ed. Ned O'Gorman (New York: Random House, 1969); Thomas Merton, *Love and Living*, ed. Naomi Burton Stone and Patrick Hart (New York: Harcourt, Brace, Jovanovich, 1979), acknowledgments, 118–19; Paul Elie, *The Life You Save May Be Your Own: An American Pilgrimage* (New York: Farrar, Straus and Giroux, 2013), 390–92.

27. Michael Mott, *The Seven Mountains of Thomas Merton* (Boston: Houghton Mifflin Harcourt, 1984), xxvi; Merton, *The Hidden Ground of Love*, 151–52.

CHAPTER SEVEN

1. Renee Gadoua, "Calling on Thomas Merton for Racial Justice and Healing," *Sojourners*, May 20, 2015, https://sojo.net/articles/calling-thomas-merton-racial-justice-and-healing; Jim Forest to Thomas Merton, March 2, 1967, and Thomas Merton, "To Whom It May Concern," June 17, 1967, Nazareth College Archives, Rochester, New York; Thomas Merton, *The Hidden Ground of Love: Letters on Religious Experience and Social Concerns*, ed. William H. Shannon (New York: Farrar, Straus and Giroux, 1985), 299; Thomas Merton to Tom Cornell, February 28, 1967, Thomas Merton to John Wu Jr., June 9, 1967, Thomas Merton Center, Bellarmine University, Louisville, Kentucky (hereafter "TMC").

2. Tom Cornell to Thomas Merton, September 17, 1966, Thomas Merton Collection, Nazareth College Archives, Rochester, New York; Dorothy Day, *All the Way to Heaven: Selected Letters of Dorothy Day*, ed. Robert Ellsberg (Milwaukee: Marquette University Press, 2010), 329–30; Marty Corbin to Thomas Merton, n.d. (September 1966), D-1, Box 15, DD-CW; Dorothy Day, *The Duty of Delight: The Diaries of Dorothy Day*, ed. Robert Ellsberg (Milwaukee: Marquette University Press, 2008), 393.

3. Thomas Merton, "Albert Camus and the Church," in *A Penny a Copy: Readings from the* Catholic Worker, ed. Thomas C. Cornell, Robert Ellsberg, and Jim Forest (Maryknoll, NY: Orbis Books, 1995), 150–62; accessed June 15, 2018, http://www.easyessays.org/blowing-the-dynamite/; Day, *All the Way to Heaven*, 329–30; "The Promised Land," *Eyes on the Prize: America's Civil Rights Years*, directed by Jacqueline Schearer and Paul Strekler (Blackside Productions, 1990).

4. Dorothy Day, "On Pilgrimage—December 1965," *Catholic Worker*, accessed June 18, 2018, http://www.catholicworker.org/dorothyday/articles/248.html; Dorothy Day, "Reflections during Advent," *Ave Maria*, December 17, 1966, 20–23, accessed June 18, 2018, https://www.catholicworker.org/dorothyday/articles/562.html; Dorothy Day, "In Peace Is My Bitterness Most Bitter," *Catholic Worker*, January 1967, accessed July 2, 2018, http://www.catholicworker.org/dorothyday/articles/250.html.

5. Day, *All the Way to Heaven*, 329–30; Merton, *The Hidden Ground of Love*, 152.

6. "We owe a debt of gratitude to Thomas Merton, Trappist monk and scholar," Day would write in her foreword to his posthumously published book *Ishi Means Man*. The cover would feature a fine woodcut of Ishi by Catholic Worker artist Rita Corbin. Merton, *The Hidden Ground of Love*, 152; Day, "In Peace Is My Bitterness Most Bitter"; Thomas Merton, *Ishi Means Man*, foreword by Dorothy Day (Greensboro, NC: Unicorn Press, 1976), cover and 1, 26–32.

7. Merton, *The Hidden Ground of Love*, 93; Day, *The Duty of Delight*, 400–401; Cornell interview.

8. Day, *All the Way to Heaven*, 331–33, and note by the editor, Robert Ellsberg, 334; Merton, *The Hidden Ground of Love*, 301–3, and note by the editor, William H. Shannon, 300–301; Dorothy Day, *The Long Loneliness* (New York: Harper and Bros., 1952), "Postscript."

9. Michael J. Kramer, "Summer of Love, Summer of War," *New York Times*, accessed July 1, 2018, https://www.nytimes.com/2017/08/15/opinion/vietnam-san-francisco-1967-summer.html; Day, *The Duty of Delight*, 407; Merton, *The Hidden Ground of Love*, 93; Joanna Moorehead, "Corita Kent: Pop-art Nun," *Guardian*, April 22, 2018, https://www.theguardian.com/artanddesign/2018/apr/22/corita-kent-the-pop-art-nun.

10. Merton, *The Hidden Ground of Love*, 93; Daniel Berrigan to Thomas Merton, March 19, 1967, Daniel Berrigan Collection, "Outgoing Correspondence of Daniel Berrigan," Box 90, Daniel and Philip Berrigan Collection, Division of Rare and Manuscript Collections, Cornell University Library; Thomas Merton, *Learning to Love: Exploring Solitude and Freedom, The Journals of Thomas Merton*, vol. 6, *1966–1967*, ed. Christen Bochen (San Francisco: HarperSanFrancisco, 1997), 234–35; Dorothy Day, "The Case of Cardinal McIntyre," *Catholic Worker*, July–August 1964, accessed July 1, 2018, https://www.catholicworker.org/dorothyday/articles/196.html; Day, *The Duty of Delight*, 407.

11. Merton, *The Hidden Ground of Love*, 95, 152–53, 424–26, 500–505; Merton, *Learning to Love*, 214; William H. Shannon, ed., "The Correspondence of Dorothy Day and Thomas Merton," in *American Catholic Pacifism: The Influence of Dorothy Day and the Catholic Worker Movement*, ed. Anne Klejment and Nancy L. Roberts (Westport, CT: Praeger, 1996), 117; editor's note appended to "The Wild Places," by Thomas Merton, *Catholic Worker*, June 1968, accessed August 5, 2019, https://thecatholicnewsarchive.org/?a=d&d=CW19680601-01.2.8&srpos=7&e=01-01-1968-31-11-1968--en-20-CW-1-byDA.rev-txt-txIN-merton------; Thomas Merton to Amiya Chakravarty, April 25, 1967, "Thomas Merton Correspondence with Amira Chakravarty," TMC.

12. Day had obtained her copy of *Conjectures of a Guilty Bystander* from former Catholic Worker Fr. Charles English, who was one of the Trappist censors for the book, which he told Day was "maybe his best book yet." Jack English (Fr. Charles English, OCSO) to Dorothy Day, n.d. (1966), D-1, Box 15, DD-CW; Thomas Merton, *Conjectures of a Guilty Bystander* (New York: Doubleday Image, 1968), 314–15; Merton, *The Hidden Ground of Love*, 151–52; Thomas Merton, *The Road to Joy: Letters to New and Old Friends*, ed. Robert L. Daggy (New York: Farrar, Straus, Giroux, 1989), 95–97; Dorothy Day, "On Pilgrimage—September

1947," *Catholic Worker,* accessed June 29, 2018, http://www.catholicworker.org/dorothyday/articles/455.html; Dorothy Day, "On Pilgrimage—December 1949," *Catholic Worker,* accessed June 29, 2018, http://www.catholicworker.org/dorothyday/articles/497.html; Dorothy Day, "The Case of Father Duffy," December 1949, *Catholic Worker,* accessed June 29, 2018, http://www.catholicworker.org/dorothyday/articles/683.html.

13. *Catholic Worker,* "Spring Mobilization," May 1967, accessed July 3, 2018, http://www.catholicworker.org/dorothyday/articles/849.html; Merton, *Learning to Love,* 214, 233.

14. Eileen Egan to Thomas Merton, April 4, 1967, and Thomas Merton to Eileen Egan, April 10, 1967, both in "Thomas Merton Correspondence with Eileen Egan," TMC; "Pax Group Scores Draft Law," *Catholic Worker,* May 1967.

15. The author observed the Carnaby Street scene in August 1967. Day, *All the Way to Heaven,* 337–38; George Dugan, "Catholic Bishops Open Meeting: Celibacy of Priests Is Key Topic," *New York Times,* November 14, 1967, https://timesmachine.nytimes.com/timesmachine/1967/11/14/90417533.pdf; Day, *The Duty of Delight,* 413; Eileen Egan, *Peace Be with You: Justified Warfare or the Way of Nonviolence* (Maryknoll, NY: Orbis Books, 1999), 286–89.

16. Thomas Merton, *The School of Charity: The Letters of Thomas Merton on Religious Renewal and Spiritual Direction,* ed. Patrick Hart (New York: Harper Collins, 1990), 329–30; Day, *All the Way to Heaven,* 340–41; Day, *The Duty of Delight,* 414–15, 437, 526.

17. Thomas Merton, *The Other Side of the Mountain: The End of the Journey,* ed. Patrick Hart (New York: HarperCollins, 1998), 286, 288; Merton, *The Hidden Ground of Love,* 455–58.

18. Jim Forest, *At Play in the Lion's Den: A Biography and Memoir of Daniel Berrigan* (Maryknoll, NY: Orbis Books, 2017), 103–4.

19. Daniel Berrigan to Thomas Merton, April, 1967, and October 6, 1967, both in "Thomas Merton Correspondence with Daniel Berrigan," TMC; Merton, *The Hidden Ground of Love,* 94–95; Merton, *Learning to Love,* 76; Jim Forest, *Living with Wisdom: A Life of Thomas Merton* (Maryknoll, NY: Orbis Books, 2008), 215; Merton, *The Hidden Ground of Love,* 94–100.

20. Daniel Berrigan, *To Dwell in Peace: An Autobiography* (New York: Harper and Row, 1987), 172–73; Daniel Berrigan, *Portraits of Those I Love* (New York: Crossroad, 1982), 82–86; Jim

Dwyer, "Remember Daniel Berrigan: A Powerful, Penniless Voice for Peace," *New York Times*, May 5, 2016; Jim Forest, *All Is Grace: A Biography of Dorothy Day* (New York: Orbis Books, 2011), 302–3.

21. Thomas Merton, "Thich Nhat Hanh Is My Brother," in *Faith and Violence* (Notre Dame, IN: University of Notre Dame Press, 1968), v, 106–8; Merton, *The Hidden Ground of Love*, 99; Berrigan, *Portraits of Those I Love*, 19–21.

CHAPTER EIGHT

1. Thomas Merton and Jean Leclercq, *Not Survival but Prophecy*, ed. Patrick Hart (New York: Farrar, Straus and Giroux, 2002), v; Thomas Merton to Gordon Zahn, April 3, 1968, "Merton's Correspondence with Gordon Zahn," the Thomas Merton Center, Bellarmine University, Louisville, Kentucky (hereafter "TMC").

2. William Apel, "Terrible Days: The Merton/Yungblunt Letters and MLK Jr.'s Death," *Merton Annual* 21 (2008): 29.

3. Passion Week is the week before Holy Week, which leads into Easter. Merton had yet another shock at this time: one of his few surviving relatives, his Aunt Kit, died in a shipwreck. Merton, *The Other Side of the Mountain: The End of the Journey*, ed. Patrick Hart (New York: HarperCollins, 1998), 77–79, 84–85, 123; Jeff Shesol, *Mutual Contempt: Lyndon Johnson, Robert Kennedy, and the Feud the Defined a Decade* (New York: W. W. Norton, 1998), 439–42; Thomas Merton, *Witness to Freedom: Letters of Thomas Merton in Times of Crisis*, ed. William H. Shannon (New York: Farrar, Straus and Giroux, 1995), 242; Thomas Merton, *The Hidden Ground of Love: Letters on Religious Experience and Social Concerns*, ed. William H. Shannon (New York: Farrar, Straus and Giroux, 1985), 443–44, 448, 640–46 and note by the editor, 635.

4. Appel, "Terrible Days"; Merton, *The Other Side of the Mountain*, 79.

5. Patrick Jordan, "Dorothy Day, the Catholic Worker, and the Liturgy," *Yale ISM Review* 4, no. 1 (Winter 2018), http://ismreview.yale.edu/article/dorothy-day-the-catholic-worker-and-the-liturgy/#_edn16; Merton, *The Hidden Ground of Love*, 587–606; William H. Shannon, ed., "The Correspondence of Dorothy Day and Thomas Merton," in *American Catholic Pacifism: The Influ-*

ence of Dorothy Day and the Catholic Worker Movement, ed. Anne Klejment and Nancy L. Roberts (Westport, CT: Praeger, 1996), 119–20; Merton, *The Other Side of the Mountain*, 80.

6. Paul Elie, *The Life You Save May Be Your Own: An American Pilgrimage* (New York: Farrar, Straus and Giroux, 2003), 406; Dorothy Day, "On Pilgrimage—April 1968," *Catholic Worker*, accessed January 13, 2019, https://www.catholicworker.org/dorothy day/articles/252.html.

7. Shattered by his brother John F. Kennedy's assassination in 1963, Robert Kennedy began to heal only when he started identifying with other wounded souls, notably those on the margins of society. Ghetto and barrio residents, sensing this emotional connection, embraced Kennedy as he campaigned in their neighborhoods. (Studies of RFK have posited that his agony over John Kennedy's murder may well have been exacerbated by guilt over having championed CIA assassination plots against Fidel Castro and worry that the Cuban leader might have retaliated.) Shesol, *Mutual Contempt*, 130–31; "Promised Land" episode of *Eyes on the Prize: America's Civil Rights Years*, directed by Jacqueline Schearer, Paul Stekler (Blackside, 1990); Merton, *The Other Side of the Mountain*, 80; "Audio Clips of Thomas Merton," TMC, accessed May 15, 2019, http://merton.org/Research/AV/audioclip.aspx.

8. Merton, *The Hidden Ground of Love*, 443–49; Ethel Kennedy to Thomas Merton, n.d. (1963) and January 18, 1965, "Merton Correspondence with Ethel Kennedy," TMC.

9. The funeral was held in New York because RFK represented New York in the U.S. Senate. Dorothy Day, "On Pilgrimage—March 1969," *Catholic Worker*, accessed July 23, 2018, https://www .catholicworker.org/dorothyday/articles/896.html; Dorothy Day, *All the Way to Heaven: The Selected Letters of Dorothy Day*, ed. Robert Ellsberg (Milwaukee: Marquette University Press, 2010), 345; "Richard 'Whiskers' Harper," *Catholic Worker*, August 2015.

10. Philip Berrigan would leave the priesthood a few years later to marry fellow Catholic peace activist Elizabeth McAlister. Jim Forest, *At Play in the Lion's Den: A Biography and Memoir of Daniel Berrigan* (Maryknoll, NY: Orbis Books, 2017) 117–18; Murray Polner and Jim O'Grady, *Disarmed and Dangerous: The Radical Lives and Times of Daniel and Philip Berrigan* (New York: Basic Books, 1997), chap. 10, "Catonsville."

11. Merton, *The Hidden Ground of Love*, 96–98; Polner and O'Grady, *Disarmed and Dangerous*, 190–217; Thomas Merton, *Faith and Violence* (Notre Dame, IN: University of Notre Dame Press, 1968), v; "The Weather Underground," *Independent Lens*, accessed November 19, 2018, http://www.pbs.org/independentlens/weather underground/movement.html.

12. Merton, *The Other Side of the Mountain*, 110; Merton, *Witness to Freedom*, 117–19; Thomas Merton, *The School of Charity: The Letters of Thomas Merton on Religious Renewal and Spiritual Direction*, ed. Patrick Hart (New York: HarperCollins, 1990), 384–85.

13. Day, *All the Way to Heaven*, 343–44; Francine du Plessix Gray, *Divine Disobedience* (New York: Alfred Knopf, 1970), 50–58.

14. Forest, *At Play in the Lion's Den*, 118–20; Thomas C. Cornell, interview with Deane Mowrer, June 6, 1968, Catholic Worker Farm, Tivoli, New York, DD-CW; Thomas C. Cornell, interview with author, August 21, 1997, Peter Maurin Catholic Worker Farm, Marlboro, New York.

15. Even Robert Kennedy's mother-in-law had done some secretarial work for Merton. Thomas Merton to Ann Brannack Skakel, September 9, 1951, TMC; Thomas Merton to Eileen Egan, February 1966, October 8, 1966, December 15, 1966, April 25, 1968, June 4, 1968; and Eileen Egan to Thomas Merton, March 8, 1968, May 29, 1968; Eileen Egan to William H. Shannon, May 21, 1983: all in "Merton's Correspondence with Eileen Egan," TMC; Merton, *Witness to Freedom*, 117–20; Merton, *The Other Side of the Mountain*, 110.

16. Eileen Egan, "Are You Ready to Commit 'Instant Auchwitz'?," *Catholic Worker*, October 1968; Eileen Egan, *Peace Be with You: Justified Warfare or the Way of Nonviolence* (Maryknoll, NY: Orbis Books, 1999), 287; Dorothy Day diary entry, July 21, 1968, DD-CW.

17. Dorothy Day, *The Duty of Delight: The Diaries of Dorothy Day*, ed. Robert Ellsberg (Milwaukee: Marquette University Press, 2008), 423; Egan, "Are You Ready To Commit 'Instant Auschwitz'?"; Egan, *Peace Be with You*, 214–16; Thomas Merton, *The Road to Joy: Letters to New and Old Friends*, ed. Robert E. Daggy (New York: Farrar, Straus and Giroux, 1989), 115–17; Douglas P. Lackey, *Moral Principals and Nuclear Weapons* (New York: Rowan and Littlefield, 1984), 206–7; Eileen Egan to Thomas Merton, August 3, 1968, "Correspondence of Thomas Merton with Eileen Egan"; Shannon,

"Correspondence of Dorothy Day and Thomas Merton," 119–20; Day, "On Pilgrimage—March 1969"; Merton, *The Other Side of the Mountain*, 142.

18. Eileen Egan to Thomas Merton, May 29, 1968, "Merton's Correspondence with Eileen Egan," TMC.

19. Julie Leininger Pycior, *LBJ and Mexican Americans: The Paradox of Power* (Austin: University of Texas Press, 1997), 219; Dorothy Day, "Strike Leader Comes East," *Catholic Worker*, May 1967, accessed July 23, 2018, https://www.catholicworker.org/dorothyday/articles/920.html; Dorothy Day, "On Pilgrimage—April 1951," *Catholic Worker*, accessed August 3, 2019, https://www.catholicworker.org/dorothyday/articles/621.html; Dorothy Day, "On Pilgrimage—June 1960," *Catholic Worker*, accessed August 3, 2019, https://www.catholicworker.org/dorothyday/articles/765.html; Day, *The Duty of Delight*, 422; "César Chávez at Dorothy Day's Funeral," accessed May 8, 2019, https://merton.bellarmine.edu/items/show/90.

20. For Merton's thoughts on the prophetic significance of Latin American social change and poetry, see, for example, his correspondence with his former novice student and the future Sandinista, poet, and priest Ernesto Cardenal. Thomas Merton and Ernesto Cardenal, *From the Monastery to the World: The Letters of Thomas Merton and Ernesto Cardenal*, ed. and trans. Jessie Sandoval (Berkeley: Counterpoint Press, 2017), introduction by Robert Haas; Dorothy Day, "Day after Day," *Catholic Worker*, November 1934, accessed July 23, 2018, http://www.catholicworker.org/dorothyday/articles/283.html; Joseph Engleberg to Committee on Peace Education, University of Kentucky, May 27, 1968, "Merton's Correspondence with Joseph Engleberg," TMC, accessed July 23, 2018, http://merton.org/Research/Correspondence/z-d.aspx?ITEMid=4667&counter=1.

21. Like Chávez, Joan Baez was Mexican American, and although from a very different socioeconomic background, this daughter of a Stanford physicist nonetheless also had faced some discrimination in her youth on account of her Mexican heritage. Thomas Spencer, "Joan Baez, Ira Sandperl, and Thomas Merton's Nonviolent Activism," *Merton Seasonal* (2009), accessed May 15, 2019, http://merton.org/ITMS/Seasonal/34/34.1Spencer.pdf; Patrick Hart and Jonathan Montaldo, eds., *The Intimate Merton: His Life in Journals* (New York: HarperCollins, 1999), 304, 305; Julie Leininger Pycior, "Precursors: Mexicans in New York before 1970,"

CUNY Institute of Mexican Studies, "Mexico–New York: Thirty Years of Migration," May 10, 2013, New York City, accessed September 10, 2017, http://www.lehman.edu/cuny-mexican-studies-institute/2013-conference.php.

22. The autographed smock is preserved in the Dorothy Day–Catholic Worker Collection at the Marquette University Archives. Kate Hennessy, *Dorothy Day: The World Will Be Saved by Beauty* (New York: Scribner's, 2017), 278; Dorothy Day, "On Pilgrimage—January 1973," *Catholic Worker*, accessed May 15, 2019, https://www.catholicworker.org/dorothyday/articles/527.html; "Dorothy Day Memorabilia," Series D-9, DD-CW, accessed May 15, 2019, https://www.marquette.edu/library/archives/Mss/DDCW/DDCW-sc.php.

23. Dorothy Day, "On Pilgrimage—November 1967," *Catholic Worker*, accessed September 22, 2018, http://www.catholicworker.org/dorothyday/articles/857.html; Paul VI, *Humanae Vitae*, July 25, 1968, accessed May 8, 2019, https://w2.vatican.va/content/paul-vi/en/encyclicals/documents/hf_p-vi_enc_25071968_humanae-vitae.html.

24. Dorothy Day, "On Pilgrimage—December 1961," *Catholic Worker*, accessed September 22, 2018, https://www.catholicworker.org/dorothyday/articles/788.html; Dorothy Day, "A Midsummer Retreat at Maryfarm," *Catholic Worker*, August 1954, accessed September 22, 2018, http://www.catholicworker.org/dorothyday/articles/671.html; Brian Terrell, "Dorothy Day: We Are Not Going into the Subject of Birth Control at All, as a Matter of Fact," *National Catholic Reporter*, September 12, 2015, accessed September 22, 2018, https://www.ncronline.org/news/people/dorothy-day-we-are-not-going-subject-birth-control-all-matter-fact.

25. Merton, *Witness to Freedom*, 173–74, 298; Merton, *The Hidden Ground of Love*, 348–49; Day, *All the Way to Heaven*, 352, 453; General Federation of Women's Clubs (North Carolina), "March Is National Women's History Month," *Federation Friday* 1, no. 35 (March 1, 2019), https://gfwcnc.org/federation-friday/march-is-national-womens-history-month/.

26. Merton, *The Road to Joy*, 117, 121; Thomas Merton, *Asian Journal of Thomas Merton* (New York: New Directions, 1975), 234–35; Thomas Merton, *Zen and the Birds of Appetite* (New York: New Directions, 1968), 89, 116–17, 120–21, 140; Tibet House US, "His

Holiness the Dalai Lama and Thomas Merton," accessed January 8, 2019, https://tibethouse.us/holiness-dalai-lama-thomas-merton/.

27. "Thomas Merton Is Dead: Monk Wrote of Search for God," *New York Times*, December 11, 1968, accessed September 27, 2018, https://timesmachine.nytimes.com/timesmachine/1968/12/11/102305538.pdf; Michael Mott, *The Seven Mountains of Thomas Merton* (Boston: Houghton Mifflin, 1984), 564–68; Jim Forest, *Living with Wisdom: A Life of Thomas Merton* (Maryknoll, NY: Orbis Books, 2008), 237–40.

28. "FBI and CIA Materials," TMC, accessed October 1, 2018, http://merton.org/Research/Correspondence/y1.aspx?id=623; Federal Bureau of Investigation, "Dorothy Day," Internet Archive, accessed October 1, 2018, https://archive.org/details/DorothyDay/page/n9; Hugh Turley and David Martin, *The Martyrdom of Thomas Merton* (Hyattsville, MD: McCabe Publishing, 2018), 247–55, 267–70.

29. "Recent and Forthcoming Publications," TMC, accessed September 30, 2018, http://merton.org/book.aspx; "Reviews of: *The Martyrdom of Thomas Merton*," TMC, accessed August 22, 2019, http://www.merton.org/Research/reviews/detail.aspx?id=594; Paul Dekar, "A Challenge to the Standard Account" (review of *The Martyrdom of Thomas Merton*), *The Merton Seasonal* 43, no. 4 (Winter 2018): viii, 309, http://merton.org/ITMS/Seasonal/43/43-4DekarRevTurley.pdf; Anthony Donavan, review of *The Martyrdom of Thomas Merton: An Investigation*, *Catholic Worker*, August–September 2019; Phil Gibbs, "What Is Occam's Razor?" (1996; last updated 1997), accessed August 20, 2019 http://www.math.ucr.edu/home/baez/physics/General/occam.html.

30. Dorothy Day, "Thomas Merton, Trappist, 1915–1968," *Catholic Worker*, December 1968, accessed September 27, 2018, https://www.catholicworker.org/dorothyday/articles/901.html.

CODA

1. Dorothy Day, *The Duty of Delight: The Diaries of Dorothy Day*, ed. Robert Ellsberg (Milwaukee: Marquette University Press, 2008), 561.

2. That *New York Times* profile of Dorothy Day was written by prominent journalist of religion John Cogley, a former Catholic Worker. The following year he announced that he was leaving the Catholic Church over its birth control teaching and related issues. John Cogley, "Dorothy Day, Comforter," *New York Times*, November 8, 1972, https://www.nytimes.com/1972/11/08/archives/dorothy-day-comforter.html; Edward B. Fiske, "John Cogley Dies at 60; Expert on Catholicism," *New York Times*, March 30, 1976, https://www.nytimes.com/1976/03/30/archives/john-cogley-dies-at-60-expert-on-catholicism.html; Office of the President, University of Notre Dame, "The Laetare Medal: Dorothy Day" (1972), accessed October 8, 2018, https://laetare.nd.edu/recipients/people/dorothy-day/; Bob Graf, "What Is the Story behind Dorothy Day Accepting the Laetare Medal from the University of Notre Dame?," accessed October 8, 2018, http://www.nonviolentworm.org/TeachWarNoMore/WhatIsTheStoryBehindDorothyDayAcceptingTheLaetareMedalFromNotreDame; television program listing, *New York Times*, May 10, 1973, accessed October 8, 2018, https://www.nytimes.com/1973/05/10/archives/television-morning-afternoon-cable-tv-evening.html.

3. Eileen Egan, *Peace Be with You: Justified Warfare or the Way of Nonviolence* (Maryknoll, NY: Orbis Books, 1999), 295–300; cover, *Jubilee*, May 1960; cover, *Jubilee*, December 1960.

4. Eileen Egan herself asked the audience to observe a moment of silence "in protest against the holocaust which we perpetrated in Hiroshima and Nagasaki"—this, according to Dorothy Day, who told her readers that Egan's gesture had "a profound effect. Even the *New York Times* mentioned it." Lou Baldwin, "World Meeting Was Big, but Was It the Biggest in Philadelphia History?," CatholicPhilly.com, posted October 13, 2015, accessed October 6, 2018, http://catholicphilly.com/2015/10/news/local-news/world-meeting-was-big-but-was-it-the-biggest-event-in-philadelphia-history/; Egan, *Peace Be with You*, 148–49, 296–97, 300–301; Dorothy Day, "On Pilgrimage—October/November 1976," *Catholic Worker*, accessed October 7, 2018, http://www.catholicworker.org/dorothyday/articles/574.html; Day, *The Duty of Delight*, 561–62; Dorothy Day, "Bread for the Hungry," *Catholic Worker*, September 1976, accessed October 8, 2018, http://www.catholicworker.org/dorothyday/articles/258.html.

5. The abbot wanted the monastery's donation kept quiet, and it was not discussed publicly for several years. Day, *The Duty of Delight,* and editor's note, 532; author description, John Eudes Bamberger, OCSO, *Thomas Merton: Prophet of Renewal* (Collegeville, MN: Cistercian Publicans, 2005); John Eudes Bamberger, OCSO, interview with author, August 11, 1997, Abbey of Our Lady of the Genesee, Piffard, New York.

6. The Ade Bethune statue, Mary, Seat of Wisdom, is the copy of one at the Marian Gardens of the University of Dayton. Photograph by author, *Seat of Wisdom* statue by Ade Bethune, Abbey of Our Lady of the Genesee, Piffard, New York; Ade Bethune, interview with author, June 18, 1999, Newport, Rhode Island; "Benedictine Oblates of Portsmouth Abbey," Portsmouth Abbey, accessed February 21, 2020, https://www.portsmouthabbeymonastery.org/oblates; "Ade Bethune," accessed February 21, 2020, http://mothermarysflowergarden.blogspot.com/2013/09/ade-bethune_5502.html; e-mail and attachment, Melanie Zambrowski (University of Dayton Marian Library) to author, August 3, 2019.

7. John Eudes Bamberger, OCSO, to Dorothy Day, July 1, 1974, D-1, Box 15, and August 24, 1974, D-1, Box 16, both in DD-CW; Day, *The Duty of Delight,* 536, 541, 544, 618, 635; Dorothy Day, "On Pilgrimage—October/November 1976."

8. "The Catholic Worker Movement," accessed May 9, 2019, https://www.catholicworker.org/; Arthur J. Laffin, "Plowshares Disarmament Chronology," accessed February 21, 2020, https://web.archive.org/web/20130919164138/http://www.craftech.com/~dcpledge/brandywine/plow/Chronology.html; John Dear, telephone interview with author, February 17, 2017; "Security Questions Are Raised by Break-In at Nuclear Site," *New York Times,* August 7, 2012; Jim Dwyer, "Remembering Daniel Berrigan: A Penniless, Powerful Voice for Peace," *New York Times,* May 5, 2016.

9. Pope Francis presented a copy of his historic peace statement to President Donald Trump on his official visit to the Vatican later that year. Philip Pullella and Steve Holland, "Pope Asks Trump to Be a Peacemaker," *Reuters,* May 27, 2017, https://www.reuters.com/article/us-usa-trump-pope-idUSKBN18K001; Pope Francis, "Nonviolence: A Style of Politics for Peace," January 1, 2017, accessed May 9, 2019, https://w2.vatican.va/content/francesco/en/messages/peace/documents/papa-francesco_20161208_messaggio-l-giornata-mondiale-pace-2017.html; Joshua McElwee, "Landmark Vatican

Conference Rejects Just War Theory, Asks for Encyclical on Nonviolence," *National Catholic Reporter*, April 14, 2016, https://www.ncronline.org/news/vatican/landmark-vatican-conference-rejects-just-war-theory-asks-encyclical-nonviolence; Joshua J. McElwee, "Francis Calls on Christians to Embrace Nonviolence in World Day of Peace Message," *National Catholic Reporter*, December 12, 2016, https://www.ncronline.org/news/vatican/francis-calls-christians-embrace-nonviolence-world-day-peace-message.

10. Dorothy Day, *All the Way to Heaven: Selected Letters of Dorothy Day*, ed. Robert Ellsberg (Milwaukee: Marquette University Press, 2010), 351; Dear interview.

11. Sharon Otterman, "In Hero of the Catholic Left, a Conservative Cardinal Sees a Saint," *New York Times*, November 26, 2012, https://www.nytimes.com/2012/11/27/nyregion/sainthood-for-dorothy-day-has-unexpected-champion-in-cardinal-timothy-dolan.html; Robert Barron, *Bridging the Great Divide: Musings of a Post-Liberal, Post-Conservative Evangelical Catholic* (Lanham, MD: Sheed and Ward, 2004), 207: Julie Leininger Pycior, "'We Are All Called to Be Saints': Dorothy Day, Thomas Merton, and Friendship House," *Merton Annual* 13 (2000): 27–62.

12. Robert Giroux, "Bookend: Thomas Merton's Durable Mountain," *New York Times Book Review*, October 11, 1998, https://archive.nytimes.com/www.nytimes.com/books/98/10/11/bookend/bookend.html; Mark Van Doren, obituary for Thomas Merton, *America*, January 4, 1969, republished December 10, 2018, https://www.americamagazine.org/faith/2018/12/10/thomas-mertons-obituary-1969; Bill Griffin, review of Thomas Merton, *Peace in the Post-Christian Era* (Maryknoll, NY: Orbis Books, 2004), *Catholic Worker*, June 2005.

13. On a random week in May 2019, most rooms at Our Lady of the Genesee, the Trappist monastery in New York, were taken. "Book a Room at Genesee Abbey Retreats," accessed May 9, 2019, https://www.abbeyretreats.org/booking; "Dorothy Day, Oblate," St. Procopius Abbey, accessed May 9, 2019, https://www.procopius.org/dorothy-day-oblate; "Our Vision," Transfiguration Monastery, accessed May 9, 2019, http://www.transfigurationmonastery.org/.

14. Center for Action and Contemplation, "History," accessed May 10, 2019, https://cac.org/about-cac/history/; Anne M. Windholtz, "For Better or Worse, a Lot of Richard Rohr," *National Association of Catholic Chaplains*, September–October 2018, accessed

May 11, 2019, https://www.nacc.org/vision/september-october-2018/for-better-or-for-worse-a-lot-of-richard-rohr/; Barron, *Bridging the Great Divide*, 207.

15. The most numerous such groups, mainly influenced by Thomas Keating, OCSO, call their practice Centering Prayer. "Centering Prayer," accessed February 21, 2020, http://www.centeringprayer.com/centering_prayer.html; Contemplative Outreach, "History of Centering Prayer," accessed February 21, 2020, https://www.contemplativeoutreach.org/history-centering-prayer.

16. Technically Fr. Byrne was a monsignor, but he brushed away that honorific. "Msgr. Raymond J. Byrne," *Catholic New York*, January 24, 2013, accessed August 4, 2019, http://www.cny.org/stories/msgr-raymond-j-byrne,8750.

17. Dorothy Day, "Poverty and Pacifism," *Catholic Worker*, December 1944, accessed December 30, 2018, http://www.catholicworker.org/dorothyday/articles/223.html.

18. Thomas Merton, *Asian Journal of Thomas Merton* (New York: New Directions, 1975), 235, 282, 296; Dorothy Day, *The Long Loneliness* (New York: Harper & Row, 1952), "Postscript."

Bibliography

ARCHIVAL COLLECTIONS

Archives and Special Collections, Burns Library, Boston College: Jim Forest Papers.

Columbia University Rare Books and Manuscripts: John Howard Griffin Papers, Robert Lax Papers, Thomas Merton Papers.

Cornell University Archives and Special Collections: Daniel and Philip Berrigan Collection.

David Levine Archive, Bedminster, Pennsylvania.

Loretto Heritage Center, Nerinx, Kentucky: Mother M. Luke Tobin Papers.

Madonna House Archives, Combermere, Ontario.

Marquette University Archives and Special Collections: Dorothy Day–Catholic Worker Collection.

Nazareth College Library, Rochester, New York: Thomas Merton Papers.

Stanford University Archives and Special Collections: Bob Fitch Collection.

Thomas Merton Center, Bellarmine University, Louisville, Kentucky.

University of California, Santa Barbara Special Collections: Center for the Study of Democratic Institutions Papers.

University of Dayton: John Stokes and Mary's Gardens Collection, Marian Library.

University of Notre Dame Archives: Catholic Peace Fellowship Collection, *Commonweal* Collection, Eileen Egan Collection.

BOOKS AND ARTICLES

Allitt, Patrick. *Religion in America since 1945: A History*. New York: Columbia University Press, 2005.

Apel, William. "Terrible Days: Merton/Yungblunt Letters and MLK Jr.'s Death." *The Merton Annual* 21 (2008): 25–32.

Bamberger, John Eudes. *Thomas Merton: Prophet of Renewal*. Collegeville, MN: Cistercian Publications, 2005.

Belcastro, David Joseph. "Praying the Questions: Merton of Times Square, the Last of the Urban Hermits." *Merton Annual* 20 (2007). http://merton.org/ITMS/Annual/20/Belcastro123-150.pdf.

Berrigan, Daniel. *No Bars to Manhood*. New York: Bantam, 1970.

———. *Portraits of Those I Love*. New York: Crossroad, 1982.

———. *To Dwell in Peace*. Eugene, OR: Wipf and Stock, 2007.

Chomsky, Noam, and Howard Zinn, eds. *The Pentagon Papers*. Boston: Beacon Press, 1971.

Cooper, David D., ed. *Thomas Merton and James Laughlin: Selected Letters*. New York: W. W. Norton, 1997.

Day, Dorothy. *All the Way to Heaven: The Selected Letters of Dorothy Day*. Edited by Robert Ellsberg. Milwaukee: Marquette University Press, 2010.

———. *The Duty of Delight: The Diaries of Dorothy Day*. Edited by Robert Ellsberg. Milwaukee: Marquette University Press, 2008.

———. *From Union Square to Rome*. Silver Spring, MD: Preservation of the Faith Press, 1938.

———. *The Long Loneliness*. New York: Harper and Bros., 1952.

———. *Loaves and Fishes: The Story of the Catholic Worker Movement*. New York: Harper and Row, 1963.

———. *On Pilgrimage: The Sixties*. New York: Curtis Books, 1972.

Dear, John. *Thomas Merton, Peacemaker*. Maryknoll, NY: Orbis Books, 2015.

Dekar, Paul. "A Challenge to the Standard Account" (review of *The Martyrdom of Thomas Merton*). *The Merton Seasonal* 43, no. 4 (Winter 2018): viii, 309. http://merton.org/ITMS/Seasonal/43/43-4DekarRevTurley.pdf.

Dolan, Timothy. *Called to Be Holy*. Huntington, IN: Our Sunday Visitor Press, 2005.

Douglass, James. *The Nonviolent Cross: A Theology of Revolution and Peace*. New York: Macmillan, 1966.

Egan, Eileen. *Peace Be with You: Justified Warfare or the Way of Nonviolence*. Maryknoll, NY: Orbis Books, 1999.

Elie, Paul. *The Life You Save May Be Your Own: An American Pilgrimage*. New York: Farrar, Straus and Giroux, 2003.

Forest, Jim. *All Is Grace: A Biography of Dorothy Day*. Maryknoll, NY: Orbis, 2010.

———. *At Play in the Lions' Den: A Biography and Memoir of Dan Berrigan*. Maryknoll, NY: Orbis Books, 2017.

———. *Living with Wisdom: A Life of Thomas Merton*. Maryknoll, NY: Orbis Books, 2008.

———. *The Root of War Is Fear: Thomas Merton's Advice to Peacemakers*. Maryknoll, NY: Orbis Books, 2016.

Garvey, Margaret, and Michael Quigley, eds. *The Dorothy Day Book*. Springfield, IL: Templegate, 1982.

Griffith, Sidney H. "Introduction to Thomas Merton." In *Pre-Benedictine Monasticism*, edited by Patrick O'Connell. Collegeville, MN: Cistercian Publications, 2007.

Hannan, Philip, Nancy Collins, and Peter Finney. *The Archbishop Wore Combat Boots*. Huntington, IN: Our Sunday Visitor Press, 2010.

Harford, James. *Thomas Merton and Friends*. New York: Continuum, 2007.

Hart, Patrick, and Jonathan Montaldo, eds. *The Intimate Merton: His Life in Journals*. New York: Harper Collins, 1999.

Hemmer, Kurt, ed. *Encyclopedia of Beat Literature*. New York: Infobase Publishing, 2010.

Hennacy, Ammon. *The Book of Ammon*. New York: Catholic Worker Books, 1965.

Hennessy, Kate. *Dorothy Day: The World Will Be Saved by Beauty*. New York: Scribner, 2017.

Horn, Gerald Rainer. *The Spirit of Vatican II: Western European Progressive Catholicism in the Long 1960s*. New York: Oxford University Press, 2015.

Kachka, Boris. *Hothouse: The Art of Survival and the Survival of Art at America's Most Celebrated Publishing House, Farrar, Straus, and Giroux*. New York: Simon and Schuster, 2013.

Martin, Eric. "The Long Formation of Daniel Berrigan." In *Crossings and Dwellings: Restored Jesuits, Women Religious, American

Experience, 1814–2014, edited by Kyle Roberts and Stephen Schloesser. Leiden, Netherlands: Brill, 2017.

Martin, James. *Building a Bridge: How the Catholic Church and the LGBT Community Can Enter into a Relationship of Respect, Compassion, and Sensitivity*. New York: Harper One, 2017.

McNamara, Robert. *In Retrospect: The Tragedy and Lessons of Vietnam*. New York: Knopf Doubleday, 2017.

Merriman, Brigid O'Shea. *Searching for Christ: The Spirituality of Dorothy Day*. Notre Dame, IN: University of Notre Dame Press, 1994.

Merton, Thomas. *The Asian Journal of Thomas Merton*. New York: New Directions, 1973.

———. *Cold War Letters*. Maryknoll, NY: Orbis Books, 2006.

———. *Conjectures of a Guilty Bystander*. New York: Doubleday, 1966.

———. *Contemplation in a World of Action*. Notre Dame, IN: University of Notre Dame Press, 1998.

———. *Dancing in the Waters of Life: Seeking Peace in the Hermitage, The Journals of Thomas Merton*. Vol. 5, *1963–1965*. Edited by Robert Daggy. San Francisco: HarperSanFrancisco, 1997.

———. *Darkness before Dawn: New and Selected Poems*. Edited by Lynn Szabo. New York: New Directions, 2005.

———. *Emblems of a Season of Fury*. New York: New Directions, 1963.

———. *Faith and Violence: Christian Teaching and Christian Practice*. Notre Dame, IN: University of Notre Dame Press, 1968.

———. *The Hidden Ground of Love*. Edited by William H. Shannon. New York: Farrar, Straus and Giroux, 1985.

———. *Learning to Love: Exploring Solitude and Freedom, The Journals of Thomas Merton*. Vol. 6, *1966–1967*. Edited by Christen Bochen. San Francisco: HarperCollins, 1997.

———. *Love and Living*. Edited by Naomi Burton Stone and Patrick Hart. New York: Harcourt, Brace, Jovanovich, 1979.

———. *New Seeds of Contemplation*. New York: New Directions, 1962.

———. *The Nonviolent Alternative*. Edited by Gordon Zahn. New York: Farrar, Straus and Giroux, 1971.

———. *The Other Side of the Mountain: The End of the Journey*. Edited by Patrick Hart. New York: HarperCollins, 1998.

———. *A Passion for Peace: The Social Essays*. Edited by William H. Shannon. New York: Crossroad, 1997.

———. "Peace and Protest." *Continuum* 3 (Winter 1966): 509–12.

———. *Pre-Benedictine Monasticism*. Edited by Patrick F. O'Connell. Initiation into the Monastic Tradition 2. Collegeville, MN: Cistercian Publications, 2007.

———. *The Road to Joy: Letters to New and Old Friends*. Edited by Robert E. Daggy. New York: Farrar, Straus and Giroux, 1989.

———. *The School of Charity: The Letters of Thomas Merton on Religious Renewal and Spiritual Direction*. Edited by Patrick Hart. New York: HarperCollins, 1990.

———. *Seasons of Celebration*. New York: Farrar, Straus and Giroux, 1965.

———. *Seeds of Destruction*. New York: Farrar, Straus and Giroux, 1964.

———. *The Seven Storey Mountain*. New York: Harcourt, Brace and Co., 1948.

———. *The Sign of Jonas*. New York: Harcourt, Brace and Co., 1953.

———. *A Thomas Merton Reader*. Edited by Thomas McDonnell. New York: Image Books, 1974.

———. *Thoughts in Solitude*. New York: Farrar, Straus and Giroux (reprint), 2011.

———. *Turning toward the World: The Pivotal Years, The Journals of Thomas Merton*. Vol. 4, *1960–1963*. Edited by Victor A. Kramer. San Francisco: HarperSanFrancisco, 1997.

———. *The Way of Chuang Tzu*. New York: New Directions, 1965.

———. *The Wisdom of the Desert*. New York: New Directions, 1960.

———. *Witness to Freedom*. Edited by William H. Shannon. New York: Farrar, Straus and Giroux, 1994.

———. *Zen and the Birds of Appetite*. New York: New Directions, 1968.

Miller, William. *Dorothy Day: A Biography*. New York: Harper and Row, 1972.

Millett, Kate. *Sexual Politics*. New York: Doubleday, 1970.

Montiero, George. "The Literary Uses of a Proverb." *Folklore Enterprises* 87, no. 2 (1976): 216–18.

Mott, Michael. *The Seven Mountains of Thomas Merton*. Boston: Houghton Mifflin Harcourt, 1984.

O'Gorman, Ned. *The Other Side of Loneliness*. New York: Arcade Publishing, 2006.

———, ed. *Prophetic Voices*. New York: Random House, 1969.

Oyer, Gordon. *Pursuing the Spiritual Roots of Protest: Merton, Berrigan, Yoder, and Muste at the Gethsemani Abbey Peacemakers Retreat*. Eugene, OR: Wipf and Stock, 2014.

Paterson, Thomas, J. C. Clifford, and K. J. Hagan. *American Foreign Policy since 1900*. Lexington, MA: D. C. Heath, 1991.

Polner, Murray, and Jim O'Grady. *Disarmed and Dangerous: The Radical Lives and Times of Daniel and Philip Berrigan*. New York: Basic Books, 1997.

Pycior, Julie Leininger. *LBJ and Mexican Americans: The Paradox of Power*. Austin: University of Texas Press, 1997.

———. "'We Are All Called to Be Saints': Dorothy Day, Thomas Merton, and Friendship House." *The Merton Annual* 13 (2000): 27–62.

Rice, Edward. *The Man in the Sycamore Tree: The Good Times and Hard Life of Thomas Merton*. New York: Doubleday, 1970.

Shannon, William H., ed. "The Correspondence of Dorothy Day and Thomas Merton." In *American Catholic Pacifism: The Influence of Dorothy Day and the Catholic Worker Movement*, edited by Anne Klejment and Nancy L. Roberts. Westport, CT: Praeger, 1996.

Shesol, Jeff. *Mutual Contempt: Lyndon Johnson, Robert Kennedy, and the Feud That Defined a Decade*. New York: W. W. Norton, 1998.

Spencer, Thomas. "Joan Baez, Ira Sandperl, and Thomas Merton's Nonviolent Activism." *The Merton Seasonal* 34, no. 1 (2009). http://merton.org/ITMS/Seasonal/34/34.1Spencer.pdf.

Stern, Karl. *Pillar of Fire*. New York: Noonday/Farrar, Straus and Giroux, 1951.

Stoessel, Scott. *Sarge: The Life and Times of Sargent Shriver*. Foreword by Bill Moyers. Washington, DC: Smithsonian Books, 2004.

Turley, Hugh, and David Martin. *The Martyrdom of Thomas Merton*. Hyattsville, MD: McCabe Publishing, 2018.

Ward, James Arthur. *Ferrytale: The Career of W. H. "Ping" Ferry*. Palo Alto, CA: Stanford University Press, 2001.

Wild, Robert. *Catherine's Friends: Some Famous People in the Life of Catherine De Hueck Doherty*. Ottawa: Justin Press, 2011.

PERIODICALS

America
Ave Maria
The Catholic Advocate
Catholic Peace Fellowship Bulletin
The Catholic Worker
The Christian Century
Crisis
The Daily American (Rome)
The Danville Bee
Friendship House News
Harpers
Jubilee
Louisville Courier-Journal
The Merton Seasonal
The Nation
National Catholic Reporter
The New York Review of Books
The New York Times
The New York Times Book Review
The New Yorker
Pax Bulletin
Scientific American
St. Louis Review
The Tablet (London)
USA Today
The Washington Post
Worldview

INTERVIEWS BY AUTHOR

Eric Anglada, June 11, 2011, Chicago, Illinois.
John Eudes Bamberger, OCSO, August 11, 1997, Abbey of Our Lady of the Genesee, Piffard, New York.
Ade Bethune, June 18, 1999, Newport, Rhode Island.
James Conner, OCSO, June 11, 2011, Chicago, Illinois.
Mary Donald Corcoran, OSB, March 27, 2012, Transfiguration Monastery, Windsor, New York.
Monica Durkin Cornell, May 7, 2006, Peter Maurin Catholic Worker Farm, Marlboro, New York.
Thomas C. Cornell, August 21, 1997, and May 7, 2006, Peter Maurin Catholic Worker Farm, Marlboro, New York.
John Dear, telephone interview with author, February 17, 2017.
Eileen Egan, May 10, 2000, New York City.
Mark Filip, OCSO, June 11, 2011, Chicago, Illinois.
Jim Forest, April 17, 1997, and June 12, 2008, Hastings-on-Hudson, New York.
Patrick Hart, OCSO, July 4, 1999, Gethsemani, Kentucky.
Anna Koop, SL, telephone interview, March 16, 2012.
Robert Lax, tape recorded answers to written questions, May 1999.
William Meninger, OCSO, November 30 and December 1, 2011, East Elmhurst, New York.
Jeanette Noel, June 19, 1998, Maryhouse Catholic Worker, New York City.
Ned O'Gorman, March 31, 2012, New York City.
Roger O'Neill, March 17, 2013, New York City.
William H. Shannon, August 12, 1997, Nazareth College, Rochester, New York.
John Stanley, March 4, 2012, New York City.
Robert Steed, March 26, 2012, Hobart, New York.
Mary Luke Tobin, SL, July 4, 1999, Sisters of Loretto Motherhouse, Nerinx, Kentucky.

INTERNET AND MEDIA SOURCES

Baltimore Catechism. "Lesson 13—On the Sacraments in General." http://www.baltimore-catechism.com/lesson13.htm.

Benedict XVI. "Address to Romano Guardini Congress." October 29, 2010. https://w2.vatican.va/content/benedict-xvi/en/speeches/2010/october/documents/hf_ben-xvi_spe_20101029_fondazione-guardini.html.

Brooklyn Museum. "Vivian Cherry, Working Street Photographer, 1940s to 1960s." https://www.brooklynmuseum.org/opencollection/exhibitions/2663.

CBS News. "The Fallout Shelter Gun Debate." https://www.youtube.com/watch?v=vW5TyPrvw2U.

Catholic Peace Fellowship. http://www.catholicpeacefellowship.org.

Catholic Relief Service. https://www.crs.org.

Center for Action and Contemplation. "History." https://cac.org/about-cac/history/.

Children's Hospital of Philadelphia. "Fetal Surgery Continues to Advance." CHOP News. June 22, 2011. http://www.chop.edu/news/fetal-surgery-continues-advance.

Christopher Closeup. "Dorothy Day." 1971. https://www.avemariapress.com/resources/22/2800/.

Cole, Audrey H. "The Catholic Worker Farm, Tivoli, New York, 1964–1978." Hudson River Valley Institute. https://www.yumpu.com/en/document/read/22354183/the-catholic-worker-farm-tivoli-new-york-1964-1978.

The Daily Catholic. http://www.dailycatholic.org.

Day, Dorothy. "Union Square Speech." November 6, 1965. http://voicesofdemocracy.umd.edu/day-union-square-speech-speech-text/.

Drescher, Jack. "De-pathologizing Homosexuality." *Behavioral Sciences* 5, no. 4 (December 2015). https://www.ncbi.nlm.nih.gov/pmc/articles/PMC4695779/.

Eyes on the Prize: America's Civil Rights Years. Directed by Jacqueline Schearer and Paul Strekler. Blackside Productions, 1990.

Forest, Jim and Nancy. http://www.jimandnancyforest.com.

Francis. "Nonviolence: A Style of Politics for Peace." January 1, 2017. https://w2.vatican.va/content/francesco/en/messages/peace/documents/papa-francesco_20161208_messaggio-l-giornata-mondiale-pace-2017.html.

General Federation of Women's Clubs (North Carolina). "March Is National Women's History Month." https://www.library

.georgetown.edu/exhibition/women-champion-peace-justice-through-nonviolence.

Holocaust Encyclopedia. United States Holocaust Museum. https://encyclopedia.ushmm.org.

Inside Schools. "Addie Mae Collins." https://insideschools.org/school/05MAXF.

Jordan, Patrick. "Dorothy Day, the Catholic Worker, and the Liturgy." *The Yale ISM Review* (Fall 2018). http://ismreview.yale.edu/article/dorothy-day-the-catholic-worker-and-the-liturgy/#_edn16.

Laffin, Arthur J. "Plowshares Disarmament Chronology." https://web.archive.org/web/20130919164138/http://www.craftech.com/~dcpledge/brandywine/plow/Chronology.html.

Merton, Thomas. "For My Brother—Reported Missing in Action, 1943." https://www.poemhunter.com/poem/for-my-brother-missing-in-action-1943/#content.

"Moral Conscience." *The Catechism of the Catholic Church*. http://www.vatican.va/archive/ccc_css/archive/catechism/p3s1c1a6.htm.

Paul VI. *Humanae Vitae*. July 25, 1968. https://w2.vatican.va/content/paul-vi/en/encyclicals/documents/hf_p-vi_enc_25071968_humanae-vitae.html.

The Personalist. "Catholic Worker Odds and Ends: Letter to Robert Steed from Thomas Merton." February 28, 2007. https://personalist.livejournal.com/10249.html.

Planned Parenthood. "Abortion." https://www.plannedparenthood.org/learn/abortion.

Poetry Foundation. https://www.poetryfoundation.org.

"Pope Asks Trump to Be a Peacemaker." *Reuters*. March 23, 2017. https://www.reuters.com/article/us-usa-trump-pope-idUSKBN18K001.

Pycior, Julie Leininger. "Catholic Nuns, the Vatican and Straight but Crooked Lines." *HuffPost*. October 5, 2012. https://www.huffpost.com/entry/the-nuns-the-vatican-and-straight-but-crooked-lines_b_1929725?guccounter=1.

———. "Sargent Shriver." *American National Biography*. https://doi.org/10.1093/anb/9780198606697.article.1501362.

———. "U.S. Catholic Bishops Side with the Dems, Not GOP on Main Issues of 2012." *HuffPost*. September 1, 2012. Updated November 1, 2012. https://www.huffpost.com/entry/us-cath

olic-bishops-side-with-dems-not-gop-on-main-issues-of -2012_b_1847062.

U.S. Naval Institute. "The Truth about Tonkin." *Naval History Magazine* 22, no. 1 (February 2008). https://www.usni.org/magazines/naval-history-magazine/2008/february/truth-about-tonkin.

"The Weather Underground." *Independent Lens*. PBS. http://www.pbs.org/independentlens/weatherunderground/movement.html.

Windholtz, Anne M. "For Better or Worse, a Lot of Richard Rohr." National Association of Catholic Chaplains. September–October 2018. https://www.nacc.org/vision/september-october-2018/for-better-or-for-worse-a-lot-of-richard-rohr/.